P. 2
V. GOOD

P. 31

↓
TAIWAN
NEOCLASSICAL
made IT
WORK.

P. 9
V GOOD

DEVELOPMENTAL STATES IN EAST ASIA

Also by Gordon White

MICROPOLITICS IN CONTEMPORARY CHINA: A Technical
Unit during and after the Cultural Revolution
(*with M. J. Blecher*)
PARTY AND PROFESSIONALS: The Political Role of Teachers
in Contemporary China
CHINA'S NEW DEVELOPMENT STRATEGY (*with Jack Gray*)
REVOLUTIONARY SOCIALIST DEVELOPMENT IN THE
THIRD WORLD (*with R. Murray and C. White*)

Developmental States in East Asia

Edited by

Gordon White

Fellow, Institute of Development Studies,
University of Sussex

Contributors: Jack Gray, Richard Luedde-Neurath,
Mick Moore, Robert Wade, Gordon White

in association with
THE INSTITUTE OF
DEVELOPMENT STUDIES
UNIVERSITY OF SUSSEX

First published 1988

Published by
THE MACMILLAN PRESS LTD
Houndmills, Basingstoke, Hampshire RG21 2XS
and London
Companies and representatives
throughout the world

Typeset by Wessex Typesetters
(Division of The Eastern Press Ltd)
Frome, Somerset

Printed in Hong Kong

British Library Cataloguing in Publication Data
Developmental states in East Asia.
1. East Asia—Economic policy
I. White, Gordon   II. University of Sussex,
Institute of Development Studies
330.951   HC 460.5
ISBN 0-333-42398-4 (hardcover)
ISBN 0-333-42399-2 (paperback)

To the memory of a valued colleague and friend
Bernard Schaffer

Contents

Notes on the Contributors

Jack Gray is a Fellow at the IDS. He is a historian and specialist on the history of Chinese economic strategy. He taught at Hong Kong University from 1953–6, at London 1956–64, and at Glasgow 1964–79. He has written extensively on China.

Richard Luedde-Neurath is a management consultant in Germany. He was formerly a research officer at the IDS. He is an economist who has recently published a book on import controls and export-oriented development in South Korea.

Mick Moore is a Fellow of the IDS, and has conducted research on sociopolitical and administrative aspects of rural development in Sri Lanka, India and Tanzania, as well as in Taiwan and South Korea.

Robert Wade is a Fellow of the IDS, with a background in economics and anthropology. He has carried out research on agricultural development and state institutions in India, Italy and South Korea.

Gordon White is a political scientist and Fellow of the IDS working on the comparative political economy of socialist patterns of development, with a particular research focus on China.

1 Developmental States and Markets in East Asia: An Introduction[1]

Gordon White and Robert Wade

> Cosmopolitical economy . . . that science which teaches how the entire human race may attain prosperity. Political economy . . . that science which limits its teaching to the inquiry how a *given nation* can obtain (under the existing conditions of the world) prosperity, civilisation, and power, by means of agriculture, industry, and commerce.   (List, 1966 (1885), p. 119)

For Friedrich List, concerned above all with how Germany could develop manufacturing industry at a time when British manufacturers were sweeping all before them, the distinction between these two kinds of economics was vital. What we know as classical economics was List's 'cosmopolitical economy'. It operated on the Enlightenment assumption of citizens of the world as economic individuals, seeking competitive advantage in free international and internal trade. Marxian economics introduced class distinctions, but gave the division of citizens of the world into nation-states no more significance than it had in classical economics.

It is the basic thesis of this volume that the phenomenon of successful 'late development' – whether 'capitalist' (Germany, Russia, Japan, South Korea, Taiwan) or socialist (the Soviet Union, China, North Korea) – should be understood primarily in terms of Listian 'political economy', concretely as a process in which states have played a strategic role in taming domestic and international market forces and harnessing them to a national economic interest.

Indeed, the modern notion of 'development' rests on a concept of the state as the *primum mobile* of socio-economic progress. It draws on the historical argument (Gerschenkron, 1966) that successful 'late development' takes a form very different from that of the early industrialisers, notably the United Kingdom: it is less 'spontaneous', more the subject of teleological determination, with the state playing the role of historical *animateur*.

The ideology of 'developmentalism' and the idea of the

1

interventionist state are thus inseparable. Over the past three decades, development analysts and policy-makers have, implicitly or explicitly, viewed the state as the primary mechanism for overcoming certain major constraints inherent in the domestic structure and international environment of the post-colonial societies (e.g. Green, 1974). Where national states were weak or embryonic, they had to be 'built'.

Until the late 1960s at least, there was a good deal of optimism about the development potential of the new post-colonial state machines. But certain salient realities of the 1960s – pervasive authoritarianism and corruption, ineffective 'planning', disappointing socio-economic performance and international dependence – undermined simpler statist conceptions of the development process. During the 1970s, a number of key debates emerged, initiated by spokespeople on both sides of the ideological spectrum. Neoclassical analysts have questioned the advisability of widespread state intervention and emphasised the benefits of allowing relatively unfettered market forces to operate. Neo-Marxist and dependency theorists have argued the dependent nature of Third World states, concluding that radical social transformation and new socialist state institutions are necessary preconditions for 'real' development, economically more dynamic and socially more fair. These debates have helped focus attention more systematically on the idea of the developmental state – its social basis, institutional character, modes of operation and developmental potential (for further discussion, see White, 1984b, pp. 98–104).

Our intention in this book is to contribute to these debates by examining the developmental relationships between states and markets in the East Asian context. East Asia is the fastest growing region in the world. Not only have capitalist South Korea and Taiwan performed impressively but socialist China and North Korea have also turned in fast growth by international standards (Hofheinz and Calder, 1982). The resilience of the region is especially well seen in the period since 1979, when economic performance in most other parts of the Third World has deteriorated to an alarming degree.

How can the fast growth and structural transformation of the East Asian countries be explained? In the capitalist cases, there is a large body of literature which proposes that they have been so successful because they have applied the principles of neoclassical economics – that is, they have had relatively free markets.[2] In the socialist cases, there is an equally powerful counter-claim that their development achievements rest on the cardinal role of the state as agent of planned growth and transformation. It is our purpose in this book to assess the validity of these arguments through case studies of South Korea, Taiwan and China.

TAIWAN AND SOUTH KOREA – EXEMPLARS OF THE GUIDED CAPITALIST MARKET

In capitalist contexts List's 'political economy' remains to this day unelaborated. In the period since the Second World War, when the role of states in conditioning the market has become unavoidably apparent to any reader of newspapers, economics still prefers to speak of the various systems of 'political economy' mainly for the purpose of demonstrating their inefficiency. It is true that development economics has debated seriously the idea that what is best for advanced and powerful countries is not necessarily best for poor and weak countries. But even within development economics there has lately been a powerful reassertion of the argument that global production would be maximised if all countries, including the poor and weak, followed free trade principles. Compelling evidence for this proposition is said to come from the capitalist states of East Asia (Little, 1982).

The argument is usually presented in more refined form. It is said that the governments of Taiwan and South Korea *did* meddle in the economy during the 1950s, imposing the familiar battery of controls in the context of a strategy of 'import substituting industrialisation'. Since the early 1960s, however, each government has been progressively withdrawing and widening the room for untrammelled market forces (while continuing to provide goods and services which would be unlikely to appear through competitive profit-seeking but which are necessary for economic development and civil life). Progressive liberalisation has gone hand-in-hand with rapid economic progress. It is, above all, the throwing open of the economy to international markets in Taiwan and South Korea which set in motion the relentless drive for allocative efficiency which in turn produced rapid growth. Other countries are advised to learn the same lesson.

The lesson is presented as all the more urgent because it indicates a reversal of the path that many, perhaps most less developed country (LDC) governments are in fact following. 'Since 1947',

Reynolds reminds us, 'private enterprise in most Third World countries has been in retreat. Public ownership, government regulation, economic planning, and the welfare state are in vogue' (1983, p. 971). Yet here we have two of the most successful industrialisers whose success has coincided with a roll-back in government intervention and an opening up to international trade; plus a body of theory which shows why the association is not simply coincidence.

The free market/lean government theme runs through the literature on all the successful (capitalist) East Asian cases. For the Japanese case, Hugh Patrick declares:

> I am one of the school which interprets Japanese economic performance as due primarily to the actions and efforts of private individuals and enterprises responding to the opportunities provided in quite free markets for commodities and labour. While the government has been supportive and indeed has done much to create the environment of growth, its role has often been exaggerated. (1977, p. 239)

Paul Kuznets argues similarly for South Korea that:

> The coincidence of rapid growth and economic planning, and the primacy of the Economic Planning Board in the circle of economic ministries have led some observers to misconstrue the function of planning and overemphasise the role of government in the Korean economy. Planning does not entail government control of resource allocation, but, rather, involves a set of activities designed to sustain rather than to repress market functions. The government acts by providing information, reducing risks, and altering incentives rather than by fiat or by assuming market or enterprise functions. (1982, p. 85)

Referring to the East Asian five (including Singapore and Hong Kong), Chen asserts that 'State intervention is largely absent. What the state has provided is simply a suitable environment for the entrepreneurs to perform their functions' (1979, pp. 183–4). Milton and Rose Friedman make the same point on a grander scale: 'Malaysia, Singapore, Korea, Taiwan, Hong Kong and Japan – relying extensively on private markets – are thriving . . . By contrast, India, Indonesia, and Communist China, all relying heavily on central planning, have experienced economic stagnation' (1980, p. 57).

This interpretation of East Asian capitalist cases is impressively consistent with claims that liberal domestic and international regimes in trade and finance are good for poor countries as well as for the rich. Such impressive empirical support is important because, even though poor countries do not participate in the formulation of the principles or rules of international trade, they are more likely to accept them willingly if they are convinced that it is in their own interests to do so. Rich countries and international agencies will then not have to impose the principles on them. The better the evidence of beneficial effects, moreover, the better the justification for those who make the rules to impose their rules on all, to ensure that self-seeking states are restrained from meddling in domestic and international economic affairs in the name of their national interests. Not only the East Asian cases are said to support this argument; countries like Ivory Coast are also said to have liberalised and consequently performed better than similar countries which have not (World Bank, 1981, p. 26). So to have the most rapid development which their circumstances allow, LDC governments must aim to increase the trade ratio by opening the economy, and to reduce the extent of government intervention in the market. If they will not do it themselves, agencies like the IMF and the World Bank are justified in making it a condition of dealing with them.

CAPITALIST GUIDED MARKET ECONOMIES

A central weakness of the vast bulk of the literature on Taiwan and South Korea is that the concern to demonstrate the *fact* of market liberalisation has detracted attention from the character and degree of liberalisation. So much so that 'liberalisation', a direction of change, is often conflated with 'liberal', a level; as when a tariff reduction from 60 to 50 per cent is taken as evidence of liberalisation, attention being held by the 10 per cent reduction to the occlusion of the 50 per cent which remains.

The economies of Taiwan and South Korea are guided market economies. They are market economies in the sense that initiative rests mainly with the enterprise, profit remains the enterprise's main motive, and enterprises which do not make profits will in most cases go out of business. In general, but with many important exceptions, the state tries to get things done by influencing the market, by shifting the composition of what is profitable, rather than by direct regulation or direct production. The supply and demand for the vast majority of things is a by-product of market forces and the controls that impinge on them. The means of production are mostly privately owned, and profits are mostly privately appropriated. In these ways Taiwan and South Korea are fundamentally different from the economies of most socialist countries. On the other hand, they are also very different from most Western economies. Most Western economies constrain market rationality by measures to protect groups vulnerable to the consequences of the rationality (Ruggie, 1982); Taiwan and South Korea constrain market rationality by the priorities of industrialisation. Industrialisation *per se* has been the main aim, not considerations of maximising profitability based on current comparative advantage. For this purpose the governments have intervened aggressively in (parts of) the market to bring about specific allocative effects – in addition to measures designed to safeguard the self-regulating parts of the market.

The underlying logic is very similar to the approach of the Japanese government, as summarised by a senior official:

> The MITI decided to establish in Japan industries which require intensive employment of capital and technology, industries that in consideration of comparative cost of production should be the most inappropriate for Japan, industries such as steel, oil-refining, industrial machinery of all sorts, and electronics. . . . From a short-run, static viewpoint, encouragement of such industries would seem to conflict with economic rationalism. But, from a long-range viewpoint, these are precisely the industries where income elasticity of demand is high, technological progress is rapid, and labour productivity rises fast. It was clear that without these industries it would be difficult to employ a population of 100 million and raise their standard of living to that of Europe and America with light industries alone; whether right or wrong, Japan had to have these heavy and chemical industries. Fortunately owing to good luck and wisdom spawned by necessity, Japan has been able to concentrate its scant capital in strategic industries. (OECD, 1972)

The governments of Taiwan and South Korea, following this logic, have shown no inclination to limit themselves to macroeconomic policy, or to provision of infrastructure. Nor have they intervened at the industry level only when the industry is in trouble, as has been the tendency in the West. Their approach has proceeded from recognition that some industries and some products, are more

important for the future growth of the economy than others, and
they have attempted, in the Japanese official's words, 'to concentrate
. . . scant capital in strategic industries'. Some industries have
accordingly been highly subsidised and directed by the government;
others have experienced policy intervention only intermittently; the
rest have been more or less left to take care of themselves within a
broad framework of regulation. It is not that the governments have
attempted on any significant scale to *prevent* investment in non-
strategic projects; they have simply not given such projects much
help. They have also retained sufficient instruments of control to
make sure that whatever happens in the rest of the economy,
enough investment is forthcoming for the strategic projects. In this
way the market is guided by the conception of a long term national
rationality of investment formulated by government officials; the
content and pace of industrialisation is not left entirely to the
aggregate decisions of individual businessmen.

Neoclassical economics makes a basic distinction between 'inward-
looking' and 'outward-looking' regimes of trade and finance; roughly
equivalent to 'import substituting' and 'export promoting'. The two
sides of the distinction are treated as mutually exclusive and
underdeveloped countries are advised to switch from the former to
the latter (Krueger, 1983, p. 9). We find in Taiwan and South Korea,
however, that vigorous 'import substitution' has been going on
simultaneously with 'export promotion', that the trade and finance
regime has been inward and outward looking at the same time, but
with respect to different sectors. While steps have been taken to
make exporting at least as profitable as domestic market sale – and
to keep the incentives for exporting *unselective* with respect to
product or market destination – the government has taken direct
and *selective* measures to establish the industries that it thinks should
exist and guide the changes in industrial composition in line with
what the government anticipates to be sensible.

Both countries have assiduously propagated a 'liberal' economic
image, for the very good reason that they want to give as little
grounds as possible for other countries to levy restrictions against
their exports. Judging from prevailing accounts of their trade regimes
in the literature, both countries have been successful in making
many of their controls on trade disappear from view. They have
played a double game, just like Japan. Whereas it took Japan, with
its big domestic market, till 1981 to come out and declare that the
principles of free trade were the essential foundation of a rational

international economic order, Taiwan and South Korea, with their heavier dependence on trade, have been saying this for some time, even while their own practice diverges substantially from it in important sectors. And the bipolar view of the world which dominates US foreign policy makes it all the more likely that such patently anti-Communist regimes which have a critical position in the Western defence perimeter, will be seen as essentially 'like us', 'us' for this bipolar purpose being understood as the embodiment of the liberal principle of free markets (Emmerson, 1982). This helps their own propagation of the liberal image to be effective, because there is a powerful constituency which wants to believe it.

Taiwan and South Korea can hardly be blamed for playing a double game. They must sell exports to earn enough foreign exchange to finance imports needed for upgrading their industrial structures, and to overcome the constraints of small domestic market size. At the same time, they feel they cannot let their economies specialise according to current comparative advantage. One piece of evidence which suggests they are right is that none of the already industrialised countries allow their own economies to be specialised in this way. The industrialised countries have been notably willing to forego the Ricardian mutual benefits of differentiated investment, production and export sectors. Growth in trade between the industrialised countries has been overwhelmingly *intra*-sectoral rather than inter-sectoral since the Second World War (Saunders, 1982; Lipson, 1982). With an irony which daily impresses itself upon the state managers of Taiwan and South Korea, in the one area where trade has been based on something approaching Ricardian comparative advantage, the international trade regime has run into great difficulties: i.e. the trade between the industrialised countries of Europe and North America, and the new industrial countries such as Taiwan and South Korea. All kinds of groups in the West which see themselves hurt by cheap labour imports lobby for protection. To ask the leaders of Taiwan and South Korea to specialise their economies even more than at present according to comparative advantage, or according to whatever the aggregate of businessmen decide are the most profitable things to produce, seems to those state managers to be asking for the economy to be made still more vulnerable.

THE LATIN AMERICAN COMPARISON

Taiwan's and South Korea's approach to guiding the market is quite different to what we could call the typical Latin American strategy of import substituting industrialisation. The latter has been based on the belief that controls on imports, coupled with unselective support of industrial investment, would be sufficient to bring about a sensible kind of industrialisation. And it has operated in the context of a society characterised by much greater income inequalities and class differences than Taiwan or South Korea. The result has been that foreign-exchange-saving controls on non-essential imports led, in the absence of income redistribution and investment controls, to the rapid growth of a luxury consumption goods industry, hindering production of essentials. The absence of selective incentives to develop backward linkages into capital and intermediate goods production has maintained a *shallow* level of import substitution (except in Brazil and to a lesser extent Mexico); easy access to foreign credits, coupled with an overvalued exchange rate, has given domestic business an incentive to use highly capital-intensive imported equipment. Behind heavy and unselective protection, the costs of over-capacity could be passed on to consumers. Industrial exports have been promoted by selective export subsidies. Brazil, in particular, which has developed into 'upstream' sectors to the greatest extent, has tried to push exports of capital goods without having built up domestic market production first – contrary to the East Asian principle. The lack of concern for who controls production, foreigners or nationals, has resulted in much of the production for the lucrative end of the domestic market being in the hands of multinational corporations. The lack of concern for limiting the growth of financial capital (financial enterprises are treated on a par with industrial enterprises) has allowed a sizeable share of the economy's investment resources to go into financial dealings and speculation rather than into industrial production – into making money, not things.

Our main point here is that whereas the liberal analysis says that Latin American governments intervened too much in the market and that is why their countries performed less well than East Asia, we find that state intervention in the latter has been both stronger and more selective than in the former, not only at the national boundary but also in key parts of domestic industry. The aim of that intervention is to build up national powers of production, reduce national vulnerabilities and, to some extent to minimise the socially disruptive costs of market adjustment.

The nation-building strategies of the ruling élites of Taiwan and South Korea have differed greatly from those used in Latin America, and this difference helps to explain the difference in methods and aims of economic intervention. In both Taiwan and South Korea the ruling group (from 1949 onwards for Taiwan, from the arrival of Park Chung Hee in 1961 for Korea) has had a clear and urgent ideology of industrialisation, and has seen industrialisation issues in a comprehensive rather than piecemeal perspective, in a military rather than a bargaining or 'muddling through' mode. In both cases the urgency of industrialisation was directly related to the perception that the country's future was under threat from powerful external enemies. In the sense of urgency and the application of a comprehensive perspective, the regimes could be called revolutionary, though obviously they aimed at less fundamental changes of power and social structure than their counterparts on the Chinese mainland or in North Korea. It might be argued that some Latin American regimes have also, at times in their history, displayed the same characteristics (such as Mexico under Cardenas). But in both Taiwan and South Korea, these characteristics have been combined with a strategy of minimising commitments to existing groups, and preventing counter-élites from defining their opposition in politically relevant terms. Some bureaucratic-authoritarian regimes in Latin America may have *wanted* to do the same, but they came to power in situations where many existing groups already had a considerable autonomy from the state and a capacity to exercise influence against it which could only be put down by the exercise of great violence. The situation in Taiwan and South Korea was different. Both governments have been centrally concerned to prevent emerging groups from acquiring autonomy from the state, to prevent independent channels of interest aggregation from forming. The strategy has been to create groups whenever the leadership sensed needs or demands for groups in the population, in order to be able to control them. The result is that in both countries the central state managers have had unusual autonomy (in a capitalist context) to define national goals, and unusual powers to get those goals accomplished, without having to enter into the bargaining and shifting alliances such as has characterised the policy process even in the more authoritarian regimes of Latin America. In neither Taiwan nor South Korea has the organised working class been an important factor in shaping economic and social policy, whether through direct representation or fear of its disruptive potential. In neither country have industrial associations been important centres of autonomous influence on the state. In neither country has an elected legislature been important in policy making.

The next three chapters describe the distinctive ways in which the South Korean and Taiwanese states have intervened in market allocations to produce a different mix of productive activities to that which would have obtained in the absence of intervention; or at least to produce that mix in a shorter time.

In the chapter on Taiwan, Wade takes up the neoclassical argument that (1) rapid export growth since the liberalising reforms of the early 1960s has been due primarily to the fact of an undistorted price environment; and (2) rapid growth of exports has been the primary cause of mass prosperity and structural change in the economy. He concludes that two key conditions in the neoclassical explanation of Taiwan's success – an open economy and a small public sector, both together being necessary for undistorted prices – have not been present in anything like the degree they are taken to be present in neoclassical accounts.

Richard Luedde-Neurath begins his chapter on South Korea with a detailed critique of the studies which provide the basis of the claim that Korea has operated a nearly free trade regime. He then illustrates the character of state involvement in the domestic economy by looking at industrial policy, financial controls, and price controls before coming to the centrepiece of his study, a detailed examination of how the trade regime actually works. The 'actually' is important, for as in Taiwan many of the controls operate below the water-line of public visibility. The analysis is of interest not only for what it says about Korea, but also for what it shows about how to do a useful study of a trade regime using methods quite different to those of neoclassical theory, methods whose use requires detailed and patient field-work, drawing not only on statistics but also on the personal experience of people actually involved in trading.

Mick Moore compares the character of state involvement in agriculture between Taiwan and South Korea, and describes how that character has changed over time. Whereas Luedde-Neurath and Wade emphasise the 'exogenous' and 'autonomous' nature of state intervention in industry, Moore emphasises its 'endogenous' aspects, that is, the causes of changes in the aims and methods of state involvement. He finds the causes in the changing economic structure.

At an earlier point in time, the state intervened actively and directively in agriculture in both countries. Subsequently, as agriculture itself became more complex, as it became less a source of resources for other sectors and more a shrinking and subsidised part of the economy, so the state has become less actively involved, has withdrawn to the use of more parametric controls. The timing of the transition differs between the two countries: as late as about 1980 in South Korea, earlier in Taiwan. Luedde-Neurath and Wade have emphasized that state intervention in industry is very selective, and although their interest has been more in the areas of intervention than in the areas of non-intervention, they recognise that large parts of the industrial sector are the object of policy interventions only intermittently or not at all. Moore shows how the principle of selectivity has worked in agriculture, by tracing the movement from a time when agriculture was a strategic sector to one when it is not and can therefore be treated with much looser controls.

What none of the chapters on Taiwan and South Korea say much about is the basis of state power, the way it is organised, or the micro principles with which officials make allocation decisions. Still less do they talk about the organisational arrangements that coordinate activities within business firms, and those that link them to government. These are exceedingly important questions. To show why they cannot be ignored in an explanation of the industrial and agricultural success of these countries it is necessary first to establish that the prevailing understanding, as presented by neoclassical economics, is misleading. To do that we have sought to show what sorts of things the state has been doing in addition to making markets work better and providing goods which markets could not supply.

CHINA: TOWARDS A SOCIALIST GUIDED MARKET?

State and Market in Socialist Development

One of the fundamental aims of socialist development in the Marxist tradition has been that of replacing the 'anarchic' markets of competitive capitalism with the 'scientific' determination of social needs through planning (Bettelheim, 1976). Drawing on the Marxian classics, early radical theorists of Soviet socialism, such as Bukharin and Preobrazhensky, held that, while markets are not peculiar to the capitalist system, they have reached their peak of historical development therein, operating on the one hand as the underlying logic of economic processes and, on the other hand, (along with class conflict) as a fundamental source of capitalism's chronic instability and eventual collapse.[3] As the new socialist society arose, it would displace the 'economic categories' characteristic of capitalist markets (value, price, wages, profits). Economics itself would become obsolete, to be replaced by a merely technical discipline of rational economic calculation in a society organised as a single 'people's workshop' (Bukharin, 1920 (1971), p. 12; Bukharin and Preobrazhensky, 1920 (1969)). The plan would impose a 'teleological unity' on society. Economic development would become the object of conscious direction; in Bukharin's words (1920, pp. 10, 68), '(the proletariat) builds as class subject, as organised power, which possesses a plan and the highest will to realise this plan, disregarding all obstacles . . . Capitalism was not built; it built itself. Socialism, as an organised system, is built by the proletariat, as organised collective subject'. In this tradition, the relationship between socialist planning and markets is conceived of as 'zero-sum', the former competing with, and eventually displacing the latter during the period of 'socialist transition'.

This zero-sum view of the relationship between the plan (equated with socialism) and the market (linked or equated with capitalism), which we call the *competitive* position, was translated into practice in the Stalinist version of socialist political economy which emerged in the Soviet Union in the 1930s and was transmitted as orthodoxy to the new socialist countries which emerged after the Second World War, both in Eastern Europe and the ex-colonial world. The orthodox position was laid down by Stalin (1952) who admitted that 'commodity production without capitalists' continued to exist and the 'law of value' (i.e. relations of supply and demand) continued to play a limited role in socialist society, but emphasised that both were subordinate to the plan and would gradually be replaced. Later forms of revolutionary socialist ideology, such as Maoism in China and Guevaraism in Cuba, while taking issue with certain aspects of the official Soviet tradition, preserved this competitive view of plan–market relations. Radical Maoists, for example, viewed the market and its characteristic features (notably prices and profits) with suspicion, as embodying an inherent potential for the re-emergence of capitalism.

While the Soviet model sought with considerable success to

restrict or abolish markets, it demonstrated the practical difficulties involved in converting the ideal of 'scientific planning' into a mechanism capable of surpassing the economic achievements of capitalist market economies. While the founding fathers of Marxism were overly optimistic about the capacity of social planners and organised populations to assume control of economies already highly developed by capitalism, the actual conditions of revolutionary socialist success – in relatively undeveloped societies – have greatly restricted the choice of institutional embodiments of the 'plan'. In the Soviet case, and in more recent Third World contexts, the logic of socialist aims (class transformation, rapid accumulation and planned economy), of underdevelopment (low levels of savings and technology, pervasive scarcity, lack of trained personnel, economic dependence and international hostility) and of radical nationalism (requiring military expansion) have combined to create an equation between the 'social mechanism of planning' and a pervasive, hierarchical state apparatus (Senghaas, 1981). The classic model of realised socialism was thus statist in both conception and practice. It brought about not the 'withering away' of the state itself, but of the earlier Marxist conception of a democratic socialist state, based on the model of the Paris Commune and revived in uncharacteristically utopian vein by Lenin in his 'State and Revolution'.

On the one hand, this reflects the general process of '*late* development', a national phenomenon whereby weak countries attempt to 'catch up' with their more advanced competitors or oppressors. The power of the state, as prime embodiment of the nation, grows in consequence. On the other hand, statism reflects the distinctive features of *socialist* development in which the state plays a dual historical role: as a development élite supplanting the capitalist entrepreneurial class and as a system of economic coordination supplanting markets.

In this traditional model, a politically and economically pervasive state regulates industrial and agricultural accumulation, production and exchange through centralised imperative plans and procurement targets, enforced through a network of political supervisory agencies, administrative bureaux and subordinated productive units (whether state industrial enterprises or agricultural collectives). The role of markets is relatively marginal, being confined to four sectors: first, foreign trade, a relatively ancillary element of an overall development strategy aiming at self-sufficiency (Koves, 1981); second, in the distribution of consumer goods; third, in relations between the (state) industrial sector and the (collective) agricultural sector; and, fourth, in the movement of labour. All of these are highly imperfect, very different from those found in neoclassical modelling.

As an engine of rapid industrial growth, the Soviet model has succeeded in the Soviet Union and Eastern Europe in creating a second tier of industrialised nations which produce an increasing share of global manufacturing output. It is hardly surprising, therefore, that this statist conception of socialist industrialisation was very attractive to the first wave of socialist Third World countries (notably China, Korea and Vietnam). In terms of industrialisation, the model has been reasonably successful in China and North Korea. Each has maintained respectably high rates of industrial growth and established a relatively comprehensive industrial structure within a framework of import substitution. In each case one could argue that the classic pattern of socialist industrialisation brought them into the ranks of the 'new industrialised countries' (NICs) (for a review of their industrial performance, see White, 1984b).

Historical experience suggests, therefore, that in certain circumstances, for certain developmental purposes, directive planning along classical Soviet lines can play a positive role in the initial stages of industrialisation: in raising the rate of investment, generating and focusing scarce resources, defining and directing strategic changes in the industrial structure, regulating international ties, generating overall political support and establishing a social structure favourable to accumulation.

But this success is highly contingent, subject to severe limitations, is purchased at considerable cost and has very limited generalisability. Evidence from the more 'mature' socialist economies of the Soviet Union and Eastern Europe suggests several conclusions. First, success in one economic sector (heavy industry) has been purchased at the cost of other sectors (light industry, agriculture, commerce and services). The latter are demonstrably sectors in which centralised directive planning methods have limited application and effect. Second, the very success in establishing a relatively comprehensive industrial structure meant that, as the economy grew more complex and sources of extensive growth began to dwindle, the characteristic problems of directive central planning multiplied. To the extent that a more complex economy leads to greater reliance on foreign trade (especially in smaller countries such as Hungary), international competition exerts pressures for more flexible economic management and more dynamic technological progress. In successful socialist industrialisers, these pressures combine to create a new set of strategic policy challenges. As the trajectory of their development moves from extensive to intensive, from import substitution to export substitution, issues of microeconomic efficiency and technological change take on cardinal significance.

These problems have forced a reconsideration of the role of markets in socialist economies, with profound implications for the economic role of the socialist state. Economic reformers drew on another tradition of socialist political economy which argued that markets were a crucial feature of the period of socialist transition and that planning could, indeed must, be harmonised with markets to serve socialist ends. We shall call this the *complementary* view of plan-market relations. Its intellectual origins can be traced to certain important (and ultimately defeated) protagonists in the Soviet industrialisation debates of the 1920s, such as Sokolnikov, Bazarov, Kondratiev and (the later) Bukharin (Brus, 1972, pp. 41–60) and to interwar discussions among Western socialists, notably Lange and Lerner, about the ideal functioning of socialist economies (Lange and Taylor, 1938; Lange, 1936–7 (1972)). It was first put on the practical policy agenda by the Yugoslav break with Stalin in the late 1940s and the gradual evolution of 'market socialism' in that country. The 'complementary' position was the basic theoretical underpinning of the movements for economic reform which began in Eastern Europe in the mid-1950s and gathered pace in the 1960s.

Turning to the Third World, even though the Soviet model of industrialisation has scored certain successes (notably China and North Korea), the fundamental fact remains that most of its main elements clash sharply with the resource endowments and institutional capacities of most developing countries. It defined agriculture as an obstacle rather than an impetus to industrialisation and imposed an organisational form (the collective), the purpose of which was to enforce state claims on agricultural surplus rather than raising productivity and rural incomes. In predominantly agrarian societies, this strategy is highly problematic where not disastrous. Peasant agriculture has in fact proven remarkably resistant to directive planning methods. Moreover, the stress on national self-sufficiency and building a comprehensive industrial base, which made some sense in a continental economy, ill records with the realities of small, imbalanced, economies highly dependent on international markets. Moreover, these countries often lack the educated manpower and communications infrastructure necessary to establish a comprehensive and minimally effective planning system in the short and medium term.

The debate between the 'competitive' and 'complementary' views of the relations between state planning and market has double relevance to Third World countries adopting a socialist development model. First, in contexts where commodity production is weakly developed and relations of production are relatively static (subsistence household, clan or tribe based collective, or traditionalistic landlord–tenant), the central thrust of developing policy should be to stimulate commodity production rather than suppress or replace it. The development of markets is crucial here because they provide incentives for stimulating productivity and increase the density of social exchange which can underlie a dynamic, interactive process of economic growth. In such contexts the imposition of a comprehensive, centralised, directive planning system is not only exceedingly difficult, but also fundamentally unwise because it may in effect by replacing one form of 'natural economy' with another. The result would be to stifle the basic motivational and social underpinnings of the transition to a self-sustaining growth economy. There would seem to be a strong case, therefore, for incorporating vigorous markets in the earliest stages of socialist transition (Mackintosh, 1984).

Second, in the case of countries which have already applied versions of the Soviet model with some success in the early stages of industrialisation, the arguments of the Eastern European reformers and the logic of the 'complementary' position are also compelling since the very advance of industrialisation has multiplied the familiar problems of directive planning.

China and North Korea are interesting on both counts. In this volume, we examine the relations between plant and market, state and economy, in the context of Chinese industry and agriculture. An initial intention to include the North Korean case had to be abandoned since scarcity of reliable data made any balanced comparative analysis with the other three cases in this volume impossible. The two Chinese sectoral studies hopefully provide a basis not merely for understanding the dynamics of socialist development and drawing certain lessons for other Third World socialist governments, but also for comparing the Chinese economy with the guided markets operating in the two capitalist East Asian societies covered in this volume.

THE SEARCH FOR A SOCIALIST GUIDED MARKET IN CHINA

The Chinese case demonstrates the dangers of an overly pervasive pattern of directive state intervention. Though economic achievements have been creditable in both industry and agriculture since 1949, the costs – in terms of strategic distortions, allocative irrationalities and low levels of factor productivity – had been considerable and were mounting. A strong case can be made that higher levels of economic performance and popular welfare could have been achieved if central elements of the Soviet planning model had not been maintained. The comprehensive system of state controls established by 1956 in both industry and agriculture had a stifling effect on the developmental impulses generated by civil society. The state's economic bureaucracy cramped or proscribed essential commodity markets in towns and cities and pervasive political and administrative controls dominated the nominally 'cooperative' sector in commerce, industry and agriculture, converting it into an appendage of the state.

Though the CCP leadership recognised problems in the planning system as early as the First Five Year Plan, successive reforms (whether in the form of administrative decentralisation within the state machine or the establishment of nominally 'collective' rural communes) served to perpetuate the initial pattern of bureaucratic control. By the end of the Maoist era, Chinese political economy was a complex and contradictory amalgam which was neither particularly centralised, nor particularly planned. But it was certainly heavily administered, in ways which imposed increasingly chafing fetters on the efficiency of productive units and the motivations of individual and cooperative workers.

The economic reforms which were ratified by the Third Plenum in 1978 and were put in motion during the next five years focused on the crucial need to change the relationship between state agencies and economic enterprises – both public and cooperative, factories and farms – in ways which reduced the scope and changed the form of state action and expanded the decision-making power of basic-level units of production. The chapters by White and Gray provide detailed analyses and assessments of these reforms in industry and agriculture. White examines the attempt to increase the decision-making powers of industrial enterprises and to introduce greater market elements in finance, commerce and labour allocation. Gray analyses the process whereby greater powers over agricultural production and marketing have been transferred to rural households and the nature of the relationship between state and rural economy has become less directive, more based on a system of contracts.

Even though the effects of reform policies have been uneven (with far greater success in agriculture than industry), the last six years have been a period of extraordinary ideological re-evaluation and practical innovation which not only enlarges our understanding of the dynamics of socialist development in China, but has also been a fertile source of lessons and innovations relevant for socialist programmes elsewhere (not merely in the Third World). The way in which the basic issues of state and economy, plan and market have been posed, moreover, bears potentially fruitful comparison with state capitalist economies such as South Korea and Taiwan.

Let us concentrate first on the implications of the economic reforms for Chinese development and socialist development models in general. They have challenged the traditional statist model of socialist development, in ways comparable to Eastern Europe in the 1960s. At the ideological level, they attempt to redefine the basic concept of socialist development, or 'socialist transition'. Instead of the classic Soviet-derived perception of the gradual triumph of planned economy over markets, of state over cooperative or individual forms of production, another model of transition has arisen which to some extent returns to Marx's original position that true socialism could only be built on the basis of an advanced commodity economy developed by capitalism. In effect, the reform project envisages a 'replay' of the original Marxian analysis of the transition from pre-capitalist modes of production to capitalism to socialism *within a socialist integument*. The early phase of Soviet-style socialism is thus redefined as in some sense 'feudal'. While more dynamic than its pre-capitalist counterparts, the logic of statist socialism is similar, in the dominance of the political over the economic, state over society. What the reforms represent, at their deepest level, is an attempt to reproduce, within a socialist framework, the social, economic and psychological dynamics of advanced commodity production which have been achieved elsewhere within a capitalist framework.

All this seems rather airy-fairy and theoretical, but the ideological environment of economic policy is crucial since socialist development is, by its very nature, an ideocratic process. Specific policies have to be legitimised in terms of broad ideological principles and linked in some way to long-term strategy. Ideological revisions which demonstrate the limitations of the socialist state as a developmental agent and rehabilitate markets as 'socialist commody production' open up vast areas of practical policy reforms in established directive planning systems and a wider range of alternative development strategies for newly emerging socialist economies in the Third World. Let us take each of these two sets of practical implications in turn.

Recent Chinese experience reflects the desire to achieve a more productive balance between state and economy – the search for a socialist 'guided market'. As the case studies by White and Gray demonstrate, this task has been difficult in both conception and execution. First, there is the need for a new conception of the theory and practice of 'planning' which embodies a new relationship between plan and markets, state and public enterprises, state and non-state economy. There has been some movement towards clarifying the specific functions of planning as an exercise in strategic decision reflecting both national economic interests and basic socialist values: regulating interaction with the outside world in ways which avoid the irrational forms of 'self-reliance' yet set the terms of international economic ties so as to maximise potential benefits and minimise potential costs; to set strategic directions and implement basic structural changes in the national economy, both regional and sectoral; to exercise overall management by maintaining basic macroeconomic equilibria and regulating the distribution of the national income in ways which reflect economic, social and political priorities.

In terms of plan implementation, the distinction between 'directive' and 'guidance' planning is important. In this context, the economic reforms imply not merely a shift from plan to market but between *different forms of planning*. Whether the scope of each form is defined in terms of economic sectors, forms of ownership or commodities (for various attempts at definition, see White, 1983a, pp. 3–4, 122ff, 134f), the attempt to shift the balance away from directive to guidance methods can hopefully provide the selectivity, sensitivity and flexibility necessary for a more effective system of economic coordination. Clearly the continuing task for Chinese policy-makers is further to diminish the scope of directive, and enlarge the scope of guidance forms of regulation. To be successful, this requires not only a careful, programmatic approach to introducing serial changes, but also changes within the state planning institutions. Some of the faults of the previous system were due to weak or non-existent planning rather than planning properly defined. Reform of the state planning institutions has three basic aspects. First, there is a need to strengthen the technical and institutional capacities of the planning agencies as an essential underpinning for both directive and guidance planning. This not only involves obvious factors such as better statistics and communications, more sophisticated methodological techniques, etc., but also requires the recognition that a shift towards guidance planning requires new skills (for example, in tax offices or banks) and moves the state into new areas of activity (for example, the welfare system, which is an essential precondition for expanding the labour market).

Second, there is a pressing need for organisational reforms throughout the complex network of state economic administration. This entails general efforts to prune, rationalise and streamline the economic bureaucracies and to establish a more regularised system of cadre recruitment, evaluation and promotion. There is also a need to strengthen the organs of plan definition and coordination in relation to branch agencies at each level. Specifically, this means increasing the power of central and local planning commissions 'and economic commissions to regulate relations not only among industrial sectors but also between industry and the other main sectors (commerce and agriculture). To the extent that this is achieved, it would help to reduce tendencies towards fragmentation and sectoral/institutional autarky. Third, there is a need to establish a more rational, less competitive relationship between central and local governments (and between layers of local government). Progress towards a clearer definition of 'central' and 'local' decisional spheres may alleviate some of the overlapping and confusions so characteristic of 'dual leadership'.

The other side of the reform coin is the need to enliven the micro-economy and to establish a productive and equitable balance between state regulation and the autonomous initiative of state enterprises, cooperatives and individuals. As the China case studies suggest, this requires further moves towards expanding the autonomy of state enterprises, relinquishing state controls over non-state units (cooperatives and households in both city and countryside) and diversifying the ownership structure to establish a better balance between state, cooperative and household/individual sectors. These trends in turn depend upon a further extension of market relations between production units, with the state playing an increasingly indirect, 'guidance' role. Success here depends largely on the government's effectiveness in tackling the price problem, combining gradual deregulation with more sensitive and sophisticated price policies. The state's capacity to use economic legislation (especially contract law) and 'economic levers' such as taxation and credit as effective instruments of economic guidance also need to be strengthened.

The general case for moving towards a 'socialist guided market' is unassailable. Resulting improvements in economic productivity should contribute significantly to higher living standards, both material and cultural, which constitute a necessary precondition for the emergence of truly socialist forms of economic planning and cooperation. Economics aside, moreover, the resulting liberation of the forces of civil society lays the foundations for participatory and decentralised forms of socialist politics and social life.

The obstacles to economic reform are formidable, though these appear far larger in the urban sector. There are complex *technical* problems to be faced in designing specific components of the reform programme; specific policy innovations, to be effective, require radical *institutional* changes; to the extent that they challenge the existing configuration of socio-economic power, the reforms face severe *political* challenges; at the most fundamental level, their success depends on a reshaping of social *attitudes* and *ideological* predispositions.

Thus the construction of a socialist guided market is not just a question of 'economic policy', but a deeply political and social process. There is a danger that if these forces conspire to block the reforms halfway, the resulting situation may cancel out, rather than combine the complementary advantages of plan and market. Clearly reform must be 'mongered' in several senses: in policy terms, through greater expertise, forethought and coordination; in institutional terms, by rationalising and reshaping the state bureaucracy and enterprise management systems; in the political arena, by shifting the balance of power, both inside and outside the party, towards those groups and strata favouring the reforms; at the attitudinal level by redefining the ideological character of socialist development and changing patterns of social authoritarianism and economic passivity.

What, if any, lessons does the Chinese experience hold for the governments of other Third World nations essaying a socialist pattern of development? Clearly China is *sui generis* and the range of generalisation must be restricted by the peculiar characteristics which have conditioned both its failures and successes: most notably a long-standing bureaucratic tradition, a continental economy with a relatively comprehensive resource base, a strong revolutionary political leadership and sense of national identity. These factors make it difficult to draw 'lessons' for 'peripheral socialist economies' in Asia, Africa and Central America. One can argue that certain basic elements of state intervention, both direct and indirect, are crucial in the conditions of the 1980s: there is still a pressing need to establish a planning network capable of identifying national economic priorities, and implementing them by selective and flexible intervention: differentiated regulation of external economic ties, coordinated action to influence the generation of savings and the allocation of investment funds, direct control over key nascent industrial sectors, widespread mobilisation of political support for economic goals and the institutional and social transformations necessary to underpin a relatively egalitarian and democratic pattern of development.

But the Chinese case should alert socialist governments to the problems of pervasive state controls and warn against any temptation towards early and comprehensive *etatisation* which may not only bring serious economic costs but also create institutional rigidities which reduce future room for manoeuvre. This would suggest the need for a greater degree of selectivity in establishing a state sector, in industry, agriculture and commerce, and the crucial importance of establishing a guided market which combines flexible methods of economic management and considerable autonomy for factories and farms. In terms of ownership, this implies greater scope for the none-state sector, both cooperative and household/individual.

While this kind of guided market would seem to be 'sound policy' it is also advisable in a more pressing sense, that is the characteristically crushing conditions of peripheral socialist economies do not seem to offer much alternative. As Fitzgerald (1985) points out, governments in such contexts have very limited capacity for economic planning and management in the traditional 'Eastern Europe' sense. They face two crucial sectors which are unplannable (in directive terms at least): the international economy and (often predominantly peasant) agriculture. In consequence, economic planning must rest centrally on the parametric regulation of markets and relatively autonomous economic actors. In such circumstances, the traditional approach to socialist planning is not only unwise but infeasible.

GUIDED MARKETS IN EAST ASIA, SOCIALIST AND CAPITALIST

Though their ideologies and economic systems are very different, the East Asian countries covered in this book share certain basic common features and problems which cut across the political divide. They share a common Confucian heritage, a historical legacy of strong and economically active states, traditions of social and political hierarchy and strong nationalist sentiments underpinned by cultural homogeneity and reinforced by external threats. These factors have conditioned both the degree and forms of state intervention and the demonstrated developmental success of East Asian states.

As we have seen, the role of the state has been predominant in all those cases. In each case the developmental impact of the state extended far beyond economic policy to include ideological mobilisation, pervasive political controls and social engineering. Each state has sought to draw a clear line between the domestic and international economies and to define and implement national economic priorities through varying forms of strategic planning.

Both types of regime have been politically authoritarian, in ways repugnant to both liberal democrats and democratic socialists. This raises a series of difficult issues which cannot be addressed here, but have fundamental implications for conventional contemporary ideologies of development and need further inquiry. It would seem that, in East Asia at least, the success of both capitalist and socialist models of development – one informed by an ethic of 'freedom', the other of 'liberation' – depends heavily on a high degree of political authoritarianism, in their early stages at least. Is this an eluctable developmental dilemma, or can dynamic forms of capitalist and socialist industrialisation be combined with powerful participatory and representative institutions? Should authoritarianism, both capitalist and socialist, be viewed as the price that must be paid for the widespread improvements in mass living standards which have undeniably occurred under both systems in East Asia? Is it plausible to suppose that development could be initiated and sustained up to the middle stages without ruling groups having a substantial capacity to resist societal pressure, at least if development is to proceed at a pace fast enough to bring substantial material improvements in mass living standards within a lifetime? Should not then a key distinction be made between developmentally 'rational' and 'irrational', historically 'progressive' and 'reactionary' forms of authoritarianism, particularly considering that the former, whether socialist or capitalist, create the social and potential conditions for the emergence of more democratic and participatory institutions, a tendency we observe in all our East Asian cases.

Some of the simple distinctions commonly used to differentiate their economic performance make less sense in the light of our analysis and of recent trends in China. In terms of development strategy, Taiwan and South Korea are clearly not pure cases of 'export orientation' as opposed to 'import substitution'; they have combined the two strategies both sequentially and concurrently. While China exhibited high degrees of inward-oriented 'self-reliance' in the 1960s, much of this was an adjustment to international economic blockade, was already breaking down before the end of the Cultural Revolution decade and changed dramatically with the advent of 'open-door' policies after the death of Mao. While the role of the state is still more pervasive in China, our analysis demonstrates that the South Korean and Taiwanese states have been far more active than conventional accounts would allow and, to the extent that post-Mao economic reforms take hold in China, there are trends towards a partial convergence in the basic structure and dynamics of East Asian political economies, towards 'capitalist' and 'socialist' guided markets. As such, they have much to learn from each other about the efficacy of different forms and techniques of state action and the concrete methods for productively combining selective state planning with market processes, both internally and externally.

East Asian experience illustrates the crucial importance of achieving a balance between governmental regulation and market processes, state and civil society, domestic and international economies; a balance which accords a substantial role to the state as the executor of a national economic interest but encourages a vibrant micro-economy operating in a competitive market context. This basic challenge confronts both 'state capitalism' and 'state socialism' in East Africa, though the political character and social basis of the 'national economic interest' and the ownership structure of the micro-economy may be very different. The search for a 'guided market' is no mere search for 'sound' economic policies but embodies fundamental clashes of social interest and visions of the future; as such, it is a deeply conflictual process and has broad implications for the overall quality of social and political life in each society.

Viewing East Asian experience in the context of wider development debates, it should give pause to any sweeping policy generalisations based on the alleged economic omnipotence of either state planning or markets. While earlier conventional development economics can be faulted for a certain blithe optimism about the developmental capacity of states and for privileging macro- over microeconomic factors, recent critics of state intervention and the so-called '*dirigiste* dogma' can be faulted for denigrating or downgrading the positive economic potential of state action.

To return to our starting point, however, surely the most basic similarity between our capitalist and socialist cases is that they are successful examples of List's 'political economy', of development as a national endeavour guided by a strong and pervasive state. In capitalist East Asia and increasingly in socialist, the efficiencies and opportunities of market economics have been harnessed to the strategic ends of national power and prosperity, like Japan before them. The developmental dynamic seems not so much from a passive adjustment to the impersonal and porous processes of 'cosmo-political economy', but from a kind of national crusade led by an alliance of state and economic managers. These processes of 'political economy' cannot be analysed in terms of state 'intervention' in an economy which is in some sense alien or discrete. Indeed, we should be alert to the ideological roots of the language of 'intervention', as a linguistic expression of an economic liberalism which polarises state from market and is of limited utility in understanding the roots and dynamics of East Asian development. The relationship between state and economy in East Asia has been more organic and multidimensional. Moreover, the state's contribution to economic progress has depended heavily on its broader social and political impact. Thus the search for a deeper understanding of the economic role of the state poses a challenge not only to development economics but to development studies as an interdisciplinary endeavour.

Notes

1. The authors would like to thank the Gatsby Charitable Foundation for providing the financial support which made this research possible. The views expressed herein do not represent those of the Foundation.

   The editor would also like to thank the following for their assistance in preparing the final manuscript: John Jenkins, Marion Huxley, Jane Deakin and Linda Simmons.
2. We exclude here a small body of literature which calls them 'tottering neo-colonies', 'houses built on sand' and the like, which is empirically too innocent to be taken seriously (Wade, 1982, chs 1 and 7).
3. For theorists such as Bukharin, the relationship between markets varied according to the stages of capitalist development. The 'anarchy' of the early stage of capitalism was to a considerable degree superseded by the emergence of 'finance capitalism' which represented 'the fusion of the economic and political organisation of the bourgeoisie', transforming capitalism from 'a subject-less economy to an economically active subject' (1920, pp. 15–19). But this merely transferred the basic problem of irrationality and anarchy to the *world* scale, as the underlying dynamic of imperialism.

References

Bettelheim, C. (1976) *The Transition to Socialist Economy* (Brighton, Sussex: Harvester Press).

Brus, W. (1972) *The Market in a Socialist Economy* (London: Routledge & Kegan Paul).

Bukharin, N. I. (1920 (1971)) *Economics of the Transformation Period*, Moscow (New York: Bergman Publishers).

Bukharin, N. I. and E. Preobrazhensky (1920 (1969)) *The ABC of Communism*, Moscow (Harmondsworth, Middlesex: Penguin Books).

Chen, E. K. Y. (1979) *Hyper-growth in Asian Economics: A Comparative Study of Hong Kong, Japan, Korea, Singapore and Taiwan* (London: Macmillan).

Emmerson, D. (1982) 'Pacific Optimism II: Explaining Economic Growth: How Magic is the Marketplace?', *University Field Staff International Report*, no. 5.

Fitzgerald, E. V. K. (1985) 'The Problem of Balance in the Peripheral Socialist Economy: a Conceptual Note', in G. White and E. Croll, (eds), 'Agriculture in Socialist Development', special issue of *World Development*, vol. 13, no. 1 (January) 1985.

Friedman, Milton and Rose (1980) *Free to Choose: a Personal Statement*, (New York: Harcourt Brace Jovanovich).

Gerschenkron, A. (1966) *Economic Backwardness in Historical Perspective* (Harvard University Press).

Green, R. H. (1974) 'The Role of the State as an Agent of Economic and Social Development in the Least Developed Countries', *Journal of Development Planning*, no. 6, 1–40.

Hofheinz, R. and K. Calder (1982) *The Eastasian Edge* (New York: Basic Books).

Jowitt, K. (1971) *Revolutionary Breakthroughs and National Development: The Case of Rumania, 1944–1965* (University of California Press).

Koves, A. (1981) 'Socialist Economy and the World Economy', *Review*, vol. V, no. 1 (Summer) pp. 113–133.

Krueger, A. (1983) *Synthesis and Conclusions*, vol. 3 of *Trade and Employment in Developing Countries* (University of Chicago).

Kuznets, P. (1982) 'The Dramatic Reversal of 1979/1980: Contemporary Economic Development in Korea', *Journal of Northeast Asian Studies*, 1(3).

Lange, O. (1936–7 (1979)) 'On the Economic Theory of Socialism', in Nove and Nuti (eds), *Socialist Economics: Selected Readings* (Harmondsworth, Middlesex: Penguin Books) pp. 92–110.

Lange, O. with F. Taylor (1938) *On the Economic Theory of Socialism* (University of Minnesota Press).

Lipson, C. (1982) 'The Transformation of Trade: the Sources and Effects of Regime Change', *International Organisation*, 36(2), Spring.

List, F. (1966 (1885)) *The National System of Political Economy* (New York: Augustus Kelley).

Little, I. M. D. (1982) *Economic Development: Theory, Policy, and International Relations* (New York: Basic Books).

Mackintosh, M. (1985) 'Economic Tactics: Commercial Policy and the Socialisation of African Agriculture', in G. White and E. Croll (eds), 'Agriculture in Socialist Development', special issue of *World Development*, January.

OECD (1972) *The Industrial Policy of Japan* (Paris).

Patrick, H. (1977) 'The Future of the Japanese Economy: Output and Labour Productivity', *The Journal of Japanese Studies*, 3, Summer.

Reynolds, L. (1983) 'The Spread of Industrialisation to the Third World: 1850–1980', *Journal of Economic Literature*, 21(3), Sept.

Ruggie, J. G. (1982) 'International Regimes, Transitions and Change: Embedded Liberalism in the Postwar Economic Order', *International Organisation*, 36(2), Spring, pp. 379–416.

Saunders, C. (1982) 'Changes in the Distribution of World Production and Trade', in J. Pinder (ed.), *National Industrial Strategies and the World Economy* (London: Croom Helm).

Senghaas, D. (1981) 'Socialism in Historical and Developmental Perspective', *Economics*, no. 23, pp. 94–115.

Stalin, J. (1952) *Economic Problems of Socialism in the Soviet Union* (Moscow).

Wade, R. H. (1982) *Irrigation and Agricultural Politics in South Korea* (Boulder, Colorado: Westview Press).

White, G. (1983) *Industrial Planning and Administration in Contemporary China* (transcript of a research trip June–July 1983), Institute of Development Studies, University of Sussex.

White, G. (1984a) 'Urban Bias, Rural Bias or State Bias? Urban–rural Relations in Post-revolutionary China', *Journal of Development Studies*, vol. 20, no. 3.

White, G. (1984b) 'Developmental States and Socialist Industrialisation in the Third World', *Journal of Development Studies*, vol. 21, no. 1, 97–120.
World Bank (1981) *World Developmental Report 1981* (Washington DC).

2 State Intervention in 'Outward-looking' Development: Neoclassical Theory and Taiwanese Practice[1]

Robert Wade

If the wealth of any nation has multiplied miraculously, that nation must be Taiwan.[2] Taiwan has experienced real GDP growth of 10.6 per cent a year from 1965 to 1979; no deterioration in income distribution; improvement in literacy and life expectancy better than in almost all other developing countries; increases in real manufacturing earnings of 15 per cent a year from 1960 to 1979; unemployment at less than 2 per cent since 1970. Income per person is three to ten times higher than China, depending on which figures are used. In 1953 Taiwan had a per capita income below the Mediterranean countries, well below any Latin American country, and well below Malaysia. By 1982 this had reached US$2500, substantially higher than Malaysia, Brazil and Mexico, and on a par with Portugal, Argentina and Chile.

This is not a case of easy natural resource exploitation, but of labour-intensive manufacturing. In 1973 the share of manufacturing in NDP was 36 per cent, which is high even by the standards of 'industrialised' countries and extraordinarily high for a 'developing' country. With a small domestic market (population 18 million), a large part of manufactured production has been exported. Exports, which amount to over *half* of GDP, consist 90 per cent of industrial goods – including not only 'first generation' textiles, clothes, leather and wood products, but also 'second generation' radio and television sets, cassette recorders, electronic calculators, sewing machines, machine tools, semi-conductors, and last but not least, personal computers. Yet in 1955 exports were 90 per cent agricultural, mainly sugar and rice. All this transformation without, since the late 1960s, balance of payments problems, rapid inflation a fiscal crisis of the state, periodic depressive stabilisation programmes and without high levels of foreign borrowing.

If this is a miracle, it is not beyond explanation. On the contrary, according to the generally accepted view Taiwan's success is due to a thoroughgoing application of the theorems of neoclassical economics.

Ian Little, as good an exponent of neoclassical economics as one can find, has conducted research on all of the new industrial countries (NICs) of East Asia (Taiwan, South Korea, Hong Kong, Singapore). He explains Taiwan's industrial boom of 1963–73 in terms of four key elements: the creation of a virtual free trade regime for exports, conservative government budgeting, high interest rates and a free labour market (1979; p. 480). Together, the four elements produce an undistorted – or 'not seriously distorted' – price environment, in which prices reflect real scarcities. In this price environment, labour-intensive manufactured exports grew rapidly, labour-intensive export growth generated home market growth, rapid gains in employment and real wages, near elimination of poverty, and declines in income inequality. As demand pulled up labour costs and as labour-intensive exports encountered protectionist barriers, so the economy's comparative advantage has shifted towards more capital- and technology-intensive activities.[3]

Nothing miraculous about that. Far from being beyond explanation, Taiwan (and South Korea) is seen to be the 'standard' case, in the sense that it shows what any country could expect if only the same principles were followed. It is the deviations from the 'standard' case which need to be explained.

Consider the differences between the East Asian and the Latin American 'gang of four' (Brazil, Argentina, Mexico, Colombia). Industrial growth in Latin America has been accompanied by recurring foreign exchange crises, unequal income distribution, and low gains in employment. Most Latin American countries have had great difficulty weathering the global price shocks of the 1970s, and many have been forced in the early 1980s to reschedule their external debts while facing the prospect of slow growth. In contrast, the East Asian NICs have experienced no major foreign exchange problems, have achieved impressive employment gains and income distribution gains, and have had faster economic growth over the 1970s and early 1980s.

Balassa *et al.* (1982) explain the difference in performance in terms of differences in the incentives used to affect the allocation of resources and international trade. The East Asian countries, after an initial period of import substitution, adopted outward-looking policies that provided broadly similar incentives to exports and import substitution, and gave producers neutral incentives as between domestic and imported inputs. In contrast, the Latin American countries continued import substitution beyond the first and easy stage. This became increasingly costly as it was extended to capital-intensive industries with large optimum scales of production. They used quantitative controls to discourage use of imported inputs, even when cheaper than domestic substitutes; and overvalued their exchange rate to make cheaper those imports which were permitted. Such policies retarded the growth of exports, causing recurrent foreign exchange crises and 'stop-go' management of domestic demand. The East Asian countries, after eliminating anti-export bias, enjoyed rapid growth of manufactured exports which in turn had stimulated overall economic growth. Their experience thus disproves the 'export pessimism' prevalent in development economics in the 1950s and 1960s, and remains influential today.

So the basic reason for this difference in economic performance is to do with the non-interference of the state in the workings of the market mechanism, especially non-discrimination against manufactured exports. The other NICs have been held back from the development they would have achieved in the 'normal' course of events by excessive state intervention. Or in a slighly different version of the argument, John Fei claims to show that 'the basic causation of success of the [East Asian] NICs on the policy front, can be traced to the *lessening* of government interference in the market economy during the E-O [Export Oriented] phase' (1983, p. 34, emphasis added).

The neoclassical view does *not* say that the state had a negligible influence. On the contrary, Ian Little stresses that the state in Taiwan has had – and states in developing countries should have – a major role in providing the framework of roads, education, health and so on required for the private sector to operate satisfactorily. It has ensured that the labour market is kept free; that the prices of foreign exchange and of financial capital are kept near scarcity values; that monetary stability is maintained. The crucial points are that all activity which can be performed by private industry is left to private industry; and the government does not attempt to provide any *directional thrust* to the workings of the market.

The theme of lean, or minimal government runs as a leitmotif through the literature on Taiwan's development. 'State intervention is largely absent', says Edward Chen; 'What the state has provided is simply a suitable environment for the enterpreneurs to perform their functions' (1979, pp. 83–4). Little emphasises 'the restraint of [Taiwan's] government which resulted in a falling proportion of public consumption to GNP' (1979, p. 485). Myers, contrasting Taiwan with China, summarises the role of government[4] in the economic sphere as follows:

> [The] party redistributed rural property rights to give more households some claim to private property. The party stabilised prices and the value of money, thereby contributing enormously to a beneficent economic environment within which businessmen could thus make their own management decisions. Finally, the party also began building a modern infrastructure with new manufacturing industries. The state also maintained law and order, expanded educational opportunities, and provided for the national defence. But these latter activities showed a *very minimal use of state power to guide the private sector*.   (1983, p. 545, emphasis added)

The description refers specifically to the period 1949–58, but is intended *pari passu* to characterise the relationship between state and society right up to the present.

Let us accept that Taiwan is, indeed, an outstanding success story in the history of industrialisation. If the explanation of its success advanced by neoclassical economics is accepted, the implications are far-reaching. Economic theories can be classified roughly into two broad groups: on the one hand, those which say that the market is at its best an automatic mechanism which ensures an efficient and pro-developmental allocation of resources, and on the other, those that the market left unguided will in many cases fail to produce that benevolent outcome. There are thus two 'standard cases' – a self-adjusting and a non-self-adjusting market; Taiwan apparently provides resounding evidence in favour of the 'self-adjusting' view.

The evidence is all the more impressive when one considers that the economy has been highly exposed to the international market, with all its volatility and uncertainty. In 1962 exports plus imports equalled 32 per cent of GDP; in 1972, 77 per cent; by 1981, 106 per cent. In terms of total volume it is the twentieth largest trading nation in the world. One might argue that the exigencies of such a trade-dependent economy would impel governments to *expand* the role of the public sector in order to protect internal stability and employment, and maintain levels of domestic production and consumption (e.g. Myrdal, 1960, pp. 70–2). In Taiwan, it seems, the government has resisted this temptation and has been rewarded for its restraint by legitimacy-enhancing growth and mass prosperity. It is the market which has adjusted to the changing conditions and uncertainties of the international economy, reallocating resources flexibly from sector to sector as the balance of profitability changes. Thus Taiwan demonstrates that there is no tendency for dependence on trade to generate state intervention in the domestic economy. On the contrary, liberalism in the international economy and interventionism in the domestic economy are incompatible (Krauss, 1978; cf. Ruggie, 1982).

The central question is how far Taiwan's industrial growth has been a 'normal' response to market expansion. I shall argue that existing accounts exaggerate the importance of markets and underestimate the effect of promotional policies by giving curiously little attention to what the state has actually done. It is as though the very fact of Taiwan's success is sufficient evidence that attempts to *modify* (not just facilitate) the workings of the market have been unimportant.

THE LIBERALISING REFORMS OF 1958–62

The key event in the neoclassical interpretation of Taiwan is the switch from import substitution to export promotion. Throughout the 1950s until about 1958, the government operated a classic import substitution policy. Then gradually over several years a number of important reforms were made, so that by 1963 the following changes had occurred:

— Imports were liberalised: tariffs were somewhat reduced, quantitative restrictions were (it is generally believed) substantially eased, foreign exchange was no longer allocated by quotas according to import category but was automatically made available for a large number of imports.
— The multiple exchange rate system was dismantled and replaced with devalued unitary rate, giving a stronger incentive to exporters.
— Exports were further encouraged by an increase and a generalisation of tax and import duty rebates for industrial exports, and by concessional credit. The net effect was to make

the 'real effective exchange rate for exports' much more favourable for exports than in the 1950s.

— A large package of selective fiscal incentives for both domestic and foreign investors was put in place. It included a five year tax holiday for investment in government designated priority sectors, a less-than-normal tax rate thereafter, and an exemption or deferment of customs duty on imports of capital equipment to produce government-stipulated priority products.

— Foreign investors were welcomed: they could have 100 per cent equity holdings, 100 per cent remittance of profits, repatriation of initial capital at the rate of 15 per cent a year starting two years after completion of the project (but no repatriation of capital gains), and they received equal treatment with domestic producers in terms of access to investment and export incentives.

In the neoclassical view, it was these reforms that set Taiwan onto a growth trajectory altogether higher and more equable than the Latin American NICs. Many but not all neoclassical economists argue that the whole period of import substitution was a waste, that if Taiwan had adopted the same policies in the early 1950s its performance would have been much better (Myint, 1982, p. 126).

The policy changes of 1958–62 were very important to Taiwan's subsequent success, but they are not the whole story. The neoclassical account is not so much wrong as misleadingly partial. It says, to simplify, that exports expanded because prices were undistorted, and specifically because export sales were not made less profitable than domestic market sales. Prices were undistorted because, above all, the economy was relatively open and the size of the public sector was relatively small, so 'political' prices could not be imposed. The structure of the economy then changed 'endogenously' as a result of rapid growth of exports and the automatically induced effects on overall growth, wage costs, incomes, savings, etc.

I shall argue, first, that Taiwan's 'initial conditions' were more favourable for subsequent success than the neoclassical account recognises; second, that the liberalisation was less marked than the neoclassical account says; and, third, that the 'non-liberal' aspects have had a more positive effect on Taiwan's success than the neoclassical account allows.[5]

ENABLING CONDITIONS, PRE-1960

International trade theory has been too inclined to assume that, once price distortions are removed, the latent comparative advantage of a country will automatically assert itself. To know why Taiwan's manufactured exports expanded so quickly after the liberalising reforms, we need to understand something of the potentials already established.

When the Japanese colonised Taiwan in 1895, they set about developing its agriculture to supply the home market with rice and other food crops. They also aimed to make it such a model of colonial administration as to convince the peoples of South East Asia that incorporation into what was later called the 'Greater East Asia Coprosperity Sphere' might be no bad thing. They improved public health and basic education, and built a good infrastructure. They established modern banking and financial institutions to service production and trade. As part of military preparations in the 1930s, they began to develop such industries as cement, pulp and paper, textiles, chemical fertilisers, aluminium and copper refining, petroleum refining, and shipbuilding. Sustained increases in per capita output were accompanied by (smaller) increases in per capita incomes; indeed some evidence suggests that the welfare of the Taiwanese peasant in the first half of the twentieth century may have exceeded that of the Japanese peasant (Ouchi, 1976, in Amsden 1979, p. 348). By the time of retrocession in 1945 the island was probably the most agriculturally, commercially, and industrially advanced of all the provinces of China. Equally important, its people had *fifty years* experience of a growth-oriented state, which maintained public order with a penetrating administrative system backed by a strong police force, and permitted them almost no political activity.

In 1949 when the Nationalist party under Chiang Kai-shek fled to Taiwan, this island of six million people received an influx of nearly two million soldiers and civilians, many of whom were well educated, with practical experience in government, commerce or industry. They took over the government of the island, and moved quickly into commerce and industry. So Taiwan did not have to build up a competence in industry, finance, trade and government administration from scratch.

From early on, the United States encouraged the Nationalist leaders to give up their ambition of taking the mainland by force and concentrate instead on making Taiwan such a model of peaceful prosperity that the populace of the mainland would rise up against the Communist rulers and invite the Nationalists to return. Massive US aid, military and economic, poured in to help bring this about. Over the 16 years to 1965, total aid averaged $16 per person per year (economic aid alone, $6). No economic aid was disbursed after 1965, though military aid continued at least up to the late 1970s. US aid helped to buttress the power of the Nationalist party-state and to dampen inflation, thereby easing moves towards an outward orientation. But aid is not a sufficient explanation of Taiwan's success. Several other countries have received similar or larger amounts of aid *per capita* (Algeria and Chile, for example) but have not used it as effectively.

The government of Chiang Kai-shek set out to expurgate the trauma of defeat on the mainland by being successful in Taiwan. It believed that the civil war had been lost for four reasons: (1) because of party indiscipline; (2) because the government became too beholden to 'vested interests'; (3) because the bankers and financiers got out of control, fuelling a catastrophic inflation; and (4) because of rural unrest, occasioned by failure to curb exploitative relations between landlords and tenants. The Nationalists were determined to make sure that these causes did not repeat themselves on Taiwan.

(1) The Nationalist party undertook a drastic 'Party Reform' in 1950–52 to remove corrupt elements and tighten party discipline. It came to resemble a Leninist vanguard party, a single, 'democratic-centralist', élite party, exercising leadership throughout the entire political system (Jacobs, 1978). At the top extraordinary authority was concentrated in the hands of Chiang Kai-shek, chairman of the party, president of the republic, and commander of the armed forces. Only one party was allowed, but local and provincial elections were permitted, in which non-party candidates could compete (and not infrequently won). However, no significant resources or powers were at stake at these local levels. Policy making and resources were concentrated nearer the top, out of reach of elected bodies. Trade unions had only a nominal existence, and industrial associations had no autonomy. The acquiescence of the local Taiwanese reflected the fact that they had virtually no experience of political participation during the fifty years of Japanese rule.

(2) To remove 'vested interests', the government attempted to eliminate or control all potentially independent groups to ensure that opposition forces could not coalesce around them. In general, its policy was to create a group whenever it sensed a need for one, ensuring that the group had no autonomy. Businessmen certainly lobby the government, but mainly on behalf of their own companies. Industrial and trade associations are not represented as important economic groups in policy formulation; still less are trade unions. The contrast with Japan, and even with South Korea in the 1970s and 1980s, is striking. All through the period since 1949 the government has been anxious to minimise commitments which would constrain its future choices – as have the governments of many states guided by a Leninist ideology.

(3) As for banking, the government kept virtually all the modern banks in *public* ownership, and instituted very tight controls over the whole financial sector. Even as late as 1979 the four private banks had only 5 per cent of the deposits and branches of the commercial banks as a whole, and the biggest of the private banks was only nominally private. A 'grey' informal money market has existed alongside the formal banking sector, watched closely by the government. Only since the mid-1970s has the government permitted the growth of a formal money market in short-term debt and as late as 1979 non-bank financial institutions like insurance companies, trust funds and bill finance companies accounted for only 7 per cent of total financial claims outstanding (Liang and Skully, 1982, p. 189). The Stock Exchange even today is rudimentary, and out of bounds to foreigners. Foreign banks, excluded altogether until 1969, are still only allowed into those pockets of business which the locals cannot do well, in return for lending plenty of money to the country's big international borrowers.

Economists have stressed the 'rigidities', and 'inflexibilities' of Taiwan's financial system. Yet we need to raise the question of whether such a strictly supervised system might not have had some advantages for industrialisation. Perhaps the tight controls on the lending operations of all financial institutions have permitted the government better control over money supply, and so contributed to monetary stability. Monetary policy has in fact been a much more important means of regulating the tempo of economic activity than fiscal policy. Perhaps the controls reduced the profit in buying and selling shares, insurance or money, and so contributed to real investment. Perhaps the controls allowed the government more influence than otherwise over firms' investment decisions, given that there has been a traditionally heavy reliance on bank borrowing (Liang and Skully, 1982, p. 193).[6]

(4) To prevent rural unrest, the Nationalists first supervised a large-scale transfer of former Japanese lands to their tenants, and then, with American encouragement, redistributed land above a ceiling of three rented-out hectares to the tenants. The effect was to create a relatively conservative peasantry, leaving the government free to concentrate its efforts to preserve stability in the cities. As importantly, the effect was to remove any trace of a potential agro-exporting oligarchy of the Latin American kind. Economically, the effect was to make an agricultural sector which could produce a sizeable volume of exports *and* generate linkages with other sectors; for of all forms of primary export production small-scale peasant production tends to have the most spread effects.

Through all these measures, the government attempted to constrain the political and economic activities of the populace to ensure its own survival. Within these constraints it brought to its work a conception of a tutelary role. The idea of tutelary government is an old one in Chinese history, but was given a powerful modern statement in the early twentieth century by Sun Yat Sen, who was a founder and the leading theoretician of the Nationalist party. Sun was an outspoken advocate of market socialism, and looked to the examples of Bismarck's Germany, Russia's New Economic Policy and Meiji Japan, for guidance on the 'method to develop by government action the natural resources of China'. He concluded that state ownership of the means of production in key sectors was a 'practical and reliable system' (Wang, 1966, p. 152–3). Sun died long before 1949, but when the Nationalist government came to Taiwan it still took his ideas as its essential principles.

The top state managers already had experience of trying to develop modern industry on the mainland. They had a fairly clear idea of what industries ought to exist in Taiwan and – with more disagreement – in what sequence to establish them. Some wanted more use of the market and private enterprise than others, but none would have trusted the market to bring about the desired structure of its own accord, and none would have expected to take their lead from private businessmen.[7] Japan also provided them with a source of ideas, a justification for their conception of the role of the state and the main external reference economy for emulation. From the beginning the state managers spoke of 'catching up with the advanced countries' as their second goal, after the retaking of the mainland.

For both goals, industrialisation had to be the main aim, they thought, not considerations of maximising profitability based on comparative advantage. Of course, industrialisation had to be constrained by the need to keep income distribution relatively equal (otherwise resulting social unrest could be ignited by the enemy 150 kilometres away across the straits). Industrialisation had also to be constrained by the need to develop agriculture, to ensure a cheap and reliable food supply, to provide employment and, initially, exports. But agriculture was already relatively developed by the 1950s, and, given heavy population pressure on the land, could not continue to be relied upon as a source of growth in foreign exchange earnings. To raise living standards Taiwan needed labour-intensive manufacturing. To sustain an assault on the mainland it also required some upstream industries.

Commonly the state established the new industries – often single factories – itself. Then, it either handed the factories over to selected private entrepreneurs, or ran them as public enterprises. Over half of industrial production came from public enterprises throughout the 1950s. As new industries started the proportion fell; nevertheless, in line with the thinking of Sun Yat Sen, key upstream sectors tended to be put under the control of public enterprises. Other promotion measures included restrictions on imports (especially of finished manufactures), sectoral allocation of foreign exchange, concessional credit, and penalties on producers of low-quality goods.

In this way the basis was laid for production of plastics, artificial fibre, glass, cement, fertiliser, plywood, and many other industries, but above all, textiles (Scott, 1979, p. 315). Manufacturing output doubled in the period from 1952 to 1958, an annual rate of about 12 per cent. *By the late 1950s a substantial industrial sector was already in existence* – with plants well beyond the cottage industry stage, backed by simple repair and maintenance enterprises and a small but fast growing number of components suppliers. Manufacturing as a share of Net Domestic Product reached 17 per cent by 1960, unusually large compared with other LDCs.[8]

So by the late 1950s, Taiwan had an unusually productive, small-holder, food producing agriculture; an unusually large manufacturing sector; a relatively well-educated labour force, long accustomed to state-imposed discipline; a stable, authoritarian political structure; a large state in terms of its share of the economy's resources; an extraordinary degree of autonomy for state managers in defining objectives and influencing the behaviour of productive enterprises; no organised working class; no agro-exporting oligarchy; no significant private financial institutions; weak organisations of private businessmen. Moreover, state managers had their previous experience of industrialisation attempts on the mainland to draw on, and knowledge of the Japanese example. And very importantly, they had ten years of experimenting with state control and market guidance during the 'import substitution' era on Taiwan.

Given all this, it is not surprising that producers responded with alacrity to the opportunities opened up by the liberalisation. The reforms encouraged goods already being produced for the home market to be sold abroad, in order to overcome the problem of market size. The fact that manufactured exports expanded so fast cannot, though, be explained *largely* in terms of neutral incentives between export and domestic market sale; the 'price' theory leaves out phenomena which underlie the success. The reader is invited to compare the structural conditions in Taiwan described above with those typical of Latin American countries or sub-Saharan Africa, to see how much better placed Taiwan was to respond to export opportunities in manufactures. Moreover, the international situation at the time Taiwan began its export boom was extraordinarily favourable, with unprecedented expansion of world trade throughout the 1960s and easy credit availability in the late 1960s. Had the international situation been less propitious growth rates may well have been lower (Amsden, 1979). The US provided powerful assistance for Taiwan and South Korea to gain economic strength, as anti-communist outposts abutting communist Asia (as it had done earlier for post-war Japan).

STATE-LED CHANGES IN COMPARATIVE ADVANTAGE

In neoclassical accounts the state disappears from the stage once the liberalising reforms are in place. It regulates, supplies public goods, keeps macroeconomic balance; but does not seek to bring about specific allocative effects. This is not because development comes to have less priority. Only that the government recognises the truth of the paradox identified by Charles Wolf, that 'the recipes on which successful development seems to depend impose definite limits on the extent and character of government intervention' (1981, p. 91). Neoclassical accounts recognise, however, that the state became more active in the early 1970s with the move to develop heavy and chemical goods industries (Little, 1979, pp. 467, 501–7). But for the long boom period from 1963 to 1973 (till the first oil shock), the state has no important steering role. How accurate is this picture?

Throughout the 1960s and 1970s Taiwan experienced massive capital accumulation. Even in 1960, before the export boom, the rate of gross domestic investment to GDP stood at about 20 per cent, which only developing countries with large natural resource investment and a few others including China then equalled (World Bank, 1983, p. 157). The majority of this investment probably went into infrastructure and labour-intensive production during the 1960s. It is also true, however, that large amounts of investment went into the development of the heavy and chemical industries – even during the 1960s.

The start of the *petrochemicals* industry in the post-war period dates from the late 1950s (Djang, 1977). Several more products were added in the first half of the 1960s and landmark was passed in 1965 with the commissioning of a naphtha cracker to make ethylene, the important petrochemical feedstock. By the second half of the 1960s, Taiwan's petrochemical industry was producing ethylene, polyethylene, polystyrene, PVC, synthetic fibre, synthetic rubber, and many other products. Synthetic fibres soon became especially important; by 1980 Taiwan was the fourth largest producer of synthetic fibres in the world (Tanzer, 1982). The state took the leading role in petrochemical development, especially through the state-owned Chinese Petroleum Corporation. Many of the upstream projects have been carried out by public enterprises on their own or in joint venture with multinationals.

In *basic metals*, the state took the leading role in *steel* production from 1962 onwards, when it took over a large, loss-making private plant. Although the decision to build an integrated steel mill was not finally taken until 1970, the project was under active study from the mid-1950s onwards. Taiwan is now the second largest steel exporter to Japan after South Korea. The government also sponsored a big increase in capacity of *aluminium* production in 1963. In *shipbuilding*, a massive increase in the industry's capacity was made by the state-owned Taiwan Shipbuilding Corporation in 1962. Even the privately-owned *automobile* industry, begun in 1960–65, was initially under close government supervision. A small pilot *nuclear reactor* began in 1961. Construction of a full-scale commercial reactor (by a public enterprise) began in 1968 and finished in 1977.

In the 1960s the government established several research and service organisations to promote technological and managerial upgrading in industry. Examples are the Metal Industries Development Centre, started in *1963* to demonstrate improved production and quality control methods, and the China Data Processing Centre, established to push the introduction of *computers* in Taiwanese industry in *1965*. Other government-sponsored research institutes were established for chemicals, mining, energy, glass, textiles, and food processing – also, in 1955, a nuclear science research laboratory (Fong, 1968). It is particularly striking that the government should have started to promote use of computers well before the end of the 1960s.

That a rapid expansion of the heavy and chemical industries began in the 1960s can also be seen from more aggregative statistics. Between 1961 and 1970, the share of machinery and electrical machinery increased from 9.7 to 20.4 per cent of industrial production (Galli, 1980, Table 9). Chemicals and petrochemicals also increased their share from 14.6 to 21.8 per cent in the same period. Together these two branches increased their share of total industrial production from 24 per cent in 1961 to 42 per cent in 1970; by 1978 their share was up to 52 per cent. Figures on the share of domestic production in total supply tell the same story (Ho, 1978, p. 190).

The government was very successful in enlisting the help of leading US and Japanese firms to establish these industries in Taiwan. One reason for this success was that Taiwan was in the fortunate position of having close links with *two* of the leading economies in the world; most underdeveloped countries have close links with only one metropolitan country – typically one of the less dynamic Western European ones.

Even during the era of 'outward-looking' growth, then, the government was energetically promoting the development of Taiwan's production capacity in more skill- and capital-intensive industries. Export promotion and second stage import-substitution went hand in hand, targeted at *different* sectors. Taiwan could make such a rapid progress in these new sectors in the early 1970s because a basic productive structure was already in place. The basic productive facilities were in place because through the 1950s and the 1960s the government took responsibility for seeing that they were there.

The government took that responsibility because it foresaw that (1) other countries would follow Taiwan into the cheap-labour export markets, (2) the period of cheap labour would come to an end, (3) the demand for appliances and machinery would increase faster than demand for food and textiles, both at home and abroad, (4) the downstream export-oriented sectors were vulnerable to input supply disruptions if most inputs had to be imported, especially if a large part of intermediate and capital goods came from Japan. The conclusions reached by this exercise of foresight were greatly strengthened by the need for heavy and chemical industries as the bedrock of a strong military. Moreover, the point about Japan was not just foresight. From early on Japanese suppliers of critical raw materials and intermediates had shown a propensity to break long-term contracts when supplies were short at home, or to sell obsolete technology; or not sell technology at all until Taiwan began to develop its own or buy from elsewhere (Djang, 1977). Taiwan had early experience of what was to become a common dilemma for industrialising countries: the gains from trade in terms of efficiency can be offset to a greater or lesser degree by the costs of having resources vital for the development strategy controlled by foreign actors.

In the late 1970s the government moved to expand some of the heavy and chemical industry facilities established earlier. It also intensified its promotion of high technology engineering industries, including metal manufacturing, electrical and non-electrical machinery, precision engineering products. These have lower capital-intensity than steel and petrochemicals, but have high knowledge- and skill-intensity, higher value-added, higher income elasticity, and strong interindustry linkages. The government has also embarked on a drive to introduce labour-saving automation equipment in important sectors.

Neoclassical accounts tend to explain the structural changes in the economy largely in terms of the *induced* effects of the rapid rise in exports, operating through self-regulating markets (Fei, 1983, p. 31). As the economic structure changed, and as protectionist pressures from the industrial countries increased in the early 1970s, so market pressures began to indicate the need to diversify into capital-intensive and skill-intensive sectors, according to these accounts (Ho, 1981). I have argued, in contrast, that even during the export boom of 1963–73 the state exercised its considerable power actively to promote its chosen pattern of economic expansion. That pattern included the export sector as the most dynamic part of the growing economy, but it also included a substantial expansion of heavy and chemical industries.

The aim was to change Taiwan's comparative advantage in *anticipation* of changing market conditions; and thus to permit a steadily more differentiated range of export products. Both government and business have taken for granted that long-term structural change of this sort requires centralised direction. Indeed, all the major changes in the economy since the early 1950s have been instigated by the government; the land reform, the policies of import substitution and export promotion, the choice of leading sectors, the current drive for labour-saving automation and financial liberalisation. Of course, it is difficult to weigh up the relative importance of state guidance as against export expansion. But one piece of evidence is suggestive. Tyler (1974) estimates that in 1969, at the height of the export boom, only 17 per cent of the labour force in Taiwan was employed *directly or indirectly* in manufacturing for export. Though this was much more than in the seven other LDCs in his sample, it still suggests there was more to the success than simple export expansion.

THE RESOURCES AND PRODUCTIVE ACTIVITY OF THE PUBLIC SECTOR

Neoclassical accounts stress *restraint* in government expenditure, which allows the private sector more room for expansion. Since, according to Ian Little, 'government expenditure fell from 19.6 per cent of GNP in 1963 to 16 per cent in 1973, whereas current revenue rose from 21 per cent to 22.4 per cent' (1979, p. 478), Taiwan is a marvellous example of conservative budgeting.

It is true, and important, that Taiwan has run budget surpluses in most years since the early 1960s, indicating public sector behaviour rather different from that of most other countries. It is also true that welfare spending has been small (though free education is available for the first nine years, and there is a free medical service). It is not true, however, that government expenditure as a share of GNP (current prices) has fallen. It *increased* from 20 per cent in 1963 to 23 per cent in 1973, and to 27 per cent in 1980–81 (CEPD, 1982, Table 8-4). Government current revenue increased from 19.3 per cent in 1963 to 25.8 per cent in 1973.[9] According to Pathirane and Blades's careful comparison of seven developing countries, over the 1965–78 period Taiwan had a *bigger* share of government consumption to GDP than all but one other (1982, Table 7).

Adding government and public enterprise gross investment to government consumption we get a figure for 'public sector final demand'. This remained constant between 1963 and 1973 at about 25 per cent of GDP in current prices, then increased over the 1970s to about 33 per cent by 1980 (CEPD, 1982, Tables 3-8c and 3-9a). In the period 1975–8 it stood at about 30 per cent of GDP, when putatively more socialist countries such as India and Tanzania had a corresponding figure of 20 and 25 per cent, Japan 19 per cent, United States 21 per cent, Scandinavia 31–34 per cent (Pathirane and Blades, 1982, Tables 1 and 7).

The public sector as a whole (including public enterprises) employs 13 per cent of the country's seven million workforce, or 4.71 people per 100 inhabitants (DGBAS, 1983, pp. 11, 25). This is quite large by LDC standards: in a sample of 21 LDCs for which comparable statistics are available, Taiwan's figure of public sector employees per 100 inhabitants ranks number eight; the figure for Korea is 3.65, for Japan, 4.44 (Heller and Tai, 1984).

As for the state's role in direct production, neoclassical accounts tend to say little about Taiwan's public enterprises other than to note their declining importance (e.g. Little, 1979, pp. 467, 468). This is consistent with the argument that market liberalisation is the primary cause of Taiwan's success. In fact, from the early 1950s onwards, Taiwan has had one of the biggest public enterprise sectors outside the communist bloc, especially if one excludes a number of countries where large-scale mining, carried out by public enterprises, contributes a large share of GNP. Public enterprises have had a major weight in the economy all through the period of 'outward looking' growth. Short (1983) using two indicators – the percentage share of public enterprise output in GDP at factor cost, and the percentage share in gross fixed capital formation – estimates that, out of 72 developed and developing countries (excluding communist bloc and oil-exporters), Taiwan is amongst the upper quintile according to both indicators. In Asia, only India and Burma are of the same order of magnitude or more (Korea's is a good deal smaller); in Latin America, only Bolivia. To emphasise how limited is the share of public enterprise, how fast the share has declined, is misleading.[10]

Individual public enterprises are typically among the largest firms in their sector. In 1980 the six biggest industrial public enterprises had sales equal to the 50 biggest private industrial concerns. Of the largest ten industrial concerns, seven are public enterprises; of the largest 50, 19 are public enterprises. Public enterprises cover a wide range of sectors, but are concentrated on the commanding heights of petroleum refining, petrochemicals, steel and other basic metals, shipbuilding, heavy machinery, transport equipment, fertiliser – in addition to the normal electricity, gas, water, railway and telephone utilities. They are important, that is, in sectors where the efficient scale of production is large relatively to product and factor markets, capital intensive, and with high forward linkages. These are just the characteristics which, Jones and Mason suggest, give a relatively high benefit to cost ratio of public ownership in mixed-economy LDCs (1982, p. 41).

That there is less pushing and prodding of private firms in Taiwan than in South Korea or Japan is both cause and effect of the fact the government has this large public enterprise sector as an instrument of selective and discretionary intervention. The concentration of public enterprises in upstream sectors gives the government indirect influence over the private downstream sectors which depend on them for inputs. It can use public enterprise price policy to adjust raw materials prices throughout the economy, for example. Moreover, public enterprises are strongly represented in sectors where multinationals would otherwise dominate. As it is, multinationals are important in many of these sectors, often in alliance with public enterprises. In this alliance the state holds its own, keeping control over key sectors within Taiwan (Amsden, 1979).

Measuring public enterprise performance is difficult at the best of times, because governments use taxes, subsidies, regulations and orders to effect industrial policy for both public and private firms. A simple profit or loss criterion will not do on its own and comparisons of capital/output ratios for public and private enterprises must control for differences in their capital intensity. Yet Taiwan's economists have regularly used such simple criteria to argue for denationalisation (e.g. Sun Chen, 1981).

In any case, public enterprise surpluses have over the 1970s contributed an average of 10 per cent of the government's net revenue, and their profit rate has been almost always positive between 1952 and 1974 (Pluta, 1979). Economists' calls for denationalisation have not had much effect. From time to time senior politicians make public statements about the need for privatisation, but no one apart from some foreigners takes such proclamations seriously. They are for public relations.

THE MANAGEMENT OF TRADE

The state uses its sizeable share of ownership of the means of production to influence directly the overall pattern of capital accumulation. It also exerts more indirect influence through a variety of parametric policies. One very important means is the trade regime.

Neoclassical accounts of Taiwan's trade regime concentrate on its 'trade bias' (the extent to which it discriminates against either export sales or domestic market sales), and conclude that trade bias against exports has been low, in contrast to the standard import substitution case. They say little about the trade regime as a means of industry bias. They fail to recognise the role of protection not only to protect, but also to steer.

The best of the neoclassical accounts admit that Taiwan has not had a free trade regime, i.e. that the government has not allowed the use of foreign exchange, the composition of imports, to be determined by domestic demand in relation to prices set outside of Taiwan. In that sense, the economy has not been as 'open' as the large volume of trade might suggest. The virtual free trade regime has applied only to exporters, who are able, by a variety of rebates and exemptions, to get their imports of equipment and materials at near world market prices. But the idea that the dualism between export production and home market production might have been *good* for industrialisation plays no part in the neoclassical argument.

The government has maintained an elaborate apparatus of trade management, and if at times it has loosened the degree of control it has not dismantled the control apparatus itself. The aim of trade management is not to save foreign exchange, of which Taiwan has had no shortage since the late 1960s. The aims have been to build up technological and supply capacity within Taiwan; to raise government revenue (nearly a quarter of total taxes came from tariffs in the late 1970s); and to use trade as a substitute for diplomatic relations as the island has become more diplomatically isolated.[11]

In the interests of brevity, I shall concentrate on quantitative restrictions (QRs), which are generally thought to be much more of an affront to efficient resource allocation than tariffs. Great importance is attached in the literature to the removal or reduction of QRs after the 1958–62 reforms (e.g. Scott, 1979, p. 327).

All imports and exports have to be covered by a licence. Imports are classified into prohibited, controlled, and permissible. The controlled list includes luxuries, goods with security implications, and some goods subject to government monopoly procurement. It also includes, some goods produced locally in quantities satisfying domestic demand and of reasonable quality, whose factory prices is not more than a certain percentage above the price of comparable imports. The allowable margin above the *tariff-inclusive* c.i.f. import price has declined from 25 per cent in 1960 to 5 per cent by the late 1970s. This 'domestic substitutes' category of controlled imports is defined by the Industrial Development Bureau, the principal agency for promoting Taiwan's industrialisation.

All items not classed as prohibited or controlled are 'permissible'. This is generally taken to mean that licences are in most cases granted automatically. The dramatic fall in the proportion of import items classed as prohibited or controlled, the rise in the proportion of permissibles, is taken to be an important indicator of liberalisation: from 43 per cent in 1968 (well *after* the start of the liberalisation and the export boom) to 3.5 per cent in 1976 (Scott, 1979, p. 331; Lee and Liang, 1982, p. 316).

The real situation is more complicated. It is well known that some of the permissible items have origin or agency restrictions (on where they can come from and who can import them), but the significance of these restrictions for free trade is less familiar. Most garments, for example, are permissible, but only (until about 1980) from Europe or America, thus excluding the most competitive sources of such products. Scott mentions yarns, artificial fibres, fabrics, some manufactured foodstuffs, chemicals, toilet preparations, machinery, and electrical apparatus as being subject to such protective origin restrictions in the mid-1970s (1979, p. 332). Some of the biggest items in Taiwan's import bill are covered by tight restrictions on who can import them. Crude oil, for example, which accounted for 14 per cent of imports in 1976, is classed as permissible – but can only be imported by the Chinese Petroleum Corporation, the giant state-owned enterprise.

More important, however, is that not all permissibles are automatically approved for import even if the origin and agency restrictions are met. The controlled list is in fact much bigger than the official one. When an importer applies to a bank for a licence to import an officially 'permissible' but *de facto* controlled item, the bank refers the request to the Industrial Development Bureau. It is difficult to find out how the hidden list system operates. Industrial Development Bureau officials shrink from discussing it, yet they are the ones responsible for compiling it and evaluating applications.[12] Only items whose domestic production the officials wish to encourage go on the list, items which are important for the growth of the economy in desirable directions.

Typically, a would-be importer of an item on the hidden list will be asked to provide evidence that the domestic supplier(s) cannot meet his terms (on price, quality, delivery). He may be asked to furnish a letter from the relevant producers' association. This might be called the 'referral' mechanism of import control, in the sense that reference must be made to domestic producers of import substitutes.

This mechanism has been an important instrument of secondary import substitution. Its function is to provide strong domestic demand for the products of the industries which the planners consider important, especially new ones. Maintaining their capacity at full utilisation helps them to reap economies of scale and lower unit prices.

Petrochemicals, chemicals, steel, other basic metals – capital-intensive sectors, producing standardised, basic items – are covered by the referral mechanism. So also are some machinery and components industries, including some machine tools, forklift trucks, and bearings.

For machinery, the referral mechanism provides only weak protection because the planners are well aware of the importance of allowing industrialists to use the equipment they think best suited to their market. So they have usually allowed would-be importers to insist upon a specification which cannot be matched in all its particulars by a Taiwanese supplier. For more standardised capital-intensive products like chemicals, importing can be much tougher once domestic capacity exists. A manufacturer who needs a higher percentage purity in his caustic soda than the local supplier can match may become so fed up with delays in his requests to import that he decides to help one or two local producers to upgrade to the point where he can buy his requirement from them. Which is just what the Taiwanese government wants.

Because the government is able to control quantities of goods crossing the national boundary, it can use international prices to discipline the price-setting of protected domestic producers. It is very sensitive to the point that there must be good reasons why domestic prices of protected items are significantly higher than international prices, especially in the case of items to be used for export production. In this way domestic prices for goods covered by formal or hidden controls can be kept near international levels, without there being a free flow of goods. The threat of allowing in more goods can be sufficient to hold prices down.

I suspect that the 'referral' mechanism was in place during the great export boom of 1963–73. What may have happened in the liberalisation of trade controls was a switch of items from the formally controlled to the *de facto* controlled list, so as to permit the planners greater flexibility for managing quantities while appearing to liberalise. This is not to say that the whole of the increase in the list of 'permissible' items was illusory; only that part of it may have been, and a fluctuating part depending on the needs of the moment. If so, the removal of QRs during the liberalisation, which bears so much of the weight of the neoclassical explanation, may have been less real than the official figures suggest.

The other main features of trade policy according to neoclassical accounts – a virtual free trade regime for exporters – also needs qualification. It is true that they could import raw materials and intermediates at world market prices, being exempt from or having rebated the tariffs on imported inputs for domestic market production. And it is true that exporters may apply for a rebate of the tariffs and indirect taxes paid by their *domestic* suppliers on their imports of inputs. Since raw materials and intermediates constitute some 70 per cent of the selling value of typical manufactured exports in the early 1970s (Scott, 1979, p. 321), the fact that exporters do not have to pay duty is clearly important in explaining their international competitiveness.

But two further points must be made. First, exporters have had to pay duty on imports of most equipment and machinery – commonly of the order of 15–25 per cent of the c.i.f. price. They are exempted only if they produce certain items (specified by the Industrial Development Bureau). But this concession applies whether the production is exported or not, and only if the Industrial Development Bureau considers there are no domestically produced substitutes available. Second, exporters are subject to both the formal and the hidden system of quantitative import restriction described above. So it is *not* the case that they can import all inputs freely, even for intermediate goods.

It may be that these qualifications to the idea that exporters have faced a virtual free trade regime are not very important if one's question is why exports grew so rapidly. After all, equipment and machinery accounts for only a small part of selling value (about 10 per cent: Scott, 1979, p. 321), so a duty on their import has only a small effect on total costs. But the qualifications are important in explaining how Taiwan has been able to develop its own productive powers in upstream and capital goods sectors.

The other best known argument about Taiwan's trade regime is that the average level of effective protection for the industrial economy as a whole has been low compared with other LDCs. The *locus classicus* of this conclusion is the long and careful study by Lee and Liang, as part of a World Bank-sponsored project on effective protection. They conclude that the weighted average of effective protection for all sectors was 4 to 5 per cent, which is, they say, 'quite low by international standards' (1982, p. 327). Little, Scitovsky and Scott's earlier study of seven LDCs suggests that Taiwan had the second lowest level of effective protection on manufacturers, after Mexico (1970, p. 174).[13]

But this sort of evidence must be treated with caution. For one thing, the procedures of the Lee and Liang study introduce the possibility of *downward* bias into the calculation of the overall level of protection.[14] Secondly, the data is from the late 1960s, and Westphal's valuable but qualitative study (1978) suggests that bias against exports has probably increased during the 1970s. Thirdly, it is misleading to use the average level of protection as the summary figure, because the average hides great variation between protection for agriculture and for manufacturing, and within manufacturing, between protection for exporting and for domestic market sale. Protection on manufacturers for home market sale was relatively high. Lee and Liang describe the category of what they call 'import-competing manufacturing' as 'highly protected' in 1969 – it had a rate of effective protection of 155 per cent, not especially low by LDC standards (1982, p. 325; cf. Hsing, 1971, p. 244).

The important point is that protection is *selective*, and any average is misleading because variance between sectors is high. The planners have been well aware of what might be called the Latin American fallacy that indiscriminate support of any industrial investment would be a sufficient condition to promote the right kind of industrialisation.

All this suggests that even the best neoclassical accounts, which make clear that Taiwan's free trade regime applied only to exporters, need some important qualifications. Much more could be said about trade management – about the scrutiny of applications to import for new plant, about export licensing, export cartels, the export quality control programme, the role of government in providing information about domestic supply capabilities and foreign market regulations. More could be said about the other instruments of industrial policy, including controls over foreign direct investment in Taiwan; controls over foreign investment from Taiwan (growing at the rate of 25 per cent a year over the 1970s, mostly to the Philippines, Indonesia and the US: Ting and Chi, 1981); fiscal incentives for investment in priority sectors; concessional credit; and administrative guidance. All these are *selective* between activities, and their use requires government officials to make judgements about promising products of a kind which neoclassical economists say bureaucrats cannot get right. The use of these instruments would be worth an extended discussion. But enough has been said to draw some conclusions.

CONCLUSION

Taiwan is a market economy. Its experience gives no comfort to those who say that 'markets do not work', still less that economic agents do not respond to prices. But neither does it support the popular idea that the seed of industrialisation bore fruit in Taiwan because the environment that nurtured it was free of state interference. Not only in the 1950s, but also in the 1960s and 1970s, the government has pressed ahead with a guided programme of import substitution, at the same time as the economy has been 'outward-looking'. The aim has not been to allow considerations of maximising profitability based on current comparative advantage to determine the direction and pace of advance. The aim has been to create a flexible and integrated production structure within Taiwan, so that the economy can respond quickly to changes in world market conditions and be less vulnerable to interruptions in input supplies. The underlying logic is very similar to the Japanese approach (Johnson, 1982), even though the observed trade patterns have differed from Japan's because of differences in natural endowment, population, and per capita income. I have tried to illustrate how misleading – sometimes simply wrong – are many of the propositions used to construct the picture of Taiwan as an exemplar of the neoclassical logic.

Open Economy, Small Government?

I have argued that Taiwan's trade regime has been less liberal than neoclassical accounts say – exporters have faced a less-than-free-trade regime, QRs have remained important in selected sectors, and production for domestic market sale has been highly protected in selected sectors. I have argued, second, that the state sector has not been as small as the neoclassical accounts claim, has not exercised such commendable restraint in its claims on the economy's resources or in its direct production (though the government budget has indeed usually been in surplus). Compared with other mixed-economy LDCs, Taiwan has had a relatively *large* public sector. Certainly Taiwan gives no support for the drastic and immediate liberalisation often recommended in Latin America, or to the popular version of its trade and industrial policies disseminated in Latin America (Fajnzylber, 1981).

The Character and Degree of Liberalisation

Yet I accept that Taiwan's price structure has indeed been not badly distorted. It seems that relatively undistorted prices can exist with a less open economy and a larger public sector than the neoclassical accounts allow. The government has used controls over trade quantities to discipline the price-setting of domestic producers (including public enterprises), by threatening to let in more imports if their prices get too far out of line. In this way the pressures of the international market can be brought to bear on domestic producers in a government-modulated way, without necessarily allowing free trade. The government has also run its sizeable public enterprise sector at an overall profit (though profitability is not a good indicator of efficiency or effectiveness). In this sense it has generally not imposed 'political' prices.

So while the price structure may well have been relatively undistorted, the trend of liberalisation, in the sense of dismantling government influences over prices and economic agents, has not been as marked as the neoclassical accounts say. It is true that a fall in a tariff from 60 to 40 per cent, a fall in the share of public enterprises in total fixed investment from 35 to 28 per cent, can be used as indicators of liberalisation. But to focus on the decline and ignore the 'non-liberal' remainder (or dismiss it as a brake on what would otherwise have been even better performance) is to be unduly partial. The concern of the neoclassical accounts to demonstrate the *fact* of liberalisation has detracted attention from the character and degree of liberalisation. Taiwan in 1958 was an exceptionally 'unliberal' economy (by capitalist standards), and quite a lot of liberalisation could take place without its becoming a recognisably liberal one.

There is another kind of evidence that might be used to support the same conclusion. Very little is known about class formation in Taiwan. But it seems likely that *no* significant change took place around the time of the liberalising reforms in the strength of various classes, or in their relationship to the state. *If* there were signs of the ascendancy of the middle classes, then one might take this as grounds for believing that a real and substantial curbing of domestic political authority over the economy took place, as Kindleburger explains the rise of free trade in Western Europe during the nineteenth century (Kindleburger, 1975, cited in Ruggie, 1982, p. 385). There are no such signs.

Causes of Export Growth

If the economy remained throughout the export boom far from 'liberal', then the role of liberalisation in the explanation of the fast growth of exports must also be smaller. A whole series of conditions which existed prior to the reforms of 1958–62 helped to increase export supply elasticities, to enable suppliers to respond to new opportunities, and to make alternative uses of resources less profitable (financial dealings or luxury goods production, for example). 'Getting prices right' when little is being done to enable suppliers to respond, however rational and profit-seeking they may be, is like pushing on a piece of string.[15] Moreover, even with more 'distorted' incentives as between exporting and import, substitution, a capitalist Taiwan would still have had large amounts of trade, for reasons to do with its resource endowment, population size and pressure, and per capita income. Then there are the demand-side causes of export growth, to do not only with the propitious state of the international economy but also (particularly in the 1970s) with the geo-political role of Taiwan in the US's global security design (Yoffie, 1981). These several kinds of factors help explain why Taiwan was able to make an export promotion strategy work.

Causes of Prosperity and Structural Change

The fast growth of exports has been a very important reason for Taiwan's prosperity and structural change. Exports have transmitted allocative- and X-efficiency pressure through the whole economy; they have helped to keep production labour-intensive, to overcome the constraint of a small domestic market for domestic producers, and to prevent a reconcentration of income in the hands of a wealthy élite, which in Latin American countries has been allowed to happen partly because it generates a growing domestic market for domestic producers of consumer durables. More specifically, the high exposure of the economy to the international market has helped to discipline public sector interventions, especially the behaviour of public enterprises which, though mostly not export-oriented, are exposed to international competition indirectly through their sales to highly exposed downstream exporters.

Granted all this, the role of the foreign sector in Taiwan's development has still been exaggerated. Notice first that 'exports' are not just any exports; they are *manufactured* exports. If the same volume of foreign exchange had been earned by exports of natural resources, it is doubtful whether the same dynamic effects would have followed – a point which is obscured when other countries are urged to adopt an export orientation *per se*. Second, the immediate reason for the country's widespread prosperity is high employment. Manufactured exports have been a big help in generating employment, being on the whole more labour-intensive than home market production. But if in 1969 only 17 per cent of the workforce could be classed as employed directly or indirectly in export production, it is difficult to argue that exports were the *necessary* condition for rapid employment growth. Other countries with bigger domestic markets could expect a similar employment-led prosperity with a much smaller export sector, *if* they can keep manufacturing both labour-intensive and dynamic (Sen, 1981). More generally, the foreign sector has influenced only indirectly, and probably not decisively, many variables important for growth and prosperity – the land reform, the productivity of non-export agriculture, decisions to save, or to invest in education, the allocation of large parts of the economy's investment fund.[16]

Thirdly, the government has been an important source of 'exogenous' structural change, adding to and guiding changes generated 'endogenously' by fast export growth and changes in international market conditions. Fast export growth was very important in generating high profits which could be channelled into new technologies and industries. But this channelling of investible resources into productive activity within Taiwan, and specifically into industries higher up the product cycle, did *not* occur only via self-regulating markets. The government has sought to accelerate and guide capital accumulation in certain lines of activity, using both direct and indirect methods. By doing so it has sought to change the composition of exports, to shift upwards into the 'second generation' range of high technology engineering products, as well as create a solid base of heavy and chemical industries within Taiwan. On the whole it relies upon firms to respond because they see a chance of good profits, rather than because they are ordered or cajoled. But it is active in making sure that the particular activities it wishes to encourage are – within limits – profitable. The government has made the trade regime consistent with these import substituting or industry-creating intentions. Another country, equally opened to trade and trading in the same kinds of products, would probably not have had the same benefits from trade if it had used different instruments and institutions – notably if it attempted to pursue *laissez-faire* policies.

Since the late 1950s, then, the government has done two outstandingly important kinds of things. One, which is the focus of the neoclassical accounts, is to remove the anti-export bias and promote exports by other measures. The second, which has received hardly any attention in the literature, is selective promotion of certain industries and specific products. The government has identified certain key sectors which are of special importance for the economy's future growth – either to reduce the economy's vulnerability to foreign (especially Japanese) suppliers, or to generate a higher value-added, more income elastic, more closely interlinked set of productive activities. It has then recognised that where a large commitment of capital or time is required in production, prices and profits cannot be left to the vagaries of the market. Otherwise these key investments may not be made and a higher than desirable portion of the economy's investment will go into quick return projects. Individual firms on their own may be more inclined to stick within a narrow range of familiar product lines than branch into new industries and economic activities. A powerful 'exogenous' (non-market) force is needed to favour such shifts, to make sure that long-term investment plans are not abandoned in the face of short-term fluctuations in international markets.

By helping to provide relatively stable market conditions for selected domestic sectors, the state has attempted to ensure that investment in these key sectors is undertaken on a sufficiently large scale to capture the economies of scale within the national unit. By giving various incentives closely tied to particular high-performance products it has attempted to ensure that domestic producers upgrade their technology. By influencing the composition of national investment it has attempted to coordinate the development of backwards and forwards linkages to ensure that external economies from any one activity are also captured within the national unit. If one accepts that economies of scale and external economies are major sources of technological advance and productivity increase, the efforts of the state to make sure that market conditions and uncertainties do not obstruct their realisation within Taiwan take on great importance in explaining the country's industrialisation.

But state interventions have been very selective between firms and industries. The non-strategic sectors have been more or less ignored: the discriminatory nature of state intervention is taken for granted as much as the opposite is taken for granted in Britain or the US, where the declaration that an economic policy is discriminatory is an act of condemnation.

Interventions have also been subject to the criterion of international competitiveness. By being able to control the quantities of goods crossing the national boundary, the state has been able to use the threat of allowing imports to discipline the price-setting of domestic producers. Trade and industrial policies in Taiwan thus answer both to the need to keep the economy exposed to efficiency-enhancing pressure from the world market, and to the need to modulate that pressure so as to capture more value-added and more of the cumulative benefits of technological change within Taiwan. One might hypothesise that policies have been able to answer effectively to both needs because, as one important reason, the structure of basic prices has been kept relatively undistorted. In this context, government promotion policies may have been more effective in shifting resource allocation than if basic prices had been deliberately distorted. To repeat, the neoclassical explanation is not so much wrong as misleadingly incomplete, as though cutting paper were to be explained in terms only one blade of the scissors.

Effects

But how do we know that all this promoting and guiding activity by the state has really helped? Would not the free market have done it better? Are not those who think otherwise like the cock who crowed at first light and believed it had brought on the dawn (to echo Jacques Rueff's epithet for French planners)? Taiwan's hundreds of professional economists have shown little interest in researching the impact of industrial policies, preferring to believe that virtually all interventions are contrary to nature and to be deplored. Foreign economists have tended to be of the same persuasion. It is extraordinary how little evidence exists. One can show that substantial amounts of resources have been affected by industry-bias policies.[17] This tells us that the policies were not merely cosmetic, but says nothing about specific allocative *effects*. But even if we cannot say that the policies have been in some sense 'optimal', or even that the benefits have outweighed the costs, we can at least say that the policies have had the intention of channelling resources into certain lines (and scales) of production, *and* that they have accompanied one of the most successful industrialisations on record. In that sense they have 'worked'. In the same sense, similar policies seem to have worked in South Korea and Japan (Westphal, 1978, p. 265). On the other hand, the case of post-Allende Chile suggests that free market policies, close to those which the neoclassical explanation says were followed in Taiwan, have *not* been terribly successful. The onus is then on those who say that the industrial policies used in Taiwan had a negligible (even harmful) role to show that the effects were quite different to the intention. Until that is done, Taiwan cannot readily be used to support the case that free trading principles, and a government restricted to law and order, infrastructure and macro balance, are always best for generating mass prosperity. Sometimes best, maybe; but not always best, and the crucial question is what makes the difference.

If development strategy in Taiwan has been defined by state officials, if state officials have steered market forces so as to create the kind of production structure which they think Taiwan should have, then the question of the basis, organisation and operation of state authority becomes exceedingly important. Given that not a few states are little more than instruments of plunder on behalf of a small group of officials, politicians and military, why has the state in Taiwan deployed its power benignly rather than malignly?[18] How has the use of public power been disciplined? How autonomous is the state from interest groups, from the owners and managers of capital? What are the less visible patterns of influence between state officials, and the leaders of public and private enterprise? How is state guidance of the market institutionalised? What criteria have state officials used to make their judgements about which industries and products to encourage? Why have economists had so little role in economic policy formulation (other than in monetary policy)? How are all these schemes administered? With how much corruption? And so on. My concern has been to show that these questions do have to be addressed if Taiwan's remarkable industrialisation is to be understood, because the neoclassical explanation in terms of self-regulating markets is not adequate.

Notes

1. Field-work in Taiwan for five months in 1983. My thanks to Professor Paul K. C. Liu, of the Institute of Economics, Academia Sinica, to Marnix Wells, David Sainsbury, and colleagues at the Institute of Development Studies for help without which the research could not have been made. Mick Moore and Susan Joekes, colleagues in Taiwan at the same time, helped sharpen the argument; so too did Larry Westphal. Many scholars, officials and businessmen in Taiwan gave generously of their time; Julius Hung and Henry Whang helped to lift the veil. This chapter is based on part of a larger manuscript, provisionally titled *Guiding the Market: Taiwanese Industrial Policies*, which says much more about institutions and politics than space permits here.

   From Bernard Schaffer I first and most clearly heard the distinction between market and bureaucratic or authoritative allocation. From him I first heard intelligently argued the view that in matters of the social rather than the natural world there are no neat, final solutions analogous to the theorems of the natural sciences. Both ideas underlie the argument made here. He died in May 1984, and I offer this chapter as a tribute to his memory.

2. Detailed accounts of Taiwan's economic performance are plentiful. For starters, Galenson (ed.) (1979) is probably the best single source; also Hsiung *et al.* (eds) (1981), Galli (1980), Ho (1978), Fei *et al.* (1979), Ranis (1978), Lin (1979), Hsing (1971). Ho (1981) makes a very useful comparison between Taiwan and South Korea. Good statistics are available from the Council For Economic Planning and Development, which publishes an annual Taiwan Statistical Data Book. The data in this paragraph comes mostly from the latter.

   I have little sympathy for the 'impossibility' theorems of crude dependency and imperialism theories; or the related arguments that since the comparative advantage of Taiwanese suppliers to the world market is based on super-exploitation of cheap (often female) labour under the aegis of an authoritarian, non-democratic government which permits no organisation of the working class, Taiwan scores minus 100 on the scale of human progress, end of story. See Wade 1982, chs 1 and 7; Amsden, 1979.

3. For another statement of the neoclassical explanation, see Balassa (1971). The literature on Taiwan and South Korea is very prone to what might be called the Helleiner effect. 'Once in the difficult world of policy formulation, [or in the context of drawing lessons from success stories] students of economics are prone to forget all of the qualifications and assumptions, and frequently apply instead the simplest and crudest versions of the models they were taught. . . One of the certain consequences of the use of crude theory is the tendency to apply "standard recipes" to all situations which appear roughly similar' (1981, p. 541). To see the end product of this process of bowdlerisation, take *The Economist* (1983) on 'How not to develop', which contrasts the bad 'neo-Uruguayan' recipe for non-development with the 'neo-Taiwanese' recipe for development. I hope that the present chapter makes it a little more difficult to propagate such caricatures of Taiwan without challenge.

4. I shall use state, government and party more or less interchangeably, and therefore loosely.

5. Of course the neoclassical argument as I have summarised it leaves out much else in addition to the role of the state. First, the condition of the international economy, to which I refer briefly later. A second is what Myint calls institutional infrastructure, meaning chiefly marketing, credit, technical information, sub-contracting and quality control (1982, p. 120). A third set of factors has to do with the entrepreneurial ability of Taiwanese businessmen, size of firms, production organisation, competitive strategies, and the like.

   On the role of the state in Taiwan's development, the seminal article is Amsden (1979); Hofheinz and Calder (1982) is also valuable.

6. But cf. Chiu (1982, p. 431), who talks of the 'high equity position' of Taiwan's private manufacturing enterprises. He calculates an equity to total assets ratio of about 39 per cent over the 1970s. Bankers in

Taiwan tend to take as a rule of thumb an equity figure of a quarter to one-third.

7. There was in fact a long dispute between two major factions within the higher levels of government, one of which gave higher priority to monetary stability, public enterprises, and heavy industry. The 1958–62 liberalising reforms were the direct result of the victory of the other group, led by Chen Cheng and his economic adviser, K. Y. Yin, who is now hailed as the architect of Taiwan's industrialisation. I owe this information to R. H. Silin.

8. In a sample of 41 LDCs (with population greater than 10 million), Reynolds finds that even by 1980 the median share of manufacturing to GNP (note the different base to the figure given in the text) is 16 per cent, and only 12 countries reach the 20–30 per cent range (1983, p. 972). Manufacturing/NDP for Taiwan in 1980 was 34 per cent (CEPD, 1982, Table 3-7b).

9. Since Little does not give a source, it is not possible to explain the discrepancy with his figures. Official statistics suggest that government *consumption* (rather than expenditure) did fall as a share of GDP (constant prices) between 1963 and 1973, from 23.1 to 15.9 per cent, but declined little thereafter (CEPD, 1982, Table 3-8c). On the other hand, Pathirane and Blades's cross-country comparison suggests that government consumption as a share of GDP did *not* fall between 1965 and 1978, oscillating between 15 and 18 per cent. Even if government consumption did fall relatively, it remained not unusually low after the fall.

10. It is true, though, that the share of public enterprises in manufacturing output has declined sharply, from over half in 1952 to 21 per cent in 1970, to 14 per cent by 1980. In Reynolds's sample of 41 LDCs the public sector share of manufacturing is 'often', he says, in the 20–25 per cent range (1973, p. 973). Taiwan's figure was in this range during 1968–70, before when it was higher, since when it has been lower.

11. A few more figures on trade to supplement those given earlier. 'Dependence' in trade is high. For most of the period since the early 1960s, 55–60 per cent of trade has been with only two countries – the US and Japan. Commodity concentration is quite high, too: textiles and electrical goods account for about half of total exports (55 per cent in 1972, 49 per cent in 1981). Taiwan runs a big balance of trade surplus with the United States, and a big deficit with Japan, from where it imports a large proportion of its intermediate and capital goods. managing the trade surpluses and deficits with these two countries has been a major preoccupation of the central decision-makers.

12. If I had not already seen Westphal's brief discussion of it I might well have missed it (1978). I am grateful to Martin Fransman for drawing the paper to my attention.

13. Little, Scitovsky and Scott's countries included Taiwan, Argentina, Brazil, Mexico, India, Pakistan, Philippines.

14. In their 587 item price comparison, 39 per cent of the items had domestic prices *lower* than world market prices, and in 65 per cent of these cases (25 per cent of the whole sample) they set the rate of

nominal protection at zero, on the assumption that the domestically-produced item was of lower quality than the world-market-traded item. The alternative decision would be to exclude these items from the survey on the grounds that the halves of the pair are not the same item, except where it could be established that the lower domestic price was just compensated for by lower quality. That would have raised the average level of protection.

15. I take this point from Michael Lipton, personal communication.
16. Here I follow Diaz-Alejandro's formulation of the same argument in the Latin American context (1983, p. 47).
17. To take just two indicators: In 1973 the ratio of total tariff exemptions to total government revenue was 16 per cent, compared with 1.9 per cent in Thailand for the same year (Sricharaychanya, 1983). The ratio of business income tax exemptions under the five year tax holiday alone, to total tax revenue, equalled 3.2 per cent in 1976; while in the Philippines, *total* tax exemptions under the Investment Incentive Act amounted to 2.1 per cent of total tax revenue in 1975 (Sricharaychanya, 1983).
18. That the government uses state power benignly rather than malignly is of course meant relatively. There is not much doubt that some very senior members of the party-government have used their positions in the state to handsomely enrich themselves. There is also no doubt that the government has abused basic civil liberties in its treatment of opponents. Surveillance by the garrison command and other intelligence services is close, in Taiwan and overseas. And local Taiwanese are only gradually taking a sprinkling of top posts in the Mainlander-dominated government. If one puts these things in comparative perspective, I suggest that the proposition about benign use of state power still stands.

References

Amsden, A. (1979) 'Taiwan's Economic History: a Case of Etatisme and a Challenge to Dependency Theory', *Modern China*, 5(3), pp. 341–80.

Balassa, B. (1971) 'Industrial Policies in Taiwan and Korea', *Weltwirtschaftliches Archiv.*, 106(1), pp. 55–77.

Balassa, B. in association with J. Berlinski *et al.* (1982) *Development Strategies in Semi-industrial Economics* (Baltimore, for World Bank: Johns Hopkins University Press).

Barclay, G. (1954) *Colonial Development and Population in Taiwan* (Princeton University Press).

Buzo, A. (1981) 'North Korea – Yesterday and Today', *The Royal Asiatic Society Korea Branch*, 56, pp. 1–25.

CEPD (Council for Economic Planning and Development) (1982) *Taiwan Statistical Data Book* (Taipei).

Chen, E. K. Y. (1979) *Hyper-growth in Asian Economics: A Comparative Study of Hong Kong, Japan, Korea, Singapore and Taiwan* (London: Macmillan).

Chen, G. (1982) 'The Reform Movement among Intellectuals in Taiwan Since 1970', *Bulletin of Concerned Asian Scholars*, 14(3), pp. 32–54.

China Credit Information Service (1981) *Top 500: The Largest Industrial Corporations in the Republic of China 1981* (Taipei). (Refers to 1980 data.)

Chiu, P. C. H. (1982) 'Performance of Financial Institutions in Taiwan', Proceedings of Conference on *Experiences and Lessons of Economic Development in Taiwan* (Institute of Economics, Academia Sinica, Taipei, 18–20 Dec. 1981).

DGBAS (Director-General of Budget, Accounts and Statistics) (1983) *Monthly Bulletin of Labor Statistics* (Republic of China, May, Taipei).

Diaz-Alejandro, C. (1983) 'Open Economy, Closed Polity?', in D. Tussie (ed.), *Latin America in the World Economy: New Perspectives* (London: Gower).

Djang, T. K. (1977) *Industry and Labor in Taiwan*, Monograph Series No. 10 (Institute of Economics, Academia Sinica, Taipei).

The Economist (1983) 'How not to develop', April 30, p. 89.

Fajnzylber, F. (1981) 'Some Reflections on South-east Asian Export Industrialisation', *CEPAL Review*, no. 15, pp. 111–32, December.

Fei, J. C. H. (1983) 'Evolution of Growth Policies of NICs in a Historical and Typological Perspective', paper to conference on Patterns of Growth and Structural Change in Asia's Newly Industrializing Countries (NICs) and Near-NICs in the Context of Economic Interdependence, April 3–8, East-West Center, Honolulu.

Fei, J., G. Ranis and S. Juo (1979) *Growth with Equity: the Taiwan Case* (Oxford University Press).

Fong, H. D. (1968) 'Taiwan's Industrialization, with Special Reference to Policies and Controls', *Journal of Nanyang University*, vol. 2, pp. 365–425.

Galenson, W. (ed.) (1979) *Economic Growth and Structural Change in Taiwan: The Postwar Experience of the Republic of China* (Cornell University Press).

Galenson, W. (1982) 'How to Develop Successfully – the Taiwan Model', Proceedings of Conference on *Experiences and Lessons of Economic Development in Taiwan* (Institute of Economics, Academia Sinica, Taipei, 18–20 Dec. 1981).

Galli, A. (1980) *Taiwan: Economic Facts and Trends* (IFO Development Research Studies, Weltforum Verlag, Munchen).

Gates, H. (1979) 'Dependency and the Part-Time Proletariat in Taiwan', *Modern China*, 5(3).

Helleiner, G. (1981) 'The Refsnes Seminar: Economic Theory and North-South Negotiations', *World Development*, 9(6).

Heller, P. and Tait, A. (1984) *Government Employment and Pay: Some International Comparisons*, Occasional paper No. 24 (March), (Washington, DC: IMF).

Ho, S. (1978) *Economic Development of Taiwan, 1860–1970* (Yale University Press).

Ho, S. (1981) 'South Korea and Taiwan: Development Prospects and Problems in the 1980s', *Asian Survey*, 21(12), December.

Hofheinz, R. and K. Calder (1982) *The Eastasian Edge* (New York: Basic Books).

Hsing, M.-H. (1971) *Taiwan: Industrialisation and Trade Policies* (Oxford University Press).

Hsiung, J. *et al.* (eds) (1981) *Contemporary Republic of China: The Taiwan Experience* (The American Association for Chinese Studies and Praeger, New York).

Jacobs, B. (1978) 'Paradoxes in the Politics of Taiwan: Lessons for Comparative Politics', *Politics*, 13(2), pp. 239–47.

Jacobs, B. (1980) 'Taiwan 1979: "Normalcy" after "Normalization"', *Asian Survey*, 20(1).

Jacobs, B. (1981) 'Political Opposition and Taiwan's Political Future', *The Australian Journal of Chinese Affairs*, 6, pp. 21–44.

Jacoby, N. (1966) *US Aid to Taiwan: a Study of Foreign Aid, Self-Help and Development* (New York: Praeger).

Johnson, C. (1982) *MITI and the Japanese Miracle: The Growth of Industrial Policy, 1925–1975* (Stanford University Press).

Jones, L. and Mason, E. (1982) 'The Role of Economic Factors in Determining the Size and Structure of the Public Enterprise Sector in Less Developed Countries with Mixed Economies, in L. Jones (ed.), *Public Enterprises in Less Developed Countries* (New York: Cambridge University Press).

Kindleberger, C. (1975) 'The Rise of Free Trade in Western Europe, 1820–1875', *J. of Economic History*, 35 (March).

Krauss, M. (1978) *The New Protectionism: The Welfare State and International Trade* (New York: New York University Press).

Lee, T. H. and K-S. Liang (1982) 'Taiwan', in Balassa *et al.*, *Development in Semi-industrial Economies*, Ch. 10.

Liang, C. and M. Skully (1982) 'Financial Institutions and Markets in Taiwan', in M. Skully (ed.), *Financial Markets and Institutions in the Far East: A Study of China, Hong Kong, Japan, South Korea and Taiwan* (London: Macmillan).

Lin, C.-Y. (1979) *Industrialization in Taiwan, 1946–72: Trade and Import-Substitution Policies for Developing Countries* (New York: Praeger).

List, F. (1966 (1885)) *The National System of Political Economy* (New York: Augustus Kelley).

Little, I. M. D. (1979) 'The Experience and Causes of Rapid Labour-Intensive Development in Korea, Taiwan, Hong Kong and Singapore; and the Possibilities of Emulation, ARTEP (Asian Region Team for Employment Promotion), ILO–ARTEP WPII–1, Bangkok, February.

Little, I., T. Scitovsky, M. Scott (1970) *Industry and Trade in Some Developing Countries: A Comparative Study* (New York: Basic Books).

Lundberg, E. (1979) 'Fiscal and Monetary Policies', in Galenson (ed.).

Mezzetti, F. (1982) 'North Korea and its Divine Kim Il Sung', *Asian Wall St. J.*, 8 Dec.

Myers, R. (1983) 'The Contest Between Two Chinese States', *Asian Survey* 23(4), April.

Myint, H. (1982) 'Comparative Analysis of Taiwan's Economic Development with Other Countries', *Proceedings of Conference on Experiences and Lessons of Economic Development in Taiwan* (Institute of Economics, Academia Sinica, Taipei, 18–20 Dec. 1981).

Myrdal, G. (1960) *Beyond the Welfare State* (Yale University Press).

Ouchi, T. (1967) 'Agricultural Depression and Japanese Villages', *The Developing Economies*, 5(4), pp. 597–627.

Pathirane, L. and D. Blades (1982) 'Defining and Measuring the Public Sector: Some International Comparisons', *Rev. of Income and Wealth*, 28(3), Sept., pp. 261–89.

Pluta, G. (1979) 'Wagner's Law: Public Sector Patterns and Growth of Public Enterprises in Taiwan', *Public Finance Quarterly*, VII(1), pp. 25–46.

Ranis, G. (1978) 'Equity with Growth in Taiwan: How "Special" is the "Special Case"?', *World Development*, 6(3).

Reynolds, L. (1983) 'The Spread of Industrialisation to the Third World: 1850–1980', *J. Economic Literature*, 21(3), Sept.

Ruggie, J. G. (1982) 'International Regimes, Transitions and Change: Embedded Liberalism in the Postwar Economic Order', *International Organisation*, Spring 36(2), 379–416.

Sandeman, H. (1982) 'Taiwan – an Island on its Own', *Economist*, 31 July.

Sen, A. K. (1981) 'Public Action and the Quality of Life in Developing Countries', *Oxford Bulletin of Economics and Statistics* 43(4), pp. 287–319.

Short, R. (1983), *The Role of Public Enterprises: An International Statistical Comparison*, Department Memo Series 83–84 (Washington, DC: IMF).

Silin, R. (1976) *Leadership and Values: the Organization of Large-Scale Taiwanese Enterprises* (Harvard University Press).

Sricharaychanya, P. (1982) 'Investment-Hospitality Can Hurt', *Far Eastern Economic Review*, Hong Kong, 12 May.

Sun, Chen (1981) 'Inflation, Trade and Economic Growth', *Industry of Free China*, May.

Tanzer, A. (1982) 'Charge of the Bright Brigade', *Far Eastern Economic Review*, 20 April.

Ting, W.-L. and Chi Schive (1981) 'Direct Investment and Technology Transfer from Taiwan', in Kumar, Krishna and Maxwell McLeod (eds), *Multinationals from Developing Countries* (Lexington, Mass.: D. C. Heath).

Tyler, W. G. (1974) 'Employment Generation and the Promotion of Manufactured Exports in Less Developed Countries: Some Suggestive Evidence', in H. Giersch (ed.), *The International Division of Labour: Problems and Perspectives* (Tubingen: J. C. B. Mohr).

Wade, R. H. (1982) *Irrigation and Agricultural Politics in South Korea* (Boulder, Colorado: Westview Press).

Wang, Y. C. (1966) *Chinese Intellectuals and the West 1872–1949* (University of North Carolina Press).

Westphal, L. (1978) 'Industrial Incentives in the Republic of China (Taiwan)', mimeo (World Bank).

Wolf, C. (1981) 'Economic Success, Stability, and the "Old" International Order', *International Security*, 6(1), pp. 75–92.

World Bank (1981) *World Development Report 1981* (Washington DC).

World Bank (1983) *World Development Report 1983* (Washington DC).

Yoffie, D. (1981) 'The Newly Industrializing Countries and the Political

Economy of Protectionism', *International Studies Quarterly* 25(4), pp. 569–99.

Yu, T.-S. (1981) 'Foreign Trade and Export Instability', *Academic Economic Papers* 9(1), Sept, pp. 69–86.

3 State Intervention and Export-oriented Development in South Korea
Richard Luedde-Neurath

INTRODUCTION

The aim of this chapter is to contribute to the debate about the role of the state in industrial development through an examination of South Korea, which has been widely heralded as a case supporting the *opponents* of state intervention. Our research suggests, however, that the South Korean experience has been seriously misrepresented. Contrary to earlier contentions, Korea has in fact resorted extensively to 'directive' forms of state intervention over the last two decades.[1] The view taken is that the Korean experience supports the *advocates* of directive state intervention in market economics.

The chapter is divided into four sections: the first challenges the argument that South Korea pursued a liberal, market-oriented development strategy. The second and third take a more general look at directive state intervention in a number of selected key areas of the Korean economy. On the one hand, we explore how the state intervened in Korea's domestic economy through case studies of industrial policy, financial and market price intervention. On the other hand, we investigate how the state intervened in Korea's economic links with the global economy through case studies of trade; foreign exchange and foreign direct investment policy; the treatment of foreign banks and the control of technology transfer. The fourth section embarks on a more general discussion of state intervention in Korea, attempting to throw some light on the question of how and why state intervention worked in Korea.

I. SOUTH KOREA AS A LIBERAL MARKET ECONOMY: A CRITIQUE

Much of the argument that Korea's success is attributable to 'liberal market' policies can be traced to the claim that its import regime was liberal, thus allowing international market signals to guide the Korean economy towards specialisation in accordance with comparative advantage. Import controls are of crucial importance in this context, given that they act as a 'gateway' for international price signals. In an economy fully exposed to international markets, the scope for directive state intervention would be extremely limited. Hence, for the debate on directive state intervention as a whole, it is important to evaluate the validity of such claims about Korea's import regime.[2]

Accepted wisdom among free market advocates about Korea's import regime may be summed up as follows. Whereas in the late 1950s and early 1960s Korea pursued a highly restrictive trade regime, a number of reforms were undertaken about 1964 to allow much greater exposure to international market forces. Among these was a major currency devaluation and a significant liberalisation of imports. The number of importable items was greatly expanded, and quantitative controls in particular were reduced. The process culminated in the switch from the 'positive' to the 'negative' import list system in 1967. By 1968, quantitative controls were virtually insignificant, domestic prices were relatively undistorted (i.e. very close to their international counterparts), the incentive system was approximately 'neutral' between production for exports and production for the domestic market, and exporters were operating virtually under a 'free trade' regime.[3]

Such accounts are based on two types of empirical analyses: one involving general reviews of Korea's trade policy during the mid to late 1960s, such as those by Balassa (1971, p. 62), Kim (1974, p. 35), Frank *et al* (1975, p. 48) and Krueger (1979, p. 92); the other involving highly disaggregated protection analyses for a selected year using 'direct price comparison surveys', namely by Westphal and Kim (1977).

Overall, the lesson extracted from the Korean experience is that 'Korea provides an almost classic example of an economy following its comparative advantage of reaping the gains predicted by conventional economic theory' (Westphal, 1978, p. 29). In view of the spectacular growth and export record, the policy of liberalisation is singled out as a key variable explaining Korea's success (Lal, 1983, p. 46). More generally, the Korean experience appears to support those academics who believe that market forces should be left to allocate international and domestic resources (for example, Westphal, 1978, p. 29).

In response to arguments that the policy was not as liberal as this (Hong, 1979, ch. 5; Kuznets, 1977, p. 153; Datta-Chaudhuri, 1979, pp. 23–5; Sen, 1981, pp. 297–9, even Westphal, 1981), liberal market advocates have suggested, first, that those 'interventionist spots' (Lal, 1983, p. 32) which did remain in countries like Korea were not widespread – success in Korea was achieved despite rather than because of directive state intervention (Lal, 1983, p. 46); and second, that import controls in Korea were counterbalanced (and thereby neutralised) by export incentives (Lal, 1983, p. 47). Overall, therefore, the assertion that there exists a close link between the Korean success and its liberal trade regime was maintained, especially when making recommendations to other countries (Lal, 1983, p. 32).

Flaws in the Liberal Market Case

Is it correct to claim that there was a significant move towards import liberalisation in the mid to late 1960s in Korea? Did the switch from the 'positive' to the 'negative' list classification system really mark a significant step towards import liberalisation? Are Westphal and Kim (1977) correct to claim that by 1968 quantitative import controls were relatively unimportant? Let us consider each question in turn, I have discussed these questions in more detail elsewhere (Luedde-Neurath 1986) and will only summarise my arguments here.

The liberalisation 1965–7

The evidence usually cited when making the claim that imports were liberalised after 1964 is the number of items that became importable, or even automatically approved for import, during the time in question. However, several factors undermine the significance of this case. First, it would not be fair to take January 1965 as the point of departure for analysing Korea's import liberalisation, as Balassa does (1971, p. 62). Until May of 1965 at least, the change was essentially a return to the level of liberalisation attained in the early 1960s. This adjustment reduces the extent of the observed liberalisation but by no means annuls it, given that the number of importable items still more than doubled between May 1965 and July 1967 (from 1588 to 3852 items). Second, the impact of the reported import liberalisation was partially counteracted by the expansion in scope of the 'Provisional Special Customs Duties Law'. The number of import items it covered rose from 587 to 2702 during 1965 (*EPB Economic Survey*, 1966, p. 90) and during 1966 it played an 'important role in curbing indirectly the excessive import demands caused by the import liberalisation' (Bank of Korea, 1966, p. 83). Third, and most important, the impact of import liberalisation was limited by the maintenance of extremely tight foreign exchange controls. Access to foreign exchange was restricted predominantly to those earning it, making it difficult for exclusively 'domestic market oriented' firms to import. Moreover, the value of composition of total imports was fixed semi-annually in accordance with Korea's 'Foreign Exchange Requirement Programme' (Luedde-Neurath, 1964, p. 74). The implication of this programme was that even 'freely importable' import items were approved only within limits predetermined through the foreign exchange control system, a fact which appears to have escaped many writers on import liberalisation in Korea.

Despite these limitations, it is probably still correct to assert that import liberalisation occurred in Korea between 1965 and 1967. We would contend, however, that the extent of liberalisation has been much exaggerated and that it was a managed liberalisation, under the auspices and ultimate control of the government. It was certainly not a shift in policy which conceded the determination of either of the import volume or import composition to market forces.

The reorganisation of trade lists in 1967
Did the switch from the positive to the negative list import system in July 1967 constitute a 'major' step towards import liberalisation?

According to Frank and colleagues, the liberalisation in question was indeed massive. By SITC 7-digit classication (30 000 items) the old system restricted 26 484 items, and the new one only 12 872 (1975, p. 58). Thus, the liberalisation ratio – by item – rose from 11.7 per cent to 57.1 per cent literally overnight.

There are three problems with this analysis. First, these authors fail to realise that the old and new listings used different classification systems (for a detailed analysis, see Luedde-Neurath, 1985, fn. 4). This error leads Frank *et al.* vastly to overstate the liberalisation implied by the switch. Second, there is considerable doubt as to whether the switch was ever properly implemented other than by name. A contemporary business journal reported, for example, that the measure was opposed by the Ministry of Commerce and Industry (MCI) and was in fact reversed after the dismissal of Chang Key-Young, former minister of the Economic Planning Board (EPB) (*FEER*, Asia Yearbook, 1968, p. 311). Third, the reorganisation of trade lists in 1967 had a limited impact on imports, in fact a mere 4.6 per cent of total imports in 1967 and 1968 according to MCI estimates (Frank *et al.*, 1975, p. 58). Yet Frank *et al.* assert that the increase in imports directly attributable to the liberalisation represented 20 per cent of 1968 imports (1975, p. 58), thus making the import regime look more liberal than it was.

Despite the grand announcements and sweeping generalisations made at the time, the switch from the positive to the negative list system in 1967 was not a significant step towards liberalisation. Neither did the promised further steps in that direction in 1968 ever properly materialise.

Westphal and Kim's microstudy for 1968

More than any other study, Westphal and Kim's (W and K's) study of Korean import controls in 1968 has provided an empirical foundation for the liberal view of Korea's import policy. The authors rejected the use of legal tariffs and quantitative restrictions (QRs) for their analysis, relying instead on a specially commissioned 'direct price comparison' survey of domestic and international prices to estimate nominal rates of protection for Korea in 1968 (1977, Annex Table 1, col. 8).

This methodology contains problems which I have discussed in detail elsewhere (1985, pp. 103–8). The difficulties involved in attempting to convert direct price comparisons into estimates of nominal protection are formidable (Bhagwati, 1978, ch. 5). It follows that W and K's study should be treated with caution.

In particular, quality- and product-specification differentials among the items compared can generate inaccuracies; there is the problem of how to interpret 'prohibitive tariffs'; the wisdom of W and K's decisions to disregard legal tariff rates as indicators of protection and to dismiss quantitative restrictions as relatively unimportant. On the latter two points, for example, it is our view that both legal tariffs and quantitative restrictions were important and in fact made for a restrictive import regime in 1968. Taking the latter two types of controls together, we find that in 1968, 294 out of 396 commodities surveyed by W and K – or *74.2 per cent of the sample* – were subject either to quantitative import controls, to legal tariff rates of 60 per cent or more, or both (W and K, 1977, Appendix, Table 1).

We thus find that both tariff and non-tariff barriers were extremely important in Korea during the late 1960s. Though the authors did in fact refer to this point (W and K, 1977, pp. 3–58), their paper as a whole seeks to present quite the opposite picture of the Korean import regime.

In short, all the evidence used to suggest that Korea liberalised imports significantly during the 1960s is highly questionable. Since the supposedly liberal nature of the trade regime constitutes an important part of the picture of Korea as a liberal market economy, this wider picture is *ipso facto* put in doubt.

II. STATE INTERVENTION IN KOREA'S DOMESTIC ECONOMY

We now propose to illustrate the active role of the state in Korea through a number of case studies. We divide these into two broad categories, one dealing with state intervention in the domestic economy, the other dealing with state intervention in external economic relations.

Industrial policy

The most powerful challenge to the 'liberal market' characterisation of Korea to date has been Jones and Sakong's (1980) excellent study of the government's involvement in domestic industrial policy. They demonstrate that the state in Korea has not restricted itself to 'promotional' forms of intervention, and conclude:

> The 'Korean miracle' is not a triumph of laissez faire, but of a pragmatic non-ideological mixture of market and non-market forces. Where the market works, fine; where it doesn't, the government shows no hesitation in intervening by means that range from a friendly phone call to public ownership.   (1980, p. 3)

> In Korea, non-discretionary parameter manipulation has by no means been eschewed, but it has been heavily supplemented by the illiberal compliance mechanisms of command and administrative

discretion. Korea is thus interventionist in the broad sense of altering decisions of productive entities, but also in the narrower sense of using compulsion and discretion in doing so. (1980, p. 294)

This thesis can also be documented from a number of other sources. First, one can point to general evaluations made in various studies on Korea. C. Smith, for example, writes that 'Korea has had one of the "Free World's" most tightly supervised economies, with the Government initiating almost every major investment in the private sector and wielding enough power to ensure that companies which make such investment also make a profit' (1979a, p. 17). K. D. Kim notes that 'from the incipient effort for rudimentary industrialisation at the turn of the century up to the present, political factors have always played a crucial part in promoting or discouraging entrepreneurial ventures in Korea' (1979, p. 66). Studies by Cole (1979), Kang and Whang (1982), ILT (1980 and 1983), Lim (1981) or Kuznets (1977) also support the vision of Korea as a relatively tightly supervised economy.

The role of the state has been more precisely documented in a number of industry studies. Kim and Lee's (1980) study of the automotive industry illustrates how the government 'selected' firms to undertake particular activities, 'designated' certain parts and components for local production, 'allowed' specific new firms to enter the sector (1980, pp. 7–14, 44–6) and, how 'production volume was allocated according to the actual performance of the domestic content schedule' (1980, pp. 12, 45). In key industries at least, such intervention must be regarded as the rule rather than as an exception: for example, in electronics (Yu, 1982, p. 21), steel (Enos, 1984 or Yoh, 1982), machinery (Bendix *et al.*, 1978, pp. 62/80) and machine tools (Jacobson, 1983/84).

The state has also on occasion initiated major industrial restructuring programmes. For example, Chang (1980) documents the directive role of the state in the restructuring process of heavy and chemical industries since 1980,[3] which involved 'bold adjustment plans for automobiles, heavy electrical machinery, electronic switching systems, diesel engines and copper smelting as well as for power generation equipment' (1980, p. 16).

Even in 1983, when the government was ostensibly reducing its intervention in the economy, active state intervention in industrial policy could be observed: in order to foster the parts and components industry as a strategic export sector, the MCI announced that it would select one or two qualified makers for each one of 96 selected items for intensive support (*ACJ*, May/June 1983, pp. 32–3). In certain other sectors, notably electronics-, heavy construction- and power generating-equipment industries, the MCI announced it would restrict new entrants in order to ensure 'appropriate production coordination' (*ACJ*, May/June 1983, p. 21).

The above-mentioned evidence makes propositions to the effort that the state had merely a promotional function in the Korean economy untenable. We can consider the evidence conclusive: with respect to industrial policy at least, the Korean state has resorted extensively to directive intervention.

Financial Policy

Control over financial institutions has been a key element of state intervention in Korea, and must be viewed in relation to the fact that Korean firms depend heavily on borrowed funds. By European standards they are hopelessly undercapitalised, given that a firm's equity participation of 10 per cent is already considered high. Banks too are severely undercapitalised, facing interest rates fixed by the government, while competing with mutual savings unions, short-term finance corporations and the curb market for deposits. The latter offer much higher returns to investors, as a result of which the banks depend heavily on the government for operating funds (Nakarmi, 1984, p. 11).

From October 1961, when the government repossessed those shares of the commercial banks in private hands (Cole and Park, 1979, p. 56) to 1980, the government had virtually complete control over the entire financial system of Korea, primarily through its public ownership thereof (Kwack *et al.*, 1973). The government controlled the Bank of Korea, and virtually owned all five nation-wide commercial banks, the six special banks and two out of the three development institutions (the Korea Development Bank and the Export–Import bank). Throughout the 1960s and 1970s, the Ministry of Finance firmly directed the banking industry in Korea. Government control extended even to low-level personnel policy, hiring and firing, salary reviews and budgets. It also set credit ceilings for individual banks, controlled their operating funds and controlled interest rates (ILT 1980, p. 22; also Hong, 1978, p. 40, Sano, 1977, p. 52, ILT, 1980, p. 23 and ILT, 1983, p. 25).

There has recently been much talk about how the financial sector is being liberalised. It is easy to exaggerate this process, however, given that the banks still depend heavily on the government for operating funds, making them vulnerable to 'informal guidance'. Also, some reform provisions appear self-contradictory, seeking to combine both greater managerial independence and greater external supervision (Ensor, 1984, p. 81).

Extensive government intervention in the Korean financial market has been the rule rather than the exception, and is being reduced only very gradually. As Jones and Sakong put it: 'Government control of the banks is thus the single most important economic factor explaining the distinctly subordinate position of the private sector' (1980, p. 296).

Price Controls

Over the last three decades, the government has influenced prices not only through its control of public enterprises such as railways, transportation, electricity, coal, oil refining, and chemical fertilisers, but also by exerting pressure on selected private firms and agricultural producers. These controls have generally been referred to not as direct but as 'informal', in the sense that 'ceiling prices' were informally agreed between the producers' associations and the government.

The highest regulative authority has been the Economic Planning Board, assisted and advised by various ministries and *ad hoc* standing commissions (Chough, 1968, p. 57). Since 1976 the number of items controlled has ranged from 46 to 193 in any one year. A wide range of products is affected, including foods, industrial raw materials and intermediaries, consumer goods and transport equipment. The criteria for the selection of price-managed items include the importance of the product to 'people's lives', and the extent of its 'market domination', measured on the basis of a manufacturer's turnover and his market share.

Producers affected are required to report price increases to the EPB and the other relevant authorities within three days of a price increase. If the rise is deemed excessive, the government may punish them under the Price Stability Law and the Monopoly Regulation and Fair Trade Law. Violators face imprisonment of up to one year and fines up to 70 million *won*. The government has also threatened to admit more imports to combat excessive price increases.

Another interesting example of state intervention in prices was Korea's reponse to the global oil-price reductions of early 1983. Instead of handing on the decrease to consumers and industrialists, the government maintained prices and used the 'windfall' surplus to assist strategically important industries (electronics, machinery, shipbuilding, construction) and to promote energy conservation (Shiffman, *AWSJ*, 23 March, 1983, p. 1).

Whereas price controls were not always able to ensure price stability in Korea (C. Smith, 1979a), they were clearly important in shaping domestic market prices (Nam, 1981, p. 203).

III. STATE INTERVENTION AND OUTWARD ORIENTATION

The problem with the evidence on industrial policy, financial policy and price controls is that it does not confront the arguments of the 'liberal market view' directly. If the Korean economy was genuinely an 'open' one, then much of what has been said about the importance of intervention can be dismissed as irrelevant. In an open economy the scope for, and therefore the effectiveness of, directive intervention will be extremely limited. The earlier discussion raised doubts about the validity of studies claiming to show that Korea has had an open economy. We now take this discussion further, by exploring the extent to which the State has intervened in the economic relationship between Korea and the world economy. Again, we shall do this via a number of case studies covering key areas of this interaction: trade, foreign exchange control, foreign investment, banking and technology transfer.

Trade

While we cannot embark on detailed analysis of import controls here, we can point to a number of obstacles which have not generally received the attention they deserve.[4] We shall therefore minimise our comments on 'visible' controls such as quantitative restrictions (QRs) and published tariffs, and concentrate instead on other, less visible restrictions.

Trader licensing
Permission to engage in foreign trade is restricted to those parties holding a trader's licence. Eligibility for this licence is conditional

upon satisfactory export performance. Annual export requirements may be product-specific (e.g. pharmaceuticals), and may be subject to periodic, company or industry-specific revision.[5] Trader licences may also entail restrictions as to what types of products may be imported.

Informal pressures

The Korean government is currently placing much emphasis on so-called 'localisation rates'. The long list of items affected involves shipbuilding, computers, pharmaceuticals, motor vehicle manufacturing, farming implements, sewing machines, textile machinery, machine tools, electric home appliances, bulldozers, loaders etc.[6] The aim of such measures is to increase the domestic content of manufacturing output, and elaborate plans are adopted by the MCI and other government agencies to achieve set localisation targets. As a result, there exists strong and continuous pressure on manufacturers to procure an increasing share of their inputs domestically.

Very detailed plans are required by the authorities for project screening purposes. An assessment is made as to which parts of the project can be localised, and ultimately, a domestic ratio is specified. One recent example of this procedure is the construction of the Seoul subway, though practically all major construction projects are subject to such screening.

Quantitative controls

Quantitative controls in Korea, as published by the MCI in its export–import notices, are what one might call 'visible' restrictions. They generally take the form of 'discretionary licensing requirements', meaning that a special licence for import must be obtained from one or several designated agencies.[7]

But by no means everything which is classified as automatically approved for import in the MCI Export–Import notices in fact deserves that description. That is to say, apart from 'visible' restrictions there exist a considerable number of 'invisible' ones. At least four types of measures undermine or even contradict the Automatic Approval (AA) system.

(i) *Special laws*. Korea can boast an impressive array of special laws, often affecting items listed as AA by the MCI.[8] Our own estimates suggest that out of US\$14.2 bn of AA-classified imports in 1982, approximately US\$8.7 bn fell under one kind of special law or another (Luedde-Neurath, 1986, Tables 4.12, 8.12–8.14, and Table A.3). The implication of these laws is almost invariably that import permission must be obtained from a public agency, making the items affected subject to procedures not dissimilar to those governing restricted items.

(ii) *Import area diversification.* Korea has for many years now sought ways of curbing import flows from Japan. Since 1977 these efforts have taken the form of so-called 'Import Area Diversification' measures. Whereas many restricted items fall under this law, a large number of AA items are also affected. According to our estimates, about US\$ 2.1 bn worth of genuine AA imports (i.e. excluding those falling under special laws) fell under this provision in 1982 (Luedde-Neurath, 1986, Table A.4). The implication for importers is that they must obtain approval from the 'Korea Trading Agents Association' for items falling under this regulation, regardless of their origin. Again, this procedure is not dissimilar to that applying to restricted items.

(iii) *Surveillance measures.* These made their first appearance in mid-1978, and coincided with serious efforts to liberalise imports in Korea. According to official sources, 'Surveillance means that the Government monitors the effect of the liberalisation and will take the necessary action if the inflow of foreign goods is found to be causing serious problems to home-based suppliers'.[9] The products affected by surveillance measures were classified in the MCI Export–Import Notices as AA items, but listed in a separate appendix. Initially, the system was one of *ex-post* monitoring by the KTA and MCI. The system changed significantly in 1979, however, when the MCI announced that surveillance items now required *prior* approval from the 'Korea Trade Agents' Association'. The association now convenes a meeting twice a month, where import implications are considered on a case-by-case basis. In essence, therefore, the system is once again not dissimilar to that for restricted imports.

(iv) *End user imports.* Certain items, such as major raw materials, are designated 'end-user import items', even though they are generally classified as AA import items according to the Export–Import Notices. Raw cotton for example appears to be genuinely freely importable: it is classified as AA and does not fall under special laws, import area diversification or surveillance measures.[10] But if one takes a close look at how cotton imports are handled in Korea, one regularly encounters references to the 'Spinners and Weavers Association of Korea' (SWAK for short), which 'decides' to import certain amounts of cotton, and which specifies what share will be used for export and domestic production respectively. SWAK also allocates both KFX and credit funds, and cotton imports among its 21 members. Other cases in point concern sawlogs, raw hides and raw rubber.

Whenever rationing arrangements of the types described are invoked, market forces are over-ruled; instead of dealing with an AA import system, we are in fact witnessing quantitative controls on imports. The 'pressure point' in such a system derives from the fact that the government can legitimately curtail import plans that have been submitted, whenever it deems this necessary. These measures combine to make the published AA import lists rather deceptive indicators of what is 'freely importable' into Korea.

Inspection requirements

Import rules may also specify 'inspection requirements'. In June 1982, the 'Industry Advancement Administration' raised from 34 to 54 the number of items subject to its inspection for import, among them selected auto parts, machine tools, metallic, electric, and sundry goods. The fact that only items for sale on the domestic market are inspected gives rise to the suspicion that the aim of the inspection agency (as its name suggests) is to advance domestic industry. Similarly, the 'Fine Instruments Center' carries out inspections of textile machinery imports. As of July 1983, moreover, imports of finished pharmaceuticals required inspection by the National Health Institute prior to customs clearance. This coincided with the liberalisation of at least some pharmaceutical imports, raising the inevitable suspicion that such inspections were to be highly obstructive, 'Japanese style'.[11]

Advance deposits

Korea has resorted to advance deposits throughout the last two decades (though they were much de-emphasised after 1978), with the express purpose of 'suppressing the demand for imports, particularly of commodities considered luxurious or non essential' (KEB, 1973a, pp. 104–5).

Customs and excise duties

It is widely accepted that throughout the period under review, legal tariffs have been relatively high in Korea, particularly with respect to manufacturers (Hong, 1979, p. 100; Westphal and Kim, 1977, pp. 2–21). Tariff reforms have on the whole been marginal rather than substantial, though tariff restrictions have shown a tendency to decline over time. The government has traditionally maintained the right to raise tariffs by 50 percentage points and to invoke 30 per cent surcharge on imports quite legally without changes in the basic law. Instead of focusing on 'visible' published tariff rates, we propose to consider other, less predictable, charges a trader might be asked to pay.

To anyone familiar with the fact that tariffs in Korea do not currently exceed 150 per cent (formerly 200 per cent), even on the most luxurious of import items, it must come as somewhat of a surprise to hear references to 400 per cent duties on golfclubs, 500 per cent on French wines, and 933 per cent on imported whisky.

The explanation lies in an array of 'other' taxes which crawl out of the woodwork when the import of non-essential items is actually attempted: education tax, defence tax, special expense tax, etc. Their effect, in combination with high tariffs, is thoroughly to discourage undesirable imports.

This should clarify why the customs hurdle is reputed to be far from straightforward among practical businessmen operating in Korea. It also prompts us to be sceptical of moves towards import 'liberalisation'. While 'visible' tariff- and non-tariff barriers may in fact come down, this may not hold true for 'invisible' restrictions.

On the basis of the above survey it should be clear that the government directly or indirectly plays a crucial role at virtually all stages of the import cycle, controlling importers, imports, and the taxes levied upon imports.

Foreign Exchange

In Korea, foreign exchange regulations are extremely tight. Indeed, the Foreign Exchange Control Law has been described as one of the tightest in the world, and far more restrictive than the Trade Control Law.[12]

Our focus in this section is one the requirement that foreign exchange banks in Korea must approve the allocation of foreign funds for intended uses in accordance with the so-called Foreign Exchange Demand and Supply Plan. Many accounts of Korea's trade regime overlook the fact that imports involve both the flow of

products and funds. Any liberalisation of imports can be seriously
undermined if restrictions on the flow of funds to pay for them are
maintained.

The Foreign Exchange Demand and Supply Plan is established
annually by the Minister of Finance, and distinguishes both between
visible and invisible expenditures (or receipts) on the one hand, and
between government and private expenditures (or receipts) on the
other. The executive agencies are generally the foreign exchange
banks. The Plan is based on information supplied annually by the
various producers' associations on behalf of their members, often
specifying imports by type of funding and whether they are for
domestic or export use. Once the overall plan is finalised, it is the
associations which relay its content back to the producers and which
ration imports if necessary.

While this system can effectively cover major industrial inputs, it
is unlikely to work with respect to every possible import item,
particularly AA imports. But with banks to control foreign exchange
outflows, in fact it becomes possible to restrict any import type if
necessary, simply by instructing the banks to limit the issue of
licences for specified import types, whether restricted or AA.

Official statements make it clear that the Plan is not intended to
be merely indicative, but to have 'absolute binding force'. Annual
IMF reports between 1977 and 1982 testified to the Plan's role in
limiting imports.[13] Moreover, one lawyer interviewed confirmed
that, until the late 1970s at least, importers had to confirm the
availability of foreign exchange for intended purposes on an '*ex ante*'
basis through their banks.

Interesting also is a comparison of projected and actual foreign
exchange expenditures in Korea.[14] We see from Table 3.1 that the
Koreans planned their foreign exchange payments (current and
capital transactions) rather well. Over the eight years for which data
were obtainable, they kept to within 10 per cent of the original
payments plan in five (1972, 1974, 1976, 1977, 1978), and spent less
than planned in two years (1975, 1979). Only in 1973 – the year of
the oil crisis – did the payments plan give a totally misleading
indication of actual payments. On the receipt side, the Koreans
generally seemed to underestimate their actual income, except in
1975.

To achieve such impressively accurate results, Korean planners
must have been extremely competent at predicting the future,
extremely lucky, or they must have had ways of ensuring that the

Table 3.1   Planned versus actual foreign exchange payments in Korea: 1969–1979. Unit: US$ million

Year	Receipts			Payments		
	Planned	Actual	Index	Planned	Actual	Index
1969	1 175	—	—	1 240	—	—
1970	1 560	—	—	1 680	—	—
1971	—	—	—	—	—	—
1972	1 972	2 252	114.2	2 032	2 206	108.6
1973	2 592	4 358	168.1	2 507	5 041	201.1
1974	5 716	6 315	110.5	6 574	6 811	103.6
1975	7 239	7 219	99.7	7 924	6 957	87.8
1976	7 353	10 004	136.1	8 450	8 932	105.7
1977	11 907	12 803	107.5	12 780	12 592	98.5
1978	15 639	16 295	104.2	19 690	17 987	91.4
1979	22 065	22 225	100.7	31 560	23 261	73.7

Source: *Korea Annual*, various issues 1970–80.

Notes:
Planned=initial plan at the beginning of the relevant year.
Subsequent revisions are excluded.
Actual=refers to receipts/payments on a settlement basis.
Index=(planned receipts/payments=100).

constraints imposed by the plan in question are adhered to. The view taken here is that foreign exchange allocation via selected banks acted as a measure of this kind, together with others such as end-user import systems and more or less informal instructions to screening agencies.

The bottom line of our findings is not that the Foreign Exchange Supply and Demand Plan rigidly rationed foreign exchange for all imports at all times. Instead, it was used to set provisional ceilings on the use of foreign exchange. Whenever these were reached, senior government officials either reorganised the existing plan, expanded it, or restricted expenditures for lack of foreign exchange. The plan thus acted as a major tool to manage the balance of payments, and as an effective pressure point to restrict undesirable types of foreign exchange spending if and when necessary.

Foreign Direct Investment

South Korea's foreign direct investment policy, like its trade regime, is widely believed to have been extremely liberal (S. Kim, 1979,

p. viii, also Westphal *et al.*, 1979, pp. 365–6). The Korean government has actively promoted a 'liberal' image of its economy and its investment laws. A review of the Foreign Capital Inducement Law and its various enforcement decrees, however, casts doubt on such claims. We find that considerations with respect to management control, the balance of payments, technology transfer and employment loom large in the screening process. We also find an emphasis on ensuring the complementarity between foreign direct investment (FDI) and domestic firms in both export and domestic markets, and on ensuring the compatibility of such investments with Korea's development plans (Laws . . . 1979). It also transpires that Korea used a 'positive list' system with respect to FDI, according to which all sectors were closed to foreign investment unless otherwise specified (ILT, 1983 and MOF, 1982).

But are Korea's regulations anything unusual by international standards, and are they actually enforced in practice? The evidence is scant, but revealing. Some years ago the UN Centre on Transnational Corporations conducted a survey of investment legislation in selected LDCs. It found that:

(i) Out of 37 countries considered, only Korea and 10 others explicitly emphasised balance of payments considerations among their screening criteria.

(ii) Out of a sample of 36, only Korea and 8 others explicitly granted preferential consideration to joint ventures.

(iii) Out of 27 countries, only Korea and 2 others considered all investment areas closed unless otherwise specified. Indeed, 11 countries did not explicitly specify any restricted areas (UN, 1978, pp. 36–40).

We suggest therefore, that by international comparison Korea's legislation towards FDI does not stand out as particularly liberal, even if it is true that some types of investment have been granted very generous incentives.

Turning to the question of policy enforcement, a comparative survey of 187 US multinationals in 66 countries (Curhan, Davidson and Suri, 1977, p. 315) suggests that Korea has been relatively strict in enforcing its policy with respect to local participation in FDI. Out of all the investments made by these forms in Korea as of January 1976 (37 cases), only 29.7 per cent took the form of wholly owned subsidiaries. The corresponding share in Japan was 33.1 per cent and the average ratio for all countries in the sample was 69.1 per cent. Indeed, Koo calculates that Korea has the lowest share of wholly owned subsidiaries in the entire sample (1982, p. 38).

A case study of a major US pharmaceutical firm which considered but abandoned plans to invest in Korea suggests that a major stumbling block was precisely the tough negotiating stand taken by the Korean government (United States Council . . ., 1979, pp. 214–16). The firm confronted – in some cases unacceptable – demands with respect to local participation, management control, product specification, exports, technology transfer and duration of service fees.

Instructive is also the 'look behind the rhetoric' of Korea's investment policy by Coolidge, a businessman with extensive practical experience there. He argues that Korea made the 'eye of the needle' for FDI rather narrow, thereby making it fit with national priorities (1980, p. 376). Foreign investors were expected by their partners and by the Korean government to make a continuing contribution to Korean development, one which was complementary to, rather than at the expense of domestic manufacturing interests. In his view, the Korean government has been 'consistent and successful' in attracting the FDI it considered desirable.

Meanwhile, informal interviews conducted by the author in Seoul in 1982, and internal documents made available by foreign businessmen, suggest three basic realities of foreign investment in Korea:

(1) *Tight investment screening.* In Korea there exists a gap between the law on paper and in practice, which more often than not works against the foreign investor rather than in his favour. Most investment applications, though officially handled by the Ministry of Finance as the 'one stop' clearing agency, require the approval of various ministries. These in turn base their decisions not merely on the Foreign Capital Investment Inducement Law, but also on a number of unpublished internal regulations and guidelines. The latter are often more important and more restrictive than the law itself.

Moreover, Korean bureaucrats at the working level enjoy a considerable degree of 'administrative freedom' with respect to how they interpret a given law. The bureaucrat, viewing patriotism as his personal duty, will raise objections to applications he does not believe to be in the best interest of Korea, even if the law or senior officials label such investments as permissible. To make matters worse, there are no formal procedures to appeal against the rejection of applications.

Finally, there is the problem of disagreement and strife among ministries. Quite regularly, headlines announce policy liberalisations and uninitiated foreigners take these at face value, assuming that they signal the successful conclusion of interministerial negotiations. In fact, given the rivalries and limited contacts among ministries, such announcements often signal only the beginning of the debate among them. Gradually and quietly the original proposals are watered down – often beyond recognition – in response to domestic opposition, while no serious effort is made to dispel the myth generated by the original announcement.

The net result of these factors is not only considerable uncertainty among potential foreign investors but also a foreign investment regime which is much stricter in practice than it appears. The question of course is whether such administrative obstacles are intentional, or merely a reflection of bureaucratic inefficiency. Most people interviewed felt that there was considerable method behind the obstruction, precisely to stall foreign interests and to protect domestic ones.

(2) *Extensive government interference.* Foreign firms regularly complain about the high degree of restrictions and interference to which they are subject while operating in Korea.

Manufacturing enterprises, for example, are often given precise instructions as to which products or product lines they may produce and what share of these may be sold on the domestic market. Guidelines on pricing (e.g. of export inputs) are not uncommon. Foreign insurance and leasing firms are also severely restricted.

Foreign enterprises are often also denied the service and support functions they consider necessary. Samples, spare parts, training aids and business technology are importable only with great difficulty, if at all. Thus, foreign firms can generally not compete on equal terms with local firms on the domestic market.

Another area of interference with foreign investors in Korea relates to the 'sanctity of contract'. When negotiating joint ventures or contracts with local partners, foreign firms often assume that once an agreement has been signed, the contract is final. Not so. In Korea, the government reserves the right to review and – where necessary – demand changes in agreed contracts. Such attempts to renegotiate signed contracts occur not only during the pre-investment phase, but on occasion also once an agreement has been in place for some time. Foreign firms may be asked to increase their exports, raise the domestic content of their output, expand output, or even to restructure their operations entirely. Contracts may be unilaterally abrogated when the assumptions underlying them change, and Korea's extremely tight Foreign Exchange Control Laws have in some cases been used to block the payment of agreed service charges. The basic government attitude appears to be that business (whether domestic or foreign) should serve the government and not vice versa.

(3) *Extensive reporting requirements and control.* Foreign firms further complain about the reporting requirements and bureaucratic control to which they are subjected. They are required to disclose considerable amounts of 'sensitive' information about their accounts and operations to Korean officials and screening agencies. Sometimes such information ends up in the hands of domestic competitors or has otherwise been used against the foreign firm.

Tax and customs officials in particular have a number of independent means of monitoring company activities. The statutory auditor, whose mission is to check annually the integrity of company accounts, acts as a powerful independent watchdog over all major companies operating in Korea. Tax officials conduct independent assessments of company tax-liabilities and compare them against submitted accounts. Customs officials have at their disposal not only very detailed international price lists, but detailed records of virtually all international commercial transactions involving Korea (a list is compiled daily). This intensive monitoring is said to be extremely effective in curbing transfer pricing in Korea.

We do not wish to suggest that all investors are at all times confronted with problems of the kind discussed. But the problems are sufficiently common to support the proposition that foreign investors in Korea do not operate in a liberal environment. Although the revised Foreign Capital Inducement Law of July 1984 promised to remove many of these restrictions, caution is in order.

The revised law will remove tax incentives for foreign enterprises not considered of strategic importance to the Korean economy. There also exists some confusion as to what the term 'automatically approved' for foreign investment will mean in practice (*Business Asia*, 17 February 1984, p. 49). In addition, a number of proposals are currently under discussion which would substantially increase the export requirements of foreign invested firms in Korea. Developments of this kind suggest that the active role of the state with respect to foreign direct investment is being reduced only very slowly.

Foreign Banks

We demonstrated above that the state exercised strict control over Korea's domestic financial institutions. We propose to argue that this is also true for foreign banks operating in Korea.[15]

For example, their access to the domestic credit market is restricted by the requirement that they have to obtain their *won* through 'swap transactions' with the Bank of Korea. According to this system, foreign bank branches obtain *won* in return for US dollars; ceilings for such transactions are set by the government through the Bank of Korea.

A number of other restrictions have been the source of bitter complaints among foreign bankers. For example, foreign banks, as of 1983:

(1) Do not have access to Bank of Korea lending/rediscounting facilities. This in turn heavily discourages them in the provision of export financing and the rediscounting of commercial bills.

(2) Are effectively barred from competing for local currency deposits, given that they are prohibited from issuing debentures or certificates of deposit to raise *won* funds. This provision has kept the share of total *won* held by foreign banks to around 3 per cent in recent years (Ensor, 1984, p. 82).

(3) Are severely restricted in owning, or in taking mortgages on real estate, thus inhibiting their ability to hedge capital or to accept real security.

(4) Permitted only minority ownership in leasing companies, merchant banks or other commercial entities.

(5) Are barred from membership in a major policy-making organisation, the Bankers' Association.

(6) Are subject to a definition of capital which takes into account only operating funds of the bank in Korea and not those of their head office abroad.

(7) Are subject to separate capitalisation and reporting requirements for each branch they operate in Korea. These factors (6) and (7)

discourage the setting up additional branches and restrict the loan and guarantee business of already established foreign-bank branches.

(8) Are subject to informal limitations in the repatriation of non-banking profits (e.g. from asset appreciation, leasing and trust services).

Much of the regulatory framework within which foreign banks operate is not anchored in written laws and regulations, but in unwritten policies. Often, banks are informed orally that certain permits or licences would be refused and are discouraged from submitting the relevant applications. Written rejections are consequently rather rare, making it difficult to prove that certain restrictions apply.

Government regulation extends far into the everyday workings of foreign as well as of local banks. Areas of detailed regulation include loan transactions, exchange transactions, funding- and securities transactions, these measures being designed to limit the earnings of the banks.

As for the much publicised liberalisation of Korea's banking sector, a US banker recently summed up the feeling shared by many foreign businessmen: 'It's one thing to say that barriers are coming down . . . it's another to see to it that foreign bankers don't keep stumbling over them' (*AWSJ*, 28 March 1983). For our purposes, what is of greatest importance is that in this area also, an active role of the state is observable.

The Transfer of Technology

As in other areas of state intervention, the literature on technology development in Korea has tended to focus on promotional types of government activity, such as incentives, educational and institutional support (Choi, 1980). While we would not dispute such accounts, we would insist that directive state intervention has been of critical importance as well. We have in mind two types of such intervention firstly, 'positive' directive intervention through screening, controlling and discouraging excessive dependence on foreign technology. Secondly, 'negative' directive intervention, which has denied protection to foreign suppliers of technology so as to promote domestic ones.

Transfer of technology: the basic system

All commercial transfers of technology are regulated by the
government, generally through the Economic Planning Board. The
EPB screens proposed contracts in consultation with the MCI,
which in turn may solicit opinions from the Ministry of Science and
Technology and from other government agencies such as the
Industrial Advancement Administration. In the case of very
expensive or long-term contracts, the EPB requests approval from
the – cabinet level – Foreign Capital Inducement Deliberation
Committee.

The basic aim of government policy is to 'encourage, protect and
manage the advanced foreign technology induced so that it may
contribute to the sound development of the national economy and
the improvement of the balance of payments' (Eckstrom, 1977,
p. 103). Under each five-year plan, the government selects certain
types of technology for import preference. During the Fourth Five-
Year Plan (1977–81), for example, 1786 types of technology were
selected for import preference, mainly to support the development
of heavy and chemical industries. The EPB will screen proposed
technological inducement contracts or licensing agreements before
granting the necessary authorisation. This process is undertaken
primarily by planners in conjunction with businessmen, rather than
by scientists and engineers (IDRC, 1980, p. 34). The EPB screens
the transfer initially in terms of its necessity, content, cost, contract
duration, economic impact (e.g. on domestic firms) and technological
impact. If the transfer meets the criteria, it will then be checked
against the basic priorities of technology transfer in Korea. At this
point, the screening considers: the potential contribution to exports;
the long-term impact on priority industries as specified under the
five-year plan; the import-substitution effect; and the 'economic
suitability'.

As a rule, the Foreign Capital Inducement Law discourages
royalty payments in excess of 3 per cent and contract periods in
excess of three years. The EPB will not authorise 'nominal' licence
agreements, that is those designed to import raw materials, partially
finished goods or brand names; nor will it approve technology which
would have a disruptive effect on the domestic market. The EPB
further reserves the right to debate or add clauses to the contracts as
necessary.

If the proposed technology transfer contract is approved, the
applicant can apply to the Office of National Taxation for selected

tax benefits and may, in principle, proceed with the transfer. In all cases, however, the applicant must apply to the Ministry of Finance for the necessary foreign exchange, which is not always forthcoming (Lee and Gallaway Jr, 1982, p. 267).

Certain types of technology transfer (e.g. certain technical assistance contracts) may require approval from several ministries (Eckstrom, 1977, p. 110); others come under the jurisdiction not of the EPB, but of the Ministry of Finance. Indeed, any type of transfer which does not fall under the Foreign Capital Inducement Law will tend to be covered by the Foreign Exchange Control Law (IDRC, 1980, p. 25).

It is fair to say, therefore, that throughout the 1970s at least, all transfers of technology to Korea have been controlled by the government and have been subject to elaborate screening. Let us now consider whether the much publicised liberalisations of the early 1980s have altered this basic picture.

Recent changes in the basic system
During 1979 to 1981, a number of changes were made regarding the control of technology transfer to Korea. As a result, all fields have become open – in principle – for such transfers, and certain technology imports have become subject to 'automatic approval'.

It is easy to overstate the importance of these reforms, however. To begin with, their main purpose has been to liberalise technology transfers to the heavy and chemical industries, though certain types of consumer goods have benefited as well (ILT, 1983, pp. 16–17). More importantly, the Automatic Approval system has by no means eliminated the screening process. The system now distinguishes between 'Class A' and 'Class B' type transfer contracts. Automatic Approval types are 'Class A', and whereas they no longer need the approval of the EPB (or now, of the MOF), they do require the approval of designated other ministries instead (Kim, 1982, p. 708). Also, certain complementary regulations governing the types of restrictive contract clauses prohibited in Korea have recently been strengthened (for example, in the Monopoly Regulation and Fair Trade Law of 1981) (ILT, 1983, p. 13).

One area where there has been a significant change is in the protection of patents and trademarks. In March of 1979 Korea joined the UN World Intellectual Property Organisation (WIPO), and in May of 1980 it became a member of the Paris Union Convention for the Protection of Industrial Property.

Despite this change, however, the process of liberalisation of technology imports is proceeding much more slowly than official announcements would suggest and these reforms do not alter our characterisation of the basic system as restrictive and subject to extensive directive state intervention.

The practice of technology transfer in Korea

As in the case of foreign direct investment, what matters is not so much the law on paper, but in practice. Let us now look more closely at evidence on the practical operation of the technology transfer system.

The first question that arises is whether Korea was able to avoid restrictive clauses in technology import contracts. The dilemma facing all importers of technology is that if restrictive clauses are rejected outright, access to the desired technology may be refused. If, on the other hand such clauses are too readily accepted, the value of the technology might be seriously undermined.

A recent study by Kwang-Doo Kim (1981) confirms that restrictions on export markets and on raw material and component purchasing are indeed relatively common in Korea despite their formal prohibition throughout the last decade at least. In 39.6 per cent of technology import contracts export market restrictions were specified, in 20.9 per cent raw material purchases were tied, and in 15.4 per cent the development and export of similar technology was restricted.[17] Given that such clauses are now technically illegal under the Monopoly Regulation and Fair Trade Law of 1981, it would appear that they are implicitly tolerated rather than officially sanctioned. This in turn means that if and when they conflict with Korean business interests they can be 'redressed' by the government. In fact, the EPB, which polices the law's enforcement, has revised a large number of agreed contracts.

Turning now to pressures on domestic firms to absorb imported technology, the general policy of the EPB has been not to approve technical assistance contracts after the initial three-year period in order to force domestic firms to master imported technology (Eckstrom, 1977, p. 111). There are many exceptions to this rule and in general it is the less essential forms of technology licensing (e.g. in consumer goods) which are affected most by such types of pressure. The heavy and chemical sectors meanwhile can secure agreements for ten years or longer. Thus the three-year rule is applied in a selective and pragmatic fashion.

Some provisions contained in the Patent and the Trademark Law have given rise to concern among foreign business interests. For example, in the pharmaceuticals industry only chemical process, but not product patents exist (ILT, 1983, p. 15). Thus if a Korean company or research institute discovers the composition of a product (for example by 'reverse engineering') and is able to alter the process of making it slightly, it can – in principle – market a rival to the original product. This is known to have occurred in at least one case in recent years involving a major European pharmaceuticals group.[18]

Finally, let us consider what foreign businessmen see as the weaknesses of the system in practice. They frequently complain about the lack of adequate technology, trademark, industrial intellectual property protection in Korea. Pirating and copying is relatively common and the relevant laws are not enforced sufficiently. In some cases, sensitive information about the composition and ingredients of products must be disclosed to the authorities, and it ends up in the hands of domestic competitors. Some companies have also reported difficulties in securing agreed royalties. In some cases, royalty payments have been blocked under the Foreign Exchange Control Law; in others the licensors had difficulty in assessing the royalties owned by the Korean firm, because accurate sales figures could not be obtained. It is also pointed out that the requirements under the Trademark Law effectively rule out licensing possibilities for most foreign trademarks.

Thus foreign companies complain predominantly about the lack of protection they are offered in Korea, rather than about the screening process as such. Other types of evidence suggest that restrictive clauses have not been totally avoided, but that the government has the potential to redress such contracts if and when necessary. We also discovered that in the simpler types of technology at least, pressures are brought to bear on Korean firms over time to cut links with their foreign partners.

To summarise the last two sections have sought to demonstrate that in any key area of the Korean economy one wishes to investigate, extensive government intervention is observable. Liberal market characterisations are generally mistaken and contradicted by a whole host of available evidence. We now turn to consider how and why intervention appears to work in Korea.

IV. STATE INTERVENTION IN KOREA: A GENERAL DISCUSSION

How It Works

Any investigation of how intervention works in Korea, must recognise that the 'Blue House', the President and his staff, is the central source of political power in this respect. Though South Korea can boast a selection of active democratic institutions, their power is in fact severely constrained.

According to the Constitution of 1948, for example, the National Assembly was envisaged as the single most important governmental body. In practice, however, 'the National Assembly became subsequently a weak institution, dominated and manipulated by ambitious Presidents' (Kim and Pai, 1981, p. 4). The weakening culminated with the adoption of the 'Yushin' constitution of 1972, which revoked the Assembly's powers of investigation and in effect, its budgetary powers. One-third of Assembly membership was now government appointed rather than elected, making overall government a relatively easy task. The tenure of government-party posts depended almost entirely on continuously demonstrated loyalty to the President. Moreover, the President could now circumvent the legislature completely by invoking emergency decrees, the National Security or martial law (Kim and Pai, 1981, pp. 25/30/33). The President deals not only with his ministers and with the heads of governmental agencies such as the Bank of Korea, but also surrounds himself with a small number of trusted policy advisers. These 'Advisers to the President' are often more influential than high ranking public officials, simply because they have greater ease of access to the President. The President also has regular contacts with Korean business leaders, for example through monthly export promotion meetings.

It is the President, as influenced by his closest advisers, who gives more or less detailed directives on broad policy directions. He is the first major link in the process of government intervention in Korea; he sets the stage for basic policy, but does not determine the precise content of that policy.

The second major link is the ministries and governmental organisations. Of foremost overall importance for Korea's industrial development have been the Economic Planning Board (EPB), the Ministry of Finance (MOF) and the Ministry of Commerce and

Industry (MCI). That is not to deny the importance of other ministries – such as Construction, Health and Social Affairs, or Science and Technology – to particular sectors.

The EPB acted as an overlord planning ministry, but also controlled the budget and administered price controls in Korea, as well as controlling foreign aid, foreign loans, foreign investment and the transfer of foreign technology. It also organised the collection of national statistics. Certain control functions (e.g. foreign investment or technology screening) were carried out in consultation with other ministries.

The Ministry of Finance controlled tax assessment and collection, but also domestic and foreign financial institutions. Moreover, it administered foreign exchange control in general, but in particular the foreign exchange supply and demand plan. Finally, it controlled the assessment and collection of tariffs through the Office of Customs Administration under its wing.

The Ministry of Commerce and Industry was in charge of export promotion, controlled industry-development plans, investment applications, project and firm designation, trader licensing, quantitative controls, industry associations, and a number of other para-governmental organisations such as KOSAMI, the Fine Instruments Center or the Korea Traders Association. On occasion, special committees will be set up to bypass the entire governmental system: an example of this was the 'Special Committee for National Security Measures', which was in charge of reorganising Korea's heavy and chemical industries. But on the whole, state intervention in Korea has operated through the above ministries.

The third major link in the system of state intervention in Korea is the producers' associations. Their function as agents for the Government to influence business is at least equal in importance to their function as a channel for consultation between producers and the Government. The MCI controls the overall working of these associations, creates new ones and merges existing ones as necessary.[19] One interviewee referred to producers' associations as 'Government Watchdogs' and Michell likens them to the 'Self Control Associations' of wartime Japan (1984, p. 34).

Detailed plans are compiled annually by the various producers' associations outlining the proposed activities of their members. This information is relayed to the appropriate ministries, and is the basis for much of their planning. If these proposals are excessive in terms of national constraints (e.g. involve excessive amounts of foreign exchange), if they are incompatible with specific national objectives (e.g. export promotion), or if they need to be changed in view of unforeseen circumstances, the producers associations are the means by which pressure is exerted by the government on producers to adjust their plans. Orderly export or import rationing arrangements, for example, tend to be operated via the producers associations.

The fourth major link in the process of intervention is the Board of Audit and Inspection, which reports directly to the President. We have already referred to its role as powerful independent watchdog over all major companies operating in Korea. However, it also inspects ministries and quasi-governmental agencies (Michell, 1984, p. 36). Whereas technically auditors are charged with the annual inspection of accounts, they may in practice mount surprise inspections at any time.

We have by no means exhausted the major links for managing state intervention. For example, the banks are important as executive agencies for the foreign exchange and demand plan, as are customs officials in the process of controlling imports. We have already discussed their importance.

Attempting a typology of decision making in Korea, the traditional view has been that of highly centralised hierarchical system, where decisions are essentially handed down from the top, while being enforced and administered by lower ranking officials, very much along organisational lines observed in the military.

In his recent analysis of Korean business organisation, Rooken-Smith (1982) found considerable evidence to support this view. For example, he pointed to the conscious efforts of Korean presidents to portray themselves as ever-vigilant 'Commanders in Chief' to the public.

Rooken-Smith further noted that not only certain structural similarities between army and business styles of organisation (1982, pp. 67–8), but also strong influences of the military upon business, both directly in the form of retired army officials in top and middle management positions and indirectly via the lengthy and compulsory military service which virtually all Korean males must complete (1982, pp. 72–5). Such influences may also be found in ministries and other governmental agencies, suggested that these too may be similar to the military in terms of their decision-making style.

This traditional hierarchical 'top-down' characterisation has been criticised by Michell (1984), who argues that 'the way in which government decisions were often, though not always, reached, involved a wide degree of opinion taking and modifications and even formulation of policy from the bottom rather than the top' (1984, p. 32). He stresses that implementation is generally left to lower ranking officials who are not normally interfered with, allowing a wide range of informal consultation to occur.

The view taken here is that the two characterisations differ more in emphasis than in essence. The process of intervention in Korea certainly displays both types of decision-making, but much depends on what kind of policy one is considering. The military style is much more likely to emerge during a crisis or an entry into new territories of industrial activity. There always exists the potential for 'military command style' intervention, if and when the President – upon the recommendation of his advisers – thinks fit. More routine policy determination and administration, meanwhile, generally take the form Michell describes.

Why it Works

Looking at the Korean experience with intervention, we see a whole host of potential recipes for disaster: extensive and very detailed intervention; a maze of often contradictory laws and regulations; considerable administrative freedom in interpreting the law; and no formal appeal procedures against administrative decisions.

So why did this system not lead to chaos? Why did bureaucratic inefficiency, corruption and misguided notions of fairness not defeat the purpose of intervention? Why did businessmen not undermine the system locally?

In attempting to pinpoint the reasons for Korea's success, we would first of all point to the highly effective channels of communication and feedback available to policy makers, which we outlined in the preceding section. Beyond this, we would focus on five main factors.

Legitimacy

In Korea, the intervention of the state in economic affairs has a long history. From the Shilla dynasty to the present, state intervention in markets has been the order of the day (Oh, 1968, p. 20 or Chough, 1968, p. 55). The legitimacy of state intervention is also an integral part of Confucianism, by which Korea has been heavily influenced since the fourteenth century. Confucian ethics prescribe a vertical as opposed to horizontal social order, with the 'supreme ruler' – as the personification of the state – at the top of a well ordered hierarchy. It should not be surprising, therefore, to find that in Korea business was expected to serve the government and not vice versa.

Nor is the concept of Adam Smith's 'invisible hand' compatible with Confucian ethics. The idea of 'natural' laws which – if allowed to operate – restore the economy to its proper order is at odds with the Confucian system where the emphasis is on the wisdom and moral ethics of the supreme ruler and ruling élite (Bun Woong Kim, 1982a, p. 47; Hahm, 1967, p. 39).

The implications of this are twofold: first, it explains the deep mistrust felt by many Korean bureaucrats towards policies which would have handed over economic control to market forces (Michell, 1982, p. 212). Second, it explains why many bureaucrats did not hesitate to stall contracts which they felt were not in the best interest of Korea, even if the law explicitly defined them as permissible. Bureaucrats often regarded it as their national duty to alter the law; intervention was regarded as a perfectly proper state activity.

The legitimacy of state intervention goes beyond the mere right to issue directives. Traditionally, private property has not been sacrosanct in Korea, given that the State was regarded as the ultimate owner of all property. The expropriation of land or – more recently – the expropriation of 'illicit profits' earned by businessmen was not only legitimate, but also very popular with the general population (Hahm, 1967, pp. 79–80; K. D. Kim, 1979, p. 70). The possibility of asset expropriation thus constituted a powerful means of keeping insubordinate businessmen in check.

Clarity/urgency of interventionist objectives
In Korea, state intervention generally revolved around three major themes: export promotion, economic growth and foreign exchange scarcity. Economic growth was to be achieved mainly through rapid industrial development. The North Korean military threat, but also the desire to catch up with Japan, acted as major motivating influences in this respect, injecting a sense of urgency into the interventionist process (Michell, 1984, p. 32). Frequently, national economic objectives were stated in military language, with development described as an economic war with national survival and the welfare of the masses at stake' (Jones and Sakong, 1980, p. 251).

Pragmatic intervention
State intervention tended not to follow ready-made textbook

prescriptions. When the market promised to produce the desired results, it was generally left to operate unhindered. When it did not function in the desired way, Koreans displayed few inhibitions in 'assisting' or 'directing' it as necessary.

Pragmatism was in turn combined with considerable flexibility. If a policy – once embarked upon – showed signs of failure or led to unanticipated problems or costs (e.g. liberalisation) the Koreans were generally quite quick to reverse it (Michell, 1981). They also frequently reorganised institutions, enterprises and entire industries to secure the success of a particular policy. Nothing in Korea was immune from sudden change.

A third important feature of Korean pragmatism was its 'offensive' orientation (cf. Cheah, 1984, Ch. 8). When Koreans opted for intervention, their purpose was generally to prepare industries for international competition not merely to protect them. Even when foreign exchange reasons necessitated the protection of industries (textiles), the producers affected were forced into international markets through export requirements.

Finally, Korean intervention was pragmatic in that it was generally based on a full awareness of the pitfalls such a strategy may encounter. Let us take one example among many from Korea's recent past. Efforts to conserve foreign exchange can seriously inhibit simultaneous efforts to earn it. This is pointed out by virtually all critiques of 'import-substitution' strategies of development. To avoid this, the Koreans adopted a 'two pronged' strategy of foreign exchange-related protection which made a fundamental distinction between products, investments, and technology destined for the domestic market on the one hand, those destined for export production on the other. Whereas the latter were treated in an extremely liberal fashion (to promote exports) the former were tightly controlled (to conserve foreign exchange).

Overall, therefore, Korean intervention was pragmatic not only in the sense that no excessive trust was placed in liberal market policies, but also in the sense that the dangers associated with state intervention were recognised.

Enforcement

Even the most thoroughly designed interventionist policy can only be as good as the state's ability to enforce it. Enforcement in turn depends, among other things, on access to information. Information is necessary not only to design and monitor the results of interventionist policies, but also to check whether enterprise is cooperating with government authorities in following its directives.

It is well known that the Koreans have a passion for collecting very detailed economic statistics. Countless statistical volumes from an array of ministries and agencies attest to this. On the whole, the quality of the collected statistics is highly impressive, even if some 'politically sensitive' figures may at times be subject to curious definitions.

More importantly, perhaps, the enforcement of interventionist policies is facilitated by the inherently vulnerable nature of enterprise in Korea. Government authorities can make life extremely difficult for 'uncooperative' firms. Firms respond to this by attempting at all times to remain in favour with the government and maintain a low public profile. The great fear of Korean businessmen is to fall out of favour with the government, to have their 'illicit profits' confiscated, or to be punished for activities which are common practice, but strictly speaking illegal.

People

It may be argued that intervention succeeds in Korea to a large extent because Koreans are honest, law-abiding people willing to follow government directives.

Whereas the honesty of the common man and woman in the street is indeed impressive, it would be wrong to credit the entire nation with such a virtue. Seoul and other cities are regularly rocked by one scandal or another involving fraud, embezzlement and other unlawful practices. There is no shortage of attempts to 'beat the system', yet on the whole the problem does appear to be contained.

The key to understanding why intervention works in Korea lies less in the honesty of the business community than in the nature and quality of the enforcing bureaucrats on the one hand, and in the tolerance of average citizens for authoritarianism on the other.

Bureaucrats are ranked relatively highly in terms of the Korean social hierarchy. They regard themselves as the guardians of the national interest, and if 'beating the system' is a favoured pastime of many businessmen, preventing this is a favoured pastime of the bureaucrats. They have extensive powers for the purpose and pursue their duties often with meticulous attention to detail.

Korean bureaucrats often also consider it their national duty to stall foreign interests. In the minds of many Koreans, foreigners come to Korea essentially to take something away, and bureaucrats see it as their duty to guard against this. This is not to deny that high profits can be made by foreigners in Korea, but they must be justified in the eyes of Korean bureaucrats if official approval is to be obtained. This stands in marked contrast with what may be observed in many other developing countries.

It would be incorrect to suggest, however, that Korean bureaucrats are never corrupt. Again, plenty of scandals involving corruption and attempts to stamp it out, suggest otherwise. Yet, two things are worth noting about bureaucratic corruption in Korea. The first is that it appears to be a modest phenomenon, at least compared with elsewhere in the developing world. The second is that corruption appears not to be such as to make nonsense of interventionist policies. Many stories about corruption in fact tell of how processes were speeded up. Yet the basic reason for the containment of corruption is probably that bureaucrats themselves live in fear of government auditors who can descend upon their offices at any moment and scrutinise their activities.

As regards efficiency, there is no doubt that Korean bureaucrats have on the whole been successful at planning, implementing, monitoring and, where necessary, modifying some highly complicated interventionist policies.[20] This alone attests to their high quality.

On the whole, therefore, we would claim that despite the occasional tendency towards corruption, Korean bureaucrats are on the whole relatively efficient, and have thereby greatly contributed to the success of state intervention in Korea.

This leaves us with a final explanatory factor: the tolerance of Koreans for authoritarianism.

No account of the Korean success is complete without a mention of the sacrifices and hard work of the Korean people at large.[21] Similarly, no account of state intervention in Korea can ignore the fact that the Korean people have – willingly and unwillingly – tolerated a level of 'military style' interference in their economic and daily affairs which would be unthinkable in many other countries. Without the ultimate cooperation of the population at large, intervention in Korea might well not have been as successful as it was.

V. CONCLUSION

The purpose of this chapter has been to explore the role of the state in South Korea's rapid industrial development and to contribute to the general debate on state intervention and economic development as a result. Our focus was on 'directive' as opposed to 'promotional' forms of state intervention.

Our research revealed not only a number of serious flaws in the widely accepted 'liberal market' account of the Korean success, but also an extensive use of 'directive' state intervention in all areas selected for closer scrutiny. Domestic industrial policy, domestic financial markets and domestic market prices were often tightly controlled, as were foreign trade, foreign exchange markets, foreign direct investment and the transfer of foreign technology. Thus, even if the precise reasons for South Korea's industrial development are still subject to intensive debate, it is now clear, firstly, that direct state intervention was an integral part of the experience and, secondly, that Korea's integration into the world economy was a far more selective phenomenon that had previously been assumed. Contrary to earlier contentions, the Korean experience supports rather than contradicts the advocates of directive state intervention in development.

In attempting to understand why intervention was successful in Korea, we selected for special emphasis the effective channels of communication and feedback available to policy makers, the legitimacy of intervention, the urgency and clarity of its objectives, its pragmatism, enforceability, and the nature of the people who administered the policy on the one hand, and who tolerated it on the other. Thus, Korea displayed an environment extremely conducive to the planning, design, implementation, monitoring and adjustment of interventionist policies.

The implications of our study are firstly, that intervention may be a necessary precondition for successful industrial development in LDCs. The fact that in Korea we observe both successful industrial development and intervention is in our view no coincidence, but symptomatic of the critical role played by the state in this context. Despite its potential pitfalls, state intervention can work, and this is demonstrated by the Korean experience.

Notes

1. We distinguish between 'promotional' and 'directive' intervention. Promotional intervention aims to restore markets to their proper function, usually through non-discriminatory incentives. It also aims to provide 'public goods', which the market cannot by itself supply efficiently, such as infrastructure, education, etc. Directive intervention, aims to achieve predetermined results through conscious interference with market forces and selective application of incentives and/or controls. Whereas promotional intervention is based on the premise that undistorted market forces 'know best' what form and direction industrial development should take, directive intervention assumes that markets do not necessarily possess this quality.

2. It should be noted that on certain issues we have no major disagreements with the free market advocates and accept their characterisations of Korea's wider trade regime. We do not dispute the importance of export incentives in Korea; nor do we wish to suggest that Korea overvalued its exchange rate as part of its development strategy. We do argue that the opponents of directive state intervention have greatly underestimated the level of protection in Korea over the last two decades.

3. Note that this is not the first time that the government initiates a major restructuring programme. Another such exercise was in 1972 (Jones and Sakong, 1980, p. 107).

4. For a much more detailed discussion of import controls in Korea see R. Luedde-Neurath, 1986, Ch. 3.

5. See Krueger, 1979, p. 59 and *ACJ*, July, 1981, p. 59. Importers may also be required to hold certain minimum bank deposits; traders may also be confronted with 'export link' or 'domestic counterpart consumption' requirements. The price of counterpart purchases is often fixed by the MCI (*ACJ*, November 1981, pp. 64/65).

6. In this context, see in particular *Business Asia*, 14 August 1981, p. 263, and 11 June 1982, pp. 187–8; also *ACJ*, April 1982, p. 59, February 1983, pp. 6–7 and March 1983, pp. 16–17.

7. For details and a list of agencies and products affected, see ACJ, February 1978, pp. 61/62. In addition to these general import rules, there exist detailed guidelines by which the decisions of the screening agency are ultimately made. These are generally not made public. Yet the decision made by the designated agency is final, and there are no formal channels for appeal against its ruling.

8. For a selective list see: MCI, Annual Export Import Notice 1981/1982 (Unofficial translation, by the KTA), pp. 4–9, and the *KTA Import Handbook, 1982* (in Korean).

9. Source: Korea Exchange Bank, *Businessman's Guide to Korea*, December 1978, p. 78. Initially, only 46 items were affected. The number then rose to 85 (*ACJ*, September 1978, p. 29) decreased to 23 by 1980 (*ACJ*, December 1979, p. 64) and increased again to around 37 times by 1982, of which 28 are AA items.

10. At least before November 1982, when raw cotton is restricted under

MCI Public Notice 82–43 (*ACJ*, November 1982, p. 62). We further find that SWAK annually formulates the 'Cotton Supply Plan' (*ACJ*, October 1981, p. 62), which in turn is integrated into the annual 'Agricultural Product Import Plan'.

11. In this context, see also MCI public notice 83–19, setting out a range of certificates that must be produced for the importation of finished pharmaceuticals (*ACJ*, August 1983, p. 57).

12. Source: interview with trade attorney. See also *Business International* 1982, p. 53. 'Just because you own foreign exchange, it does not follow that you can see it as you like', commented another interviewee.

13. See IMF *AREAR*, any issue 1977–82 (e.g. 1977, p. 281 or 1982, p. 271).

14. I am indebted to Tony Michell for pointing out this data to me.

15. This section, unless otherwise indicated, is based on interviews and on a number of confidential documents made available to the author in Korea. For more general analyses of foreign banking in Korea see K. D. Lee, KEB, *MR* April 1982, 2, pp. 12–14; Richardson, 1979, p. vi and M. J. Rhee 1981, Ch. III.

16. Our sources for this section have been: Chung (1975, pp. 11–15); Eckstrom (1977, pp. 102–5) unless otherwise specified.

17. K.-D. Kim, 1981, Tables 7–9. Unfortunately, Kim's tables, which were taken from the 'Survey of Industrial Technology Development' of the Federation of Korean Industries, do not state the year or period to which they refer, or the total number of cases considered.

18. Source: interviews. This case is different from that involving the Dow Chemical Corporation which in 1983 lost a lawsuit filed against a Korean firm concerning the use of allegedly stolen technology (*Korea Herald* and *Korea Times*, 24 April 1983 and *ACJ*, May–June 1983, p. 7).

19. For examples illustrating this see: *ACJ* July 1981, p. 62 (according to an MCI 'ruling', KOSAMI will screen certain machinery imports); *ACJ*, October 1982, p. 28 (The 'Semiconductor Research and Development Association' will be established, according to a 'plan' adopted by the MCI); or *ACJ*, September 1980, p. 23 and *ACJ* February 1978, p. 42 (The MCI 'orders' the merger of certain textile industry associations 'under its wing').

20. See, for example, Y. W. Rhee (1981) on the arrangements for export promotion.

21. According to the International Labour Organisation in Geneva, Korean labourers work the highest number of hours per week in the world (*Korea Times*, 11 February 1982). For an account of their regimentation see *AWSJ*, 26 January 1983.

References

ACJ (*American Chamber of Commerce in Korea Journal*) (monthly), various issues, Seoul, Korea.

Ahn, S.-K. (1980) *Auslaendische Privatinvestitionen in Suedkorea* (Muenchen: Kaiser Grunewald).

AWSJ (*Asia Wall Street Journal*) (daily), various issues.

Balassa, B. (1971) 'Industrial Policies in Taiwan and Korea', *Weltwirtschaftliches Archiv*, 106(1).

Balassa B. *et al.*, (1971) *The Structure of Protection in Developing Countries (IBRD)* (Baltimore: Johns Hopkins University Press).

Bank of Korea (1965–9) *Review of Korean Economy* (annual), various issues.

Bendix, P. J. *et al.* (1978) *Development and Perspectives of the Korean Machinery Industry* (Berlin: German Development Institute).

Berthomieu, C. and A. Hanaut (1980) 'Can International Subcontracting Promote Industrialisation?', *International Labour Review*, 119(3), May/June.

Bhagwati, J. (1978) *Foreign Trade Regimes and Economic Development: Anatomy and Consequences of Exchange Control Regimes* (National Bureau of Economic Research, New York) (Cambridge, Mass.: Ballinger).

Bhagwati, J. and T. N. Srinivasan (1978), *Trade Policy and Development*, World Bank Reprint Series, No 90, reprinted from R. Dornbusch and J. A. Frenkel (eds.), *International Economic Policy: Theory and Evidence* (Baltimore: Johns Hopkins University Press) pp. 1–38.

Birnbaum, R. B. (1983) 'Proposed Commercial Code Revisions: Impact on Foreign Investors', *East Asian Executive Reports* (monthly), March.

Brown, G. T. (1973) *Korean Pricing Policies and Economic Development in the 1960s* (Baltimore: Johns Hopkins University Press).

Business Asia (1973–84) (weekly), various issues. Hong Kong.

Business International (1982) 'Guide to Exchange Controls in 25 Countries', a Special *Business International* Report, New York, October.

Business International Corporation, *Investing, Licensing and Trading Conditions Abroad* (ILT), Korea: various issues.

Business Korea (monthly), Seoul, Korea.

Chang Whan-Bin (1980) 'Adjustment of Korea's Heavy and Chemical Industry Investment', Korea Exchange Bank *Monthly Review*, vol. xiv, no. 12, December, Seoul.

Charters, A. (1981) 'Controls to be Eased', *Financial Times* survey on South Korea VI, Friday 5 June.

Cheah, Hock Beng (1984) 'Policies for Upgrading Industrial Structure: the Case of the New Economic Policy in Singapore', DPhil thesis (unpublished), Sussex University.

Choi, Hyung-Sup (1980) 'Development of Technology: the South Korean Experience', *Development Digest*, vol. xviii, no. 3, July.

Chough, Soon (1968) 'The Economics of Price Supervision', Seoul National University *Economic Review*, vol. ii, no. 1, December, Seoul, Korea.

Chung, Kun Mo (1975) 'Commercial Transfer of Foreign Technology to the Electronics Industry in Korea', *Asian Economies*, no. 13, June, Seoul, Korea.

Cohen, B. I. (1972) 'The Economic Impact of Foreign Investment for the Export of Manufactures: a Tentative Study of South Korea', Yale University, Economic Growth Center, *Discussion Paper* 136, New Haven, Connecticut, January.

Cohen, B. I. (1975) *Multinational Firms and Asian Exports* (Yale University Press).

Cole, D. (1979) 'Free Enterprise vs Government Regulation: Decision Making and Regulation in the Korean Economy', *Asian Affairs*, vol. 7, no. 2, Nov/Dec.

Cole, D. and Y. C. Park (1979) 'Financial Development in Korea 1945–1978', *KDI Working Paper*, no. 7904, Seoul, Korea.

Coolidge, J. T. (1980) 'The Realities of Korean Foreign Investment Policy', *Asian Affairs*, 7(6), July/August.

Crane, P. S. (1967) *Korean Patterns*, Royal Asiatic Society, Korea Branch, Kwangjin Publishing Co, Seoul, Korea (4th edn 1978).

Curhan, J. P., W. H. Davidson and R. Suri (1977) *Tracing the Multinationals: a Sourcebook on US-Based Enterprises* (Cambridge, Mass.: Ballinger).

Darton, D. (1982) 'Foreign Investment in the Korean Economy', *Korea Exchange Bank Monthly Review*, XVI (8), August.

Datta-Chaudhuri, M. K. (1979) 'Industrialisation and Foreign Trade: an Analysis Based on the Development Experiences of the Republic of Korea and the Philippines', ILO (ARTEP) *Asian Employment Programme WP*, II-4, September.

Dell, S. and R. Lawrence (1980) *The Balance of Payments Adjustment Process in Developing Countries*, Pergamon Policy Studies on Socio-Economic Development (New York: Pergamon Press).

East Asian Executive Reports, 1983, monthly, March.

Eckstrom, L. J. (1977) *Licensing in Foreign and Domestic Operations*, vol. 2, chapter 32: 'Licensing operations in Korea' (3rd edn) (New York: Clark Boardman Company Ltd).

Economist, The, weekly, London, various issues.

Enos, J (1984) *IDS Bulletin*, vol. 15, no. 2, April.

Ensor, P. (1984) 'Staying Away from the Economic Curb', Special Survey: Banking '84, *Far Eastern Economic Review*, 26 April 1984.

EPB Economic Bulletin (bi-weekly), Economic Planning Board, Seoul, Korea, various issues.

EPB Economic Survey, Economic Planning Board, Seoul, Korea, various issues.

Epstein, B. and R. Newfalmer (1982) 'Imperfect International Markets and Monopolistic Prices to Developing Countries: a Case Study', *Cambridge Journal of Economics*, vol. 6, no. 1, March, pp. 33–52.

Far Eastern Economic Review, Asia Yearbook (1961–83) (annual), various issues. (Hong Kong).

Far Eastern Economic Review (weekly), various issues, 1962–83, Hong Kong.

Frank, C. R. Jr, Kim Kwang Suk and L. Westphal (1975) *Foreign Trade Regimes and Economic Development: South Korea*, National Bureau of Economic Research (New York: Columbia University Press).

Hahm, Pyong-Choon (1967) 'The Korean Political Tradition and Law: Essays in Korean Law and Legal History', Royal Artistic Society Korea Branch *Monograph Series* No. 1 (Seoul: Computer Press).

Hahn, F. (1982) 'Reflections on the Invisible Hand', *Lloyds Bank Review*, no. 144, April, pp. 1–21.

Hamilton, C. (1985) *Capitalist Industrialisation in Korea* (Westview Special Studies on East Asia).

Helleiner, G. K. (1980) 'World Market Imperfections and Developing Countries', in G. K. Helleiner, *International Economic Disaster: Essays in North-South Relations* (London: Macmillan).

Hone, A. (1974) 'Multinational Corporations and Multinational Buying Groups: their Impact on the Growth of Asia's Export of Manufactures', *World Development,* 2(2), February.

Hong, Wontack, (1978) 'Export Plan and Actual Export Performance in Korea', *Seoul National University Economic Review,* vol. xii, no. 1, December.

Hong, Wontack, (1979) *Trade, Distortions and Employment Growth in Korea,* Korea Development Institute, Seoul, Korea.

Hong, Wontack and L. B. Krause (1981) *Trade and Growth of the Advanced Developing Countries in the Pacific Basin* (Seoul: KDI).

IDRC (International Development Research Centre) (1980) *Science and Technology for Development,* STPI Module G: 'Policy Instruments for the Regulation of Technology Imports'.

ILT (Investing, Licensing and Trading Conditions Abroad) (1980) *Korea,* Business International Corporation, July.

ILT (1983) *Korea,* Business International Corporation, June.

IMF (International Monetary Fund) (1956–83) *Annual Report on Exchange Arrangements and Restrictions,* various issues, Washington.

Jacobsson, S. (1983) 'Industrial Policy for the Machine Tool Industries of Korea and Taiwan', Research Policy Institute, University of Lund, Sweden, mimeo.

Jacobsson, S. (1984) 'Industrial Policy for the Machine Tool Industries of South Korea and Taiwan', *IDS Bulletin,* vol. 15, no. 2.

Jeong, G.-S. (1983) 'Direct Foreign Investment in Korea', Korea Exchange Bank, *Monthly Review,* xvii(10), October.

Jo, S.-H. (1976) 'The Impact of Multinational Firms on Employment and Incomes: the Case Study of South Korea', World Employment Programme *Working Paper,* No. 12, ILO, Geneva.

Jo, S.-H. (1980) 'Direct Foreign Private Investment', in C. K. Park (ed.), *Essays on the Korean Economy Vol III: Macroeconomic and Industrial Development in Korea* (Seoul: Korea Development Institute).

Jones, L. P. and I. Sakong (1980) 'Government, Business and Entrepreneurship in Economic Development: the Korean Case', Harvard University Council on East Asian Studies, *Harvard East Asia Monographs,* no. 91, Cambridge, Mass.

Kalton, M. (1979), 'Korean Ideas and Values', *Philip Jaisohn Memorial Paper,* no. 7, Philip Jaisohn Memorial Foundation, Pennsylvania.

Kang, Kyung-Shik and In-Joung Whang (1982) 'The Role of Goverment in Korea's Industrial Development: the Extent of Planning and Implementation Mechanisms', Paper Presented at the *International Forum on Industrial Planning and Trade Policies, KDI,* Seoul, June.

KEB (Korea Exchange Bank) (1971) *Foreign Exchange and Trade Systems in Korea* (Seoul: Korea Exchange Bank).

KEB (1973a) *Foreign Exchange and Trade Systems in Korea,* (Seoul: Korea Exchange Bank).

KEB (1973b) *The Businessman's Guide to Korea* (Seoul: Korea Exchange Bank).

KEB (1978) *Businessman's Guide to Korea* (Seoul: Korea Exchange Bank).

KEB (1979) *Foreign Exchange and Trade Regulations in Korea* (Seoul: Korea Exchange Bank).

KEB, undated (1968 approx), *Foreign Exchange Control Act and Presidential Decree Thereof* (Seoul: Korea Exchange Bank).

KEB, various issues, *Monthly Review*, Seoul.

Kim, Bun Woong (1982a) 'Korean Bureaucracy in Historical Perspective', in Kim and Rho (eds), *Korean Public Bureaucracy*.

Kim, Bun Woong (1982b) 'The Korean Political Psyche and Administration', in Kim and Rho (eds), *Korean Public Bureaucracy*.

Kim, Bun Woong (1982c) 'Confucianism and Administrative Development Interventionism', in Kim and Rho (eds), *Korean Public Bureacracy*.

Kim, Bun Woong and Wha Joon Rho (eds) (1982) *Korean Public Bureaucracy*, Perspectives in Korean Social Science I, (Seoul: Kyobo Publishing Inc).

Kim, Chan Jin (ed.) (1982) *Business Laws in Korea: Investment, Taxation and Industrial Property* (Seoul: Panmun Book Company Ltd).

Kim, Chin and R. H. Rogier (1976) 'International Trade and Investment Law in the Republic of Korea', *Journal of World Trade Law*, vol. 10, no. 5, pp. 462–77.

Kim, Chong Kim and Seong-Tong Pai (1981) 'Legislative Process in Korea', The Institute of Social Sciences *Korean Studies Series*, no. 3 (Seoul National University Press).

Kim, Chuk Kyo and Chul Heui Lee (1980) 'Ancillary Firm Development in the Korean Automotive Industry', *KIEI Working Paper*, no. 13, Korea International Economic Institute, Seoul.

Kim, Kwang-Doo (1981) 'Cost and Appropriateness Analysis of Technology Imports with Reference to Korea', Paper presented to the *Korea–France Joint Symposium*, September, KIEI (Korea International Economic Institute).

Kim, Kwang Suk (1974) 'Outward-looking Industrialisation Strategy: the Case of Korea', *KDI Working Paper* 7407, Korea Development Institute, Seoul.

Kim, Kyong-Dong (1979) 'Political Factors in the Formation of the Entrepreneurial Elite in Korea', in Kyong-Dong Kim (ed.), *Man and Society in Korea's Economy Growth*, The Institute of Social Sciences Korean Studies Series no 1, Seoul National University Press.

Kim, Linsu (1982) 'Science and Technology Policies for Industrial Development', paper presented at the *International Forum on Industrial Planning and Trade Policies, KDI*, Seoul, 1–12 June.

Kim, S. (1979) 'Foreign Investment: the Rush Slows Down', *Financial Times* Survey: South Korea, Monday, 2 April.

Kim, Seung Hee (1970) *Foreign Capital for Economic Development: a Korean Case Study*, Praeger Special Studies in International Economics and Development (New York, Washington, London: Praeger).

Kim, Sooyong (1982) 'Contract Migration in the Republic of Korea', International Migration for Employment *Working Paper*, Geneva.

Koo, B.-J. (1981) 'Role of foreign direct investment in recent Korean economic growth', *KDI Working Paper* 8104, Korea Development Institute, Seoul.

Koo, B.-J. (1982) 'New Forms of Foreign Investment in Korea', *KDI Working Paper* 82–02, Korea Development Institute, Seoul.

Korea Annual (1967–82) Yonhap News Agency, Seoul, various issues.

Korea Herald, daily (English), Seoul, various issues.

Korea Legal Center (1975) *Laws of the Republic of Korea*, Seoul.

Korea Times, daily (English), Seoul, various issues.

Krauss, M. B. (1983) *Development Without Aid: Growth, Poverty and Government* (New York: McGraw-Hill).

Krueger, A. O. (1978) *Liberalisation Attempts and Consequences*, vol. x, Foreign Trade Regimes and Economic Development, National Bureau of Economic Research, New York.

Krueger, A. O. (1979) 'The Developmental Role of the Foreign Sector and Aid', *Studies in the Modernisation of the Republic of Korea: 1945–1975* (Cambridge, Mass.: Council on East Asian Studies, Harvard University Press).

KTA (Korea Traders Association) (1973) *Laws Relating to Foreign Trade* (Seoul: Korea Traders Association).

KTA (1981) 'Ministry of Commerce and Industry, Annual Export and Import Notice for Second Half of 1981 and First Half of 1982' (unofficial translation).

KTA (1982) *Import Handbook* (in Korean), Seoul.

Kuznets, P. W. (1977) *Economic Growth and Structure in the Republic of Korea.* (New Haven: Yale University Press).

Kwack, Yoon Chick *et al.* (1973) *Credit and Security in Korea: the Legal Problems of Development Finance* (St Lucia, New York: University of Queensland Press, Crane, Russak & Company).

Lal, D. (1983) *The Poverty of 'Development Economics'*, Hobart Paperback 16 (London: Institute of Economic Affairs).

Lall, S. (1981) 'Welfare Economics and Development Problems', in S. Lall, *Developing Countries in the International Economy: Selected Papers* (London: Macmillan).

Lall, S., and P. Streeten (1977) *Foreign Investment, Transnationals and Developing Countries* (London: Macmillan).

Laws on International Transactions, Banking and Finance (1979) Republic of Korea, Kumyoong-Kyungje Press Co, Seoul.

Lee, C. H. (1980) 'United States and Japanese Direct Investment in Korea: a Comparative Study', *Hitotsubashi Journal of Economics*, 20(2).

Lee, Kyung-Deok (1982) 'Foreign Banks in Korea', Korea Exchange Bank *Monthly Review*, vol. xvi, no. 4.

Lee, Man-Ki (1978) 'Ideology and Practice in Korea's Economic Development', *Korea Observer* (quarterly), vol. ix, no. 4, The Academcy of Korean Studies, Seoul.

Lee, Tae-Hee and W. H. Callaway (1982) 'Foreign Exchange Controls in Korea and Their Impact upon International Commercial Transactions', in Kim Chan Jin (ed.), *Business Laws in Korea: Investment Taxation and Industrial Property* (Seoul: Panmun Book Company Ltd).

Lim, Youngil (1981) 'Government Policy and Private Enterprise: Korean Experience in Industrialisation', *Korea Research Monograph*, no. 6, Institute of East Asian Studies, University of California, Berkeley.

Little, I. (1979) 'The Experience and Causes of Rapid Labour-intensive Development in Korea, Taiwan, Hong Kong and Singapore; and the Possibilities of Emulation', ARTEP (Asian Region Team for Employment Promotion), ILO-ARTEP *WP* II-1.

Little, I., T. Scitovsky and M. Scott (1970) *Industry and Trade in Some Developing Countries: a Comparative Study*, published for the OECD by Oxford University Press, London.

Luedde-Neurath, R. (1985) 'State Intervention and Export-oriented Development in South Korea', in White and Wade (eds), 95–189. *Developmental States in East Asia*.

Luedde-Neurath, R. (1986) 'Import Controls and Export-oriented Development: a Reassessment of the South Korea Case', Westview Special Studies on East Asia.

Luther, H. U., (1981) *Suedkorea (K)ein Modell fuer die Dritte Welt?: Wachstumsdiktatur und Abhaengige Entwicklung* (Muenchen: Verlag Simon & Hagiera).

MCI (Ministry of Commerce and Industry), *Public Note* 81–40 (in Korean), Seoul.

Michell, T. (1981) 'What Happens to Economic Growth when Neo-classical Policy Replaces Keynesian? The case of South Korea', in S. Griffith-Jones and D. Seers (eds), *'Monetarism': Its Effects on Developing Countries*, special issue of *IDS Bulletin*, 13(1), IDS, University of Sussex, Brighton, pp. 60–67.

Michell, T. (1982) 'South Korea: Vision of the Future of Labour Surplus Economies?' in M. Bienefeld and M. Godfrey (eds), *The Struggle for Development: National Strategies in an International Context* (Chicester: John Wiley and Sons).

Michell, T. (1983) 'Trade Employment and Industrialisation in South Korea', International Division of Labour Programme, *World Employment Research Programme Working Paper*, ILO, Geneva.

Michell, T. (1984) 'Administrative Traditions and Economic Decision Making in Korea', *IDS Bulletin*, vol. 15, no. 4.

MOF (Ministry of Finance) (1982) *Guidelines on Foreign Investment*, 8 October, Seoul.

Morawetz, D., 1980, 'Why the Emperor's New Clothes are Not Made in Colombia', *World Bank Staff Working Paper*, no. 368, IBRD, Washington.

Nakarmi, L. (1984) 'Banking Reforms: Repairing Cracks and Credibility', *Business Korea*, February.

Nam, Chong Hyun (1981) 'Trade and Industrial Policies and the Structure of Protection in Korea', in Wontack Hong and L. B. Krause (eds), *Trade and Growth of Advanced Developing Countries in the Pacific Basin* (Seoul: Korea Development Institute).

OECD (Organisation for Economic Co-operation and Development) (1977) *Restrictive Business Practices of Multinational Enterprises: Report of the Committee of Experts on Restrictive Business Practices*, Paris.

Oh, Sang-Lak (1968) 'The Role of Government in Korean Marketing', Seoul National University *Economic Review*, vol. 11, no. 1, Seoul.

Page, S. A. B. (1979) 'The Management of International Trade', *Discussion Paper*, no. 29, National Institute of Economic and Social Research, London.

Paik, Wan Ki (1982) 'A Psycho-cultural Approach to the Study of Korean Bureaucracy,' in Kim and Rho (eds), *Korean Public Bureaucracy*.

Park, E. Y. (1982) 'Pattern of Foreign Direct Investment, Foreign Ownership and Industrial Performance: the Case of Korean Manufacturing Industry', Korea Development Institute, Seoul, mimeo.

Philippine Labour Review (1979) 'Manpower Requisition Procedures in Korea', vol. 4, no. 2.

Purcell, G. and Yung Whee Rhee (1978) 'A Firm-level Study of Korean Exports', *Research Report*, no. 1 (preliminary); 'Some Institutional Aspects of Incentives Policy', World Bank, mimeo, December.

Rhee Kyu Ho (1983) *Struggle for National Identity in the Third World*, Hollym International Corporation, Elizabeth, New Jersey and Seoul.

Rhee, Myung-Jai (1981) *International Banks and Financial Markets in Korea*, KIEI (Korea International Economic Institute).

Rhee, Yung Whee (1981) 'Administrative Arrangements for Korean Export Promotion, World Bank, 14 June, preliminary mimeo.

Richardson, R. (1979) 'Banking: Competition and Conformity', *Financial Times* Survey on South Korea VI, Monday, 2 April.

Rooken-Smith, D. R. (1982) '"Japan Incorporated" and "The Korean Troops": a Comparative Analysis of Korean Business Organisations', MA thesis (unpublished), Department of Asian Studies, University of Hawaii.

Sano, J. (1977) 'Foreign Capital and Investment in South Korean Development', *Asian Economics*, no. 23, December.

Sen, A. K. (1981) 'Public Action and the Quality of Life in Development Countries', *Oxford Bulletin of Economics and Statistics*, November.

Sharpston, M. (1975) 'International Subcontracting', *Oxford Economic Papers*, 27(1), March.

Smith, C. (1979a) 'A Change of Direction', *Financial Times* Survey on South Korea, Monday, 2 April.

Smith C. (1979b) 'Trading Companies: Group System Wins More Exports', *Financial Times* Survey on South Korea V, Monday, 2 April.

Sunoo, H. H. (1978) 'Economic Development and Foreign Control in South Korea', *Journal of Contemporary Asia* 8(3).

Uekusa, M. (1980) 'Monopoly Regulation and Fair Trade Policy in Korea', *Consultant Paper Series*, no. 18, Korea Development Institute, Seoul.

UN (United Nations) Centre on Transnational Corporations (1978) *National Legislation and Regulations Relating to Transnational Corporations*, ST/CTC/6, New York.

UN Centre on Transnational Corporations (1983) *Transnational Corporations in World Development: Third Survey*, ST/CTC/46, New York.

United States Council of the International Chamber of Commerce (1979) *Public Policy and Technology Transfer: Viewpoints of US Business*, vol. 3: 'Host Country Environments', Fund for Multinational Management

Education, Council of the Americas, The George Washington University.

Vaitsos, C. (1976) 'The Revision of the International Patent System: Legal Considerations for a Third World Position', *World Development*, vol. 4, no. 2.

Westphal, L. E. (1978) 'The Republic of Korea's Experience with Export-led Industrial Development', *World Development*, vol. 6, no. 3, pp. 347–82.

Westphal, L. E. (1981) 'Empirical Justification for Infant Industry Protection', *World Bank Staff Working Paper*, no. 445, IBRD, Washington.

Westphal, L. E. and Kim Kwang Suk (1977) 'Industrial Policy and Development in Korea', *World Bank Staff Working Paper*, no. 263, IBRD, Washington.

Westphal, L. E., Y. W. Rhee and G. Purcell (1979) 'Foreign Influences on Korean Industrial Development', *Oxford Bulletin of Economics and Statistics*, 41(4), November.

Whang, In-Joung (1969) 'Elite Change and Program Change in the Korean Government, 1955–1967', *Korean Journal of Public Administration*, vol. vii, no. 1, April, Seoul.

White, G. and R. Wade (eds) (1985) *Developmental States in East Asia*, IDS Research Report, Brighton.

Wortzel, L. H. and H. V. (1981) 'Export Marketing Strategies for NIC and LDC-based Firms', *Columbia Journal of World Business*, Spring.

Yoh, Song Whan, (1982) 'Management of Industrial Projects: the Case of Pohang Iron and Steel Co Ltd', Paper Presented at the *International Forum on Industrial Planning and Trade Policies*, KDI, Seoul, 1–12 June.

Yoon, Woo Kon (1982) 'Korean Bureacrats Behaviour: the Effect of Personality on Behaviour', in Kim and Rho (eds), *Korean Public Bureaucracy*.

Yu, Seongtae (1982) 'The Development of the Korea Electronics Industry, with Special Reference to Samsung Electronics', paper presented at the *International Forum on Industrial Planning and Trade Policies*, KDI, Seoul, 1–12 June.

4 Economic Growth and the Rise of Civil Society: Agriculture in Taiwan and South Korea[1]
Mick Moore

1. INTRODUCTION

Interpretations of the post-war industrialisation of Taiwan and South Korea have generally understated the extent of state regulation of economic life. In their accounts of industrial policy, Leudde-Neurath and Wade have devoted considerable attention to getting the facts straight – to detailing the nature and extent of state involvement in economic decision making – as well as to assessing the consequences of this involvement. The student of *agricultural* policy in these two 'little tigers' is in a more fortunate position. Existing literature leaves little doubt that the state has intervened deeply in the agricultural economy throughout the post-war period. Liberated from the need to establish and assert basic facts about the degree of state intervention, one can devote more attention to exploring some of its dimensions.

If one were to respond to the demand for 'lessons' for other countries from the Taiwanese and South Korean experiences, this discussion would focus on the contributions, positive or negative, of state regulation for agricultural growth. While it is suggested below that state regulation of agriculture has almost certainly helped promote industrial (and thus general economic) growth, the main focus of this chapter is *not* on the causal relationship between policy and economic performance. I am concerned with a more fundamental set of issues about the connection between economic structure and forms of state regulation of the economy. My main intention is not to add to the debate about the causes of rapid economic growth in Taiwan and South Korea since the early 1950s, but to examine instead the consequences for state regulation of the economy of the major changes in economic structure which have accompanied this growth.

113

In sum, my thesis is that structural change – the diversification of the input and product structure of agriculture, and the growing market integration between sections of the agricultural economy and between agriculture and non-agriculture – has played a major role in both countries in inducing a shift from statism to pluralism in the relationship between the state and the agricultural economy and population. Trying to avoid a simple deterministic position, it is argued that in both Taiwan and South Korea a certain pattern of public economic and political regulation of agriculture, here labelled 'statist', was feasible – i.e. could be implemented without incurring excessive political and economic costs – in the early post-war period because of aspects of economic structure. Changes in economic structure and relationships have: (a) changed the objectives of the state *vis-à-vis* agriculture; (b) increased the economic and political costs of pursing established *dirigiste* economic policies which diverted material resources away from agriculture: (c) reduced the political and economic effectiveness of the established institutional framework of government–agriculture relationships. The result has been the emergence of a more pluralist relationship – 'the rise of civil society'.

The concepts of statism and pluralism are explained in Section 2. This is followed by a discussion of the East Asian context in Section 3, and of the context and purpose of the Taiwan–South Korea (henceforth Korea) comparison in Section 4. Since space constraints necessitate a very compressed presentation of the argument and the exclusion of much supporting evidence and empirical detail, structural changes in Taiwanese and Korean agriculture are summarised in Section 5, and their causal role in the transition from statism to pluralism sketched out in Section 6. Such detail as it is possible to give on individual country experience is contained in Sections 7 to 9.

2. STATISM AND PLURALISM

'Statism' and 'pluralism' refer to the balance of power, in the broadest sense, between the state and civil society. 'Statism' indicates a high degree of dominance and control by central government over polity, society and economy. There are various dimensions of such dominance, and a great deal of imprecise imagery in the language used. One cannot begin to measure the variables used on anything but an impressionistic basis. The best that can be said about the conceptual apparatus used here is that it is the best we have.[2]

For present purposes the term 'statism' is used to indicate the following primary features of the relationship between the state and the agricultural population/economy:

(i) Agencies of the central government have a high capacity to initiate changes in agricultural policy and the agricultural economy, and to impose these changes on the agricultural population. These agencies are relatively well coordinated with one another, and independent of the populations with which they interact.

(ii) While state power may be employed in part to further the individual or group interests of state personnel, it is used to an important degree to advance more collective, 'national' interests and projects, especially the strengthening of the state apparatus *vis-à-vis* civil society, and the advancement of national interests in the international arena.

(iii) The state intervenes routinely and pervasively in the agricultural economy, and in large degree through administrative regulation impinging directly on the economic behaviour of the individual citizen or enterprise. The conceptual distinction between private economic interests and *raison d'état* is barely recognised.

(iv) The agricultural population are kept powerless and unorganised. They are not effectively represented in policy-making. Autonomous political organisation is not tolerated. Even 'private' associations serving economic purposes – e.g. cooperatives, producer associations – are permitted to exist and function, if at all, only under the tutelage of state agencies.

The main characteristics of the concept of 'pluralism' can be inferred from this description of statism. They are:

(i) A degree of symbiosis between individual state agencies and the client populations with which they interact, typically leading to a greater degree of conflict between state agencies over agricultural policy as these agencies come to espouse different interests.

(ii) A greater capacity on the part of the agricultural population to resist, through both economic and political means, coercive or exploitative economic policies. The state correspondingly finds it increasingly necessary to take account of the likely responses of the agricultural population when formulating policy.

(iii) The agricultural population is more effectively organised to influence national policy.
(iv) The practice of direct administrative regulation of the private economy diminishes in favour of the use of parametric controls, i.e. indirect inducements to alter private economic decisions.

The state–pluralism continuum used here is very different from the state control-free market dichotomy which is deeply embedded in Western economic thought and which tends to dominate discussion of these broad issues of government–economy relationships. The state–pluralism continuum focuses on an issue which is pushed to the sidelines in the conventional discourse: *alternative* modes of state regulation of the 'private' economy. More fundamentally, the state control-free market dichotomy is conceptually inadequate and empirically misleading. By implying that the absence of state regulation leads to fully competitive market processes and thus to the allocation of resources through competitively-determined prices this dichotomy ignores all those occasions in (a) which market competition is stifled by the use of private economic and political power (e.g. monopoly, collusion); and (b) effective, but not total, state control of the economy is achieved through the emergence of 'corporatist' arrangements of various types between state agencies and organised private interests.

State control and free markets are not polar opposites. In many situations the relationship between the two can be symbiotic. A strong state may be needed to ensure freely-functioning competitive markets, and the resultant constraints on the emergence of private monopoly power help perpetuate the autonomy of the state. In certain respects statism in Taiwan and Korea has actually promoted competitive market processes. The muzzling of trade unions has meant that agricultural and industrial wage rates *have* been largely determined by competitive market processes. Similarly, the prohibition on independent farmers' associations has permitted competitive market processes very wide scope to shape those areas of the agricultural economy in which the state has chosen not to intervene.

The account here of the shift from statism to pluralism is emphatically not an account of the triumph of the market over the state. Our existing conceptual apparatus does not permit one to make any claim about changes in the balance between the two. Where the balance has shifted is between state and civil society.

Here there has been a change from command, domination and exploitation to a more negotiated relationship.

3. THE EAST ASIAN CONTEXT

Statist approaches to economic regulation have a long history in East Asia, and have been prevalent since the Second World War in 'capitalist' Japan, South Korea and Taiwan, as well as in communist China and North Korea (Cumings, 1984; Hofheinz and Calder, 1982). Only Hong Kong stands out as an exception, and clearly not one of great significance. In relation to agriculture, the peculiar characteristic of Taiwan and Korea is that their variants of statism have involved the almost complete exclusion of agriculturalists from the ruling coalition and from any influence on the policy making process. This distinguishes these two from Japan, with which they otherwise share many common features in terms of agrarian structure, particular agricultural policies, and the changing relationships between agricultural and other sectors of the economy in the course of economic growth. For, since 1945 at least, farmers have constituted an important if largely passive element in the coalition which has dominated the Japanese state. In this respect Japan may have more in common with China than with Taiwan and Korea. True that Chinese farmers lack organised channels for representing their interests independent of the Communist Party. Yet history, ideology and the peasant backgrounds of party, state and military cadres make the Chinese state relatively responsive to peasant interests (Nolan and White, 1984). Here China stands in marked contrast to the Soviet Union, and it is perhaps to the Soviet Union that Taiwan and Korea can most usefully be compared. The three constitute the only cases in world history of successful industrialisation programmes masterminded by ruling coalitions from which virtually all segments of the agricultural population were excluded.

4. THE TAIWAN–SOUTH KOREA COMPARISON

The Taiwan and Korea cases are being treated together here, not in order to emphasise contrasts between them, but rather to illustrate fundamental similarities in the evolution of the state–agriculture relationship. The existence of these similarities is based on a common history and context in respect of, for example; history (Japanese colonial rule, marked by a very authoritarian, and successful, approach to promoting agricultural development); agrarian structure (small family rice farms); agricultural population densities (very intensive land use); place in global geo-political struggles after the Second World War; and rapid recent industrialisation. Even more importantly, the main point of similarity, and the historical point of departure for our analysis, is the nature of the regimes which were established in Taiwan and Korea after the Second World War, liberation from Japanese rule, varying degrees of civil war, the imposition of Nationalist rule in Taiwan, social revolution in Korea, the 1961 military takeover in South Korea, and continuing intense rivalry and near-war between Taiwan and China and South and North Korea respectively.[3]

The Taiwanese and South Korea regimes were highly statist in the broadest sense of the term. The military, allied with small and unrepresentative social groups, dominated the state, and the state dominated civil society and the 'private' economy to a very high degree. The interests of groups in civil society, including the interests of the owners of capital, were closely subordinated to the interests of the groups controlling the state. Interest groups in civil society were organised and represented in policy-making only on sufferance. To ensure their own survival, domestically and in the context of international geo-political competition, the groups controlling the state were strongly motivated to adopt a *dirigiste* approach towards the management of the economy: to direct trade and investment to meet military needs; to accumulate surpluses in state hands; to accelerate the process of industrialisation; to undertake land reform to keep the peasantry politically quiescent; and to manage the local economy to ensure a reliable supply of cheap food for military, official and urban consumers.

There are inevitably differences between the two countries in various dimensions listed above, and the implications are mentioned where appropriate. One contextual difference is that Korean cultural traditions,[4] and the structures of power and forms of government action which reproduce those traditions, are more clearly congruent with statism than is the political culture of Taiwan. Individualism, familialism and a sense of moral limits to state control of private behaviour are more in evidence in Taiwan.

Another difference is that industrial development has been highly decentralised in Taiwan while concentrated around just two cities in Korea (Ho, 1982). This has made the combination of industrial employment with agriculture much more frequent in Taiwan.

A third difference is that, in agriculture as in other sectors, policy has been more stable in Taiwan than in Korea, and changed in a more incremental fashion. As many have observed, Korean policy tends to take the form of the risky 'big push'. The greater volatility of Korean policy-making is closely related to a greater commitment to 'Maoist'-type beliefs that social mobilisation and human will are the mainsprings of social and national progress. It also makes it more difficult for the observer to detect the fundamental, long-term effects on policy and polity of changes in economic structure, at least compared with Taiwan.

There is, however, one difference between the two countries which is intrinsic rather than contingent to the central argument about the evolution from statism to pluralism: while the two have followed a very similar path of growth and structural economic change, Taiwan has consistently taken the lead by virtue of its higher income levels. The changes in the state–agriculture relationship induced by economic growth have taken place earlier in Taiwan. The Taiwanese experience is therefore paid more attention here. The Korean material serves mainly to illustrate that the Taiwanese case is not *sui generis*, and that similar influences working in similar contexts have tended to produce similar results.

These 'influences' are seen mainly to reflect economic and political changes internal to Taiwan and Korea respectively – 'internal' either in the strict sense of the term or in the sense that their national economic and political structures mediate and shape the domestic impact of the common global economic and political context. Nevertheless, the two experiences are not entirely independent of one another in causal and historical senses. In agricultural as well as in industrial policy, Taiwan and Korea both appear to see the Japanese experience as a model for emulation in at least some respects. (The shift to massive agricultural protection and high public expenditure on agriculture in Japan in recent decades is, however, seen more as a warning than a model for Taiwan and Korea.) In addition, both Taiwan and Korea keep a watchful eye on one another and imitate policy where this seems appropriate. Because Korea is more clearly 'backward' in agriculture than in

industry when compared with Taiwan, Koreans tend to look to
Taiwan for ideas and models for agricultural policy rather than vice
versa.

5. STRUCTURAL CHANGE IN THE AGRICULTURAL ECONOMY

The changes which have taken place since the early 1950s in the
structure of Taiwanese and Korean agriculture and in the relationship
between agriculture and the national economy are fairly predictable.
In essence, in both countries an economy which was to a large
degree 'peasant' and agrarian has given way to one in which
agriculture is but one, rather small, economic sector which is highly
integrated with other sectors of the economy. As has already been
mentioned, Taiwan has maintained several years lead over Korea in
their common advance along almost identical pathways of structural
economic change. A few of the most significant aspects of this
structural transformation will be listed here, with only brief
comments or supporting evidence.

Firstly, the relative quantitative importance of agriculture has
declined considerably because of very rapid industrial growth,
despite an average growth rate of agricultural production of around
3.6 per cent per year in both countries. In 1953 the agricultural
sector provided 34 per cent of Taiwan's Gross National Product. By
1981 this had fallen to 7 per cent. The comparable figures for Korea
are 46 per cent and 18 per cent respectively. Over the same period
the 'farm population' – i.e. persons living in farm households –
declined from 45 per cent to 21 per cent of the population of Taiwan
and from 46 per cent to 26 per cent of that of Korea.

Secondly, there has been very substantial product diversification
within the agricultural sector, with grains (rice, plus some barley in
Korea) losing their primacy. Their place has been taken by livestock
and horticultural products. These are mainly perishable products
which require rapid and careful post-harvest handling and, in some
cases, processing, and whose profitability is heavily dependent on
their meeting consumer preferences for taste, quality, timing of
marketing, freshness, etc. Between 1953 and 1981 the ratio of the
value of production of these perishables to the value of grain
production has risen from 0.5 : 1 to 2.3 : 1 in Taiwan, and 0.4 : 1 to 1.0 : 1
in Korea. This is a consequence of changing patterns of consumer

demand stemming from increased incomes. Per capita consumption of rice peaked in 1967 in Taiwan, and began to fall steeply from 1978. Rice is no longer the dominant element in consumer budgets.

Thirdly, agricultural production is becoming more capital intensive, commercialised, and thus integrated into the non-farm economy. Whether measured in physical or value terms, land and labour have been playing a steadily diminishing role in agricultural production. The intensity of land use has declined in both countries from peak levels in the mid-1960s. Capital, and especially current capital not originating on the farm (i.e. not farm produced animal feed or organic manures) is of increasing importance. At the level of the farm enterprise this process of capitalisation manifests itself in rising asset to income ratios and increases in both the proportions of farm inputs obtained for cash and of the proportions farm income realised in cash rather than in auto-consumption. Human labour is being replaced by farm machinery. Purchased animal feed is now much more important than farm supplied feed. Farmers are purchasing pumps to supplement or substitute for canal irrigation. Pesticides, fuel, feed and fertilisers are becoming major items of expenditure for farmers.

One important aspect of this general process is that the range of farm inputs obtained from the industrial sector has widened considerably. In the early period chemical fertiliser was the dominant purchased farm input, and widely used by government as a lever to regulate and exploit agriculture. Pesticides, fuel, purchased tools, purchased seed, a diverse range of intermediate inputs, and, above all, animal feed, have become more important in both countries. In addition, chemical fertiliser mixes have become more diverse and specialised as they have increasingly come to be used for non-rice crops.

Fourthly, the sub-section of agriculture which has grown fastest over the past decade – livestock – is in both countries mainly and increasingly dominated by a relatively small number of large firms which have their roots in manufacturing, food processing or feedgrain importing, and who feed their livestock mainly on imported American feedgrain. The livestock sub-sector is increasingly distinct from the bulk of agriculture in structural terms, has very different interests in economic policy, is much better organised to influence policy, and has a much more direct and fruitful relationship with economic policy-makers.

Fifthly and finally, non-farm rural employment has spread so rapidly, especially in Taiwan, that agriculture has shrunk to a secondary income source for most of the farm population. In the 1960s the proportion of farm household income earned from non-farm sources was around 20 per cent in both countries. Because of the decentralised pattern of industrial development in Taiwan this increased rapidly, reaching 70 per cent in 1980. At this point only 10 per cent of Taiwanese farm households obtained more than half their income from farming. In Korea the proportion of farm household income earned off-farm remained around 20 per cent until 1976. Only then did it begin to increase rapidly, but had reached only 33 per cent in 1981.

In the face of these structural transformations a few things remain almost unchanged. There are two structural continuities very relevant to the general argument here. One is that, throughout the post-war period, the agricultural economies of both countries have been producing almost entirely for domestic consumption. There has thus been a very close interaction between their agricultural and non-agricultural sectors. In particular, the structure of the agricultural economy has been closely determined by the nature and speed of industrialisation, and influenced only to a relatively small degree by fluctuations in world primary commodity markets.

The second structural continuity is the persistence since land reform of an essentially small family farm system in all areas of agriculture except livestock production (see above). Although some smaller landowners have left agriculture entirely, more so in Korea than in Taiwan, non-farm rural employment has stabilised the farm population, and there is no detectable process of displacement of small landowners by agrarian capitalists.

6. THE POLITICAL CONSEQUENCES OF STRUCTURAL ECONOMIC CHANGE

The central thesis about the causal connection between structural economic change and the transition from statism to pluralism is not here subjected to any rigorous process of verification. It derives from a wide variety of sources, and is justified essentially on grounds of overall plausibility. Space constraints prohibit any 'thick description' of how the causal processes operated in each of the two countries. The main argument is therefore summarised in this section, and limited detail on Taiwan and Korea given in succeeding sections. Before presenting the central argument itself a few contextual explanations are required.

One is that structural economic change is not asked to bear the whole burden of explaining the emergence of pluralism in the government–agriculture relationship. Part of the explanation, at least in Taiwan, must lie in the gradual liberalisation of the political system. Generally speaking, authoritarianism, intolerance of any dissent, and the near-total exclusion from political power of the majority of non-Mainlander population (i.e. Taiwanese, who account for virtually all farmers, and who in the 1950s were mainly farmers) have given way to a degree of tolerance of dissent and to the increasing incorporation of Taiwanese into the policy-making process. Over some aspects of policy, including agricultural policy, public debate is relatively vigorous. Some politicians have made the defence of agricultural interests their central concern.

The second and related point is that the kind of pluralism which has emerged in both countries has not extended to the direct incorporation into the policy-making process of representatives drawn from the agricultural population. The increased bargaining power of the agricultural population is mainly of a passive and reactive nature, and spokesmen for agriculture are drawn from state agencies which have a vested interest in the allocation of public resources to agriculture.

The third point is that the shift from statism to pluralism has been paralleled by, and in part causally related to, a change in the overall impact of public policy on resource flows to and from agriculture. In sum, statism was closely associated with sets of policies which resulted in the extraction of resources from agriculture to support the state apparatus, urban food consumers, and industrialisation, while pluralism is associated with the protection of increasingly high cost agriculture against competing imports and with the subsidisation of agriculture from public funds. The causal connection between these two processes is however incomplete, and the parallelism in timing closer in Taiwan than in Korea (see Section 9).

Leaving all these reservations and qualification aside, the core of the thesis is that there are three main mechanisms through which the structural economic changes summarised in the previous section have contributed to the shift from statism to pluralism. These mechanisms, labelled 'economic diversification', 'producer choice' and 'political balance', are discussed separately below.

Economic diversification

The use of directive controls over the agricultural economy was founded on the relative simplicity of both the structure of the agricultural economy and the nature of the government's policy objectives:

(a) The predominance in the output pattern of foodgrains (mainly rice), which are easily accounted for, stored, processed, handled and marketed;
(b) The limited importance and variety of purchased production inputs, among which chemical fertilisers and publicly-provided irrigation water were the most significant;
(c) The primacy of the need to expand the output of basic foodgrains to feed the population.

The main objectives of government policy were clear and simple, and public control of fertiliser supply, irrigation and foodgrain marketing provided a few key levers through which farmers' production practices could be directly influenced by administrative means.

Agriculture has since become more complex in both policy and structural senses. Structurally it has become much more diverse. Purchased inputs like agro-chemicals, machinery and animal feed have become relatively much more important compared with land, labour and farm-produced organic fertilisers. These newer inputs are supplied mainly by commercial agencies, and in some cases, (e.g. small-scale pumps), they provide farmers with alternatives to dependence on inputs supplied by state agencies (e.g. canal irrigation). The relative importance of foodgrains in the output pattern has declined in favour of horticultural and livestock products. The marketing and processing of these products requires a degree of speed, sophistication and responsiveness to consumer needs that state agencies cannot generally provide. State agencies are obliged to give way to or compete with private traders. Taiwan has become embarrassed with a surplus of foodgrains and Korea is rapidly approaching such a situation. To increase foodgrain production is no longer an imperative, and thus it is no longer easy to set a few clear targets for individual farmers or to use control of the supply of inputs for foodgrain production and control of foodgrain markets as levers to influence individual farmers. There is something inherently ridiculous about the idea of the state setting production and delivery quotas for such newly-profitable agricultural products as frogs, flowers, and freshwater shrimps.

Overall, the provision of agricultural inputs and products is no longer taking place in a situation of physical scarcity, and has to be more responsive to the needs of the cultivator and the consumer for variety, quality and timing. The need to physically *supply* scarce commodities has been overtaken by the need to *market* them in the commercial sense of the term. Directive controls have ceded place to parametric controls over market allocations.

Producer choice

In the early period the use of directive controls and macro-level policy instruments to extract a surplus from agriculture was feasible in macroeconomic terms because farmers had limited capacity to react by switching economic resources into alternative non-agricultural uses. There were few alternative uses for the production inputs which farmers controlled themselves, i.e. land, family labour and farm-produced organic fertilisers. And farmers controlled only limited amounts of capital which might be used for other purposes. Although squeezed economically, farmers were obliged to continue to produce because of the lack of alternative sources of livelihood. This situation has changed.

In the first place, the growth of non-agricultural employment and the rising ratio of non-farm to farm labour earnings has provided farm families with alternative and more attractive uses of family labour than farm production.

In the second place, agricultural production has become increasingly dependent on farmers' willingness to reinvest in agriculture – through purchase of agro-chemicals, machinery, livestock feed, etc. – the increasing income that non-farm jobs have brought. Current and fixed capital other than land and labour have become more important in agricultural production generally, and in the livestock sector a few large accumulations of private capital have appeared. It has become increasingly possible for farmers to respond to the squeezing of agriculture in macroeconomic policy by directing their capital elsewhere.

In the third place, in Taiwan at least the decentralised pattern of industrial growth has pushed rural land values to high levels, and provided temptations to sell agricultural land for industrial or housing purposes.

Overall, the pattern of economic growth has made it possible for farmers to switch all major agricultural inputs – land, labour and capital – to non-agricultural uses if the returns from agricultural production are not attractive. Government correspondingly has less scope to determine national economic policy without taking into account the economic responses of the farming population, and their likely adverse effects on national food supplies.

Political balance

Success in industrialisation and the continual tendency for non-agricultural incomes to rise faster than agricultural incomes have created perceived political threats to which governments have felt obliged to respond. The main political threat has been an increased sense of relative deprivation on the part of the farming population. A second threat arose in Korea where, unlike in Taiwan with its dispersed pattern of industrial growth, the rising rural–urban income gap generated considerable rural–urban migration. The consequent growth of shanty towns around Seoul was seen as politically dangerous.

Both governments have responded by shifting inter-sectoral terms of trade in favour of the farming populations and by increasing levels of public spending on rural infrastructure to make rural living more attractive. Two other changes have made governments willing to contemplate making these material concessions to farmers to meet perceived threats to political stability. Rising urban incomes and the consequent declining role of foodgrains in consumer expenditures have decreased potential urban resistance to paying higher prices for foodgrains. It has also been feasible for the government to bear some of the cost of higher producer prices for foodgrains because agriculture is of diminished quantitative significance in the total economy, and the cost of subsidising it from public revenue correspondingly proportionately less than in earlier years.

7. THE TAIWANESE EXPERIENCE OF STATIST AGRICULTURE

This section deals with some of the more significant features of statism in Taiwan, mainly in relation to the 1950s and 1960s. The first sub-section illustrates the range and depth of public regulation of the agricultural economy in that period. The second sub-section demonstrates that political considerations – the establishment and consolidation of the Mainlander Nationalist regime – explain the origins of the high degree of state intervention in the agricultural economy, but that these political objectives did not conflict with the goal of economic development. The third section deals with the institutional dimensions of public intervention, focusing especially on the political dimensions of institutional efficiency.

7.1 Intervening in the Market[5]

One has it on the very best authority that *laissez-faire* and the freely-functioning market were not awarded pride of place as mechanisms for promoting agricultural progress in Taiwan in the 1950s. In the words of T. H. Lee, Cornell-trained economist, and currently Vice-President of the Republic of China:

> The price mechanism was not considered as an incentive for adopting new technology and increasing agricultural output. Government allocation of chemical fertilisers, pesticides, irrigation water, funds and subsidy compensated for the price mechanism. Government collection of rice, sugar and other important products in addition to the unfavourable terms of trade resulted in a tremendous net capital outflow from agriculture. (Lee, 1971, p. 138)

Lee's own academic work was concerned mainly with the enforced transfer of economic resources from agriculture to non-agriculture, and especially with the effects of the battery of monopolies, restrictions, barter arrangements and taxes applied to the producers of rice, the major crop grown by the great majority of farm households.

Farmers were legally required to grow rice on lands designated and recorded as paddy lands. Ownership of paddy land carried an obligation to deliver to the state a quota of rice and to pay a substantial land tax in rice. (Under the Japanese the land tax had been paid in cash.) Rents on the remaining publicly-owned rice land were collected in kind, as were tenants' repayments (to the state) for paddy land acquired under land reform. Credit from the public 'rice' agency, the Provincial Food Bureau, was repayable in rice. In addition and most importantly, fertiliser manufacture and importing were the monopoly of the Taiwan Fertilizer Corporation. Fertiliser was allocated by crop, and was only available to rice farmers in exchange for rice. The rice–fertiliser barter programme accounted for more than half of all public rice procurement. And this in turn accounted for 60 per cent of total rice releases (sales and rental payments) by producers in the period 1950–60. (By 1970 this figure had fallen to 38 per cent.)

All rice deliveries to the state were valued at a single rate. Between 1952 and 1968 this averaged 70 per cent of the 'free' market price. This residual market was far from free. The state dominated it directly or indirectly by monopolising rice imports and exports; by supplying a rice ration to all state, military and educational personnel and their families; and by setting the price at which government-procured rice was released to private traders. Private traders required a licence. The movement of rice between 'food zones' was restricted. The 'private' rice trade was closely monitored by the Provincial Food Bureau. And a range of *ad hoc* regulations were introduced from time to time to further limit the scope of private choice in food trade and consumption. For example, in 1953 a limit of two to three months on home storage of rice was declared; milling of brown rice to more than 93–94 per cent was prohibited; and a programme was launched to promote sweet potato and wheat as rice substitutes.

The Provincial Food Bureau failed in its attempt to widen the scope of the barter economy by exchanging rice for cotton cloth, bicycles, soyabean cake and other commodities. The Bureau was, however, successful in obliging the Farmers' Associations – 'private' organisations (see below) – to bear the bulk of the costs of administering this large public food system. The local Farmers Associations stored and distributed fertiliser; collected, stored and milled paddy; and distributed much of the rice ration. The fees they were paid for these activities seem never to have covered costs. Not only did the Nationalist state succeed in obliging the farmers to meet the costs of administering a system which exploited them, but it succeeded also in maintaining the appearance of a 'lean state' in personnel terms.

Sugar was the second most important crop in the 1950s and this was under even more direct state control than rice production.[6] The Taiwan Sugar Corporation, like the Taiwanese public sector as a whole, has its origins in the seizure by the Nationalists of former Japanese enterprises. The provision of sugar for Japan had been the main single economic motive for and function of Japanese colonial rule. While they produced some cane on their own estates, Japanese sugar refining firms relied mainly on small farmers, who were obliged to supply cane on terms fixed by the refiners. The refining firms were highly cartelised and firmly supported by the administration. Each had a monopoly in the procurement of cane within its operational territory. The Chinese Nationalists took over the system and continued to run it on established lines, albeit at a lesser disadvantage to farmers than under Japanese rule, and in a context in which the relative importance of sugar production declined once the monopoly over the Japanese market was lost. The Sugar Corporation maintained a monopoly over sugar exports and over refining, each contract grower being tied to the refinery serving his locality. Administrative and political pressure was used to secure supplies from growers. Levels of remuneration to growers for their sugar were well below open market sugar prices.

Just as public industrial enterprises have been used to help further the government's plans to build up new lines of production (Wade, this volume), so the Taiwan Sugar Corporation has been prevailed upon to meet state rather than its own corporate objectives in relation to agriculture. The Corporation has diversified into a wide range of agriculture-related industries. Its main activity has become livestock production; it is the largest hog producer in the island. (The livestock sector is dominated by hog production.) In recent years government has tried to stabilise the market price of hogs by asking the Corporation to regulate the timing of its market deliveries in the light of actual and expected prices. The Corporation's farms and agricultural expertise have also been called upon in pursuit of broader policy objectives. The Corporation has for example: helped small farmers diversify into livestock production; financed local drainage, flood control, irrigation, water supply and projects; and tried to promote cooperative farming as part of the 'Second Land Reform' (see below). The Sugar Corporation runs the Livestock Research Institute.

It was the desire to put pressure on farmers to grow sugarcane which had led, in the Japanese period, to the development in canal-irrigated areas of prescribed crop and irrigation rotations. These practices were continued in the Nationalist period, with an emphasis on rice as well as sugarcane. As in the case of the Farmers' Associations in relation to rice procurement and storage, the nominally private Irrigation Associations were subject to state control and employed to enforce public policy. Publicly-financed and controlled infrastructure, especially irrigation, accounted for the bulk of agricultural investment. Private agricultural investment was relatively insignificant.

Other dimensions of state regulation of agriculture included: the existence of a Wine and Tobacco Monopoly which was the sole legal licensee for cultivators of tobacco and grapes, and the monopsony purchaser of their produce; a livestock slaughter tax which was a significant source of public revenue in the 1950s; retail price controls on a range of agricultural products apart from rice, notably pork; strong state pressure on farmers in the 1960s to 'assent' to land consolidation programmes; state control of the import of virtually all agricultural products; and the use of Farmers Associations as agents for the licensing and collection of private contract production of asparagus and mushrooms on behalf of cartels of canning firms. Small wonder that Taiwanese farmers believed that they were working *for* the government, and that external observers, with a pardonable degree of exaggeration, have likened the entire Taiwanese agricultural sector to one large (state) farm (Apthorpe, 1979).

7.2 Political and Economic Objectives

The political process in Taiwan is highly secretive.[7] The identity of those who actually wield power and their perceptions and intentions are not always easy to determine. It is, however, clear that the origins of the high degree of state regulation of agriculture lie almost entirely in the immediate political and economic exigencies of the post-war period: in the need to create a domestic revenue base and a source of foreign exchange for the very fragile Nationalist state, and in the need to feed and find employment for two million Mainlander immigrants. As the Mainlanders themselves still insist, they, unlike the Taiwanese, had no land or property, and of necessity relied on the state and the military for employment. It is important to recall that the KMT leadership could not be confident of the loyalty of either the Mainlander army or the motley collection of civilian refugees which came over from the Mainland with the army. The Mainlanders had to be employed and settled as soon as possible.

The imperative needs for public revenue and for cheap food (i.e. rice) and jobs for the Mainlanders were in large part met by the agricultural policies and the public food system described above and by entrenching the Mainlander population in bureaucratic posts. The rice ration was supplied to three predominantly Mainlander groups: the public bureaucracy, teachers, and the military. The public rice, sugar and wine and tobacco monopolies generated state revenue and foreign exchange at the farmers' expense. The refining and trading operations of the Taiwan Sugar Corporation, and estate production on the lands which it successfully protected against land reform, provided jobs for Mainlanders. So too did the Provincial Food Bureau, which handled far larger volumes of material resources – and it has been suggested, provided for wider opportunities for graft – than did the other agricultural agencies, the Sino-American Joint Commission on Rural Reconstruction and the Provincial Department of Agriculture and Forestry.

One can then explain the *origins* of statist agriculture in terms of the urgent need of the nationalist regime to feed, in both literal and metaphorical senses, the Mainlander population and the state apparatus. Statist agriculture has also helped provide the political foundations of the nationalist state by supporting in rural areas a very dense network of KMT party and national security personnel whose function is to survey and thus help forestall any organised opposition to Mainlander Nationalist rule from the majority – and initially mainly rural – Taiwanese population. In addition to the KMT itself, which includes at least a third of the adult male population among its members, the regime operates a political surveillance system which is notoriously extensive and, in its own terms, so far very successful. Surveillance and control extend far beyond spheres of activity normally recognised as political. In addition to the education system, which is anyway staffed largely by Mainlanders, surveillance extends into religious organisation, religious ceremonial, and into 'private' life styles. The KMT at least exploited, if it did not consciously create, the network of parastatal institutions associated with statist agriculture in order to extend its political and security networks into the countryside.

With its large Mainlander staff and substantial presence in the countryside, the Taiwan Sugar Corporation has helped provide nuclei for KMT party activities in the rural areas. More importantly, the Corporation has provided a mechanism to buy the political support of the Taiwanese village leadership in cane-growing areas. The prevalent practice of appointing as its local agents existing or potential village leaders, including village and hamlet chiefs, has served three ends at once. First, it has given the Corporation access to political and administrative channels to help persuade farmers to grow sugarcane. Second, it has provided village leaders with material inducements to remain loyal to the regime. And third, it has furnished these leaders with material resources to bolster their personal positions within the village. As agents of the Corporation they control access to the fringe benefits provided to cane growers by the Corporation: insurance, education and health care benefits, and production loans. The latter are especially important in an environment where official credit has been relatively very scarce. The agents also exercise discretion in relation to such questions as the order in which farmers' cane will be harvested locally and who will be recruited to the harvesting teams managed by the Corporation. Sugarcane has consistently been grown by about a seventh of all farm households, all located in the south of the island, which for historical reasons has been the main locus of (passive) resistance to Nationalist rule and to the penetration of local institutions by the KMT.

Local Farmers' Associations and Irrigation Associations maintain, despite their formal non-government status, 'security' departments staffed by central Party or security personnel but financed by the Associations themselves. The utility of the Farmers' and Irrigation Associations as strategic institutions from which to maintain political surveillance at local level was enhanced by the policy towards 'private' associations pursued by the KMT in agriculture as in all spheres of public activity. Only officially recognised and registered associations may function. Those which are recognised – and closely controlled politically – are given *de facto* monopolies. Where organisations do not exist, they are created on state initiative as a preemptive measure. The only farmers' organisations officially tolerated are the Farmers' and Irrigation Associations and the marketing 'cooperatives' mentioned above.

While the *origins* of major state interventions in agriculture lie mainly in the political exigencies of the post-war period, the goal of economic development – itself closely related to the survival of the existing state in the Taiwanese case – has played a role. In some cases 'development' and more immediate political objectives appear to have harmonised. The system of licensing farmers to supply mushrooms and asparagus on contract to members of cannery cartels (see above) appears both to have benefited influential people and helped provide an efficient mechanism for maintaining quality of product supply and for encouraging potentially-competitive firms to combine to make an organised national assault on export markets. During the years that it remained a relatively low cost producer Taiwan achieved a large export trade in these products.

In other cases state interventions in agriculture appear to have been motivated more directly by the 'development' objective: for example large public investments in irrigation development and land consolidation, and the creation – or re-establishment – of relatively effective systems of agricultural research, extension, and livestock disease control. In these cases the systems and practices established by the Japanese were re-established relatively easily. The Joint Commission on Rural Reconstruction (see below) has been a source of relatively expert, technical and apolitical pressure for development-oriented agricultural policies.

The question about the objectives of state regulation of agriculture which is least easy to answer concerns the subordination of the agricultural economy to the needs of the industrial sector. The economic *consequences* are clear. There can be little doubt that the extraction of various surpluses from agriculture made important contributions to industrial development.[8] Cheap rice enabled industrial wage costs to be kept low and thus boosted industrial profits and Taiwan's competitive position in export markets. Taxes on agriculture provided the state with domestic financial resources which could be invested in industry. Monopsonistic arrangements for the procurement of agricultural export commodities from growers served to concentrate foreign currency earnings in the hands of the state (sugar and rice), well-connected private capitalists (asparagus and mushrooms) or some combination of the two (fruits). In addition, two further important sets of stimuli to industrial growth resulted from state action to skew terms of trade against farmers in an environment where (a) the agricultural sector comprised mainly family-operated farms; (b) there was, until about 1968, a clear aggregate surplus of labour; and (c) industrial development was decentralised to rural areas.

In the first place, this combination of policy and circumstances further reduced the supply price of industrial labour and thus helped provide the basis for Taiwan's take-off into low-cost industrial production and exporting. Because the returns to farm labour were lower than they would otherwise have been without state manipulation of inter-sectoral terms of trade, members of farm families were more willing than they would otherwise have been to take industrial jobs at low wage rates. And the fact that some industrial jobs were available in the countryside meant that industrial workers could survive on relatively low wages by living on the family farm.

In the second place, this combination of circumstances and policy created an industrial work-force which was relatively malleable from the employers' point of view. Relatively few farm families abandoned agriculture entirely. Household heads, i.e. older married males, tended to work the family farm and younger men and women to seek non-agricultural jobs. Maintaining a base on the family farm, these young industrial workers were less likely to claim permanent employment and resist the loss of their jobs. They could be dismissed or redeployed relatively easily. Industrial capitalists were relatively unconstrained in pursuing the flexible investment practices which seem so characteristic of at least smaller scale private business in Taiwan. (And the scale of private sector industrial enterprise in Taiwan is small in comparison with Korea and Japan.) Taiwanese businessmen appear relatively adept at changing product lines in response to new opportunities. At the macroeconomic level the farm sector has functioned as an economic safety net into which redundant industrial labour could be impelled during recessions. The fact that much of the industrial labour force has retained strong ties with the family farm – residence, social involvement, property rights and expectations of eventual return – seems, along with the high proportion of females and the surveillance and control of industrial labour carried out by the KMT, employers and official trade unions, to help explain the low levels of autonomous labour organisation, the dearth of industrial 'labour problems', and the continued attractiveness of Taiwan to local and foreign investors.

There is then little doubt that, in combination with favourable circumstantial structural features of the economy, state action to skew terms of trade against agricultural producers has played a very positive role in Taiwanese industrial development. The uncertainty referred to above concerns the extent to which this outcome was foreseen or intended by policy makers. One can certainly reject the more extreme arguments that agricultural policy has always been geared to the interests of industrial capital.[9] The KMT was not for example motivated to carry out land reform because it realised that an even 'purer' family-farm agriculture would, in a situation of labour surplus, further reduce the supply price of industrial labour and yield an economically and politically malleable industrial labour force. Had this been the intention the land reforms would have been even more radical. Like other aspects of statist agriculture, land reform can be satisfactorily explained in terms of the acute political and military insecurity of the Nationalist regime in its early years. The main motivation for land reform was an understandable if ultimately misplaced fear that agricultural tenants in Taiwan were a potential spearhead of communism, as they had been on the Chinese mainland and in Korea.[10]

However, the factors which explain the origins of statist agricultural policies do not adequately explain the persistence of these policies. Over time the Taiwanese state came to represent an alliance of the interests both of the Mainlander-dominated military/bureaucracy/KMT party and of largely non-Mainlander private industrial capital. It thus became increasingly valid to claim that the small-scale agricultural sector was directly and deliberately subordinated to the needs of industrial capital – state and private, Mainlander and Taiwanese (Amsden, 1979, p. 362; Gates, 1981).

7.3 The Institutions for Regulating Agriculture

American finance and, even more importantly, American technical experts, played a major role in the implementation of statist agricultural policy in Taiwan. Close links were forged between Taiwan and leading American universities. I have heard the agricultural policy of this period described as 'the Cornell strategy'. It is scarcely surprising that the non-Chinese literature on Taiwanese agricultural policy, which is almost entirely of American origin, is both laudatory and largely mute on the exploitative and coercive aspects. Yet, as far as one can judge in the face of the propaganda barrage, there is probably a substantial core of truth in the claim that policy was generally implemented in a technically and organisationally proficient manner. Further, it is true that the two particular agricultural institutions for which Taiwan has become well known – the Sino-American Joint Commission on Rural Reconstruction (JCRR) and the Farmers' Associations (FAs) – did indeed play a central role in policy implementation. However, to understand how they helped solve problems which have bedevilled so many other countries one has to look beyond propaganda and examine the political dimensions of their activities.

The JCRR had its origins in the Chinese mainland.[11] The sense of purpose and commitment which it was to exhibit in Taiwan stem in part from the belief that the success of communism in the mainland was due to the support of the peasantry, and to the failure of the Nationalists to take a similar pro-peasant stance.

The JCRR was commissioned to avoid a repeat of this mistake in Taiwan. The JCRR has frequently been described as the *de facto* Ministry of Agriculture. This is to a large degree true, but also both underestimates and exaggerates its influence. It is an underestimate in the sense that the JCRR had even greater capacity than a ministry to initiate and monitor action in the field and within subordinate institutions. Not formally a part of the public service, and until 1978 run jointly by Chinese and American staff – although the latter decreased in numbers over time – it has had privileged access to American aid funds, considerable *de facto* influence derived from the American connection, the ability to pay high salaries to attract good people, and a degree of freedom from the constraints which normally impinge on public bureaucracies. In the late 1940s, the 1950s and the 1960s, the JCRR controlled the bulk of public (and therefore, total) agricultural investment. It never undertook field programmes itself, but worked only in collaboration with other public or quasi-public agencies (e.g. Farmers' and Irrigation Associations). Its influence over its 'collaborators' was however immense. The Provincial Department of Agriculture and Forestry for example, was restricted solely to a subordinate role.

By virtue of its partial autonomy from and domination over parts of the regular government bureaucracy, the JCRR can be seen as an extreme example of a phenomenon which characterises both East Asian capitalist regimes and, more generally, military-bureaucratic regimes committed to the idea of 'modernisation from above' without the participation or mobilisation of the mass of the people: the independence of the bureaucracy from particularistic political pressures in policy implementation, and the correspondingly large scope given to technical expertise in the formulation and implementation of policy (Trimberger, 1978). This autonomy, combined with the political commitment to improving agriculture stemming from fear of rural communism, goes a long way to explaining why the JCRR achieved a reputation for technical competence, close links with the farming community, and rapid and flexible action.

However, despite this high degree of autonomy in respect of technical matters and the detailed implementation of policy, the JCRR was in areas of strategic economic policy relatively powerless and, as suggested above, less than a Ministry of Agriculture. It had no responsibility for foreign trade decisions affecting, for example, the degree of import protection to be given to agriculture. This fell within the sphere of the Ministry of Economic Affairs. While the JCRR influenced the details of agricultural policy, the major macroeconomic decisions affecting agriculture were taken elsewhere. While implicitly opposed to the economic exploitation of agriculture, the JCRR was unable to force a fundamental change in policy. The KMT has always kept a close eye on the JCRR by appointing senior party men as 'consultants' to the organisation. And even the JCRR, the most plausible applicant for the title of 'farmers champion', has never found place for farmer representatives on its council or on any other consultative body.

Yet any suggestion that farmers have no institutionalised representation in policy making would be vigorously challenged by spokesmen for the government of Taiwan. Apart from any reference which might be made to the very impressive facade of democratic government at all administrative levels, official spokesmen would refer to the system of FAs, organised in three tiers at the township, country and provincial levels. The notion that this comprises a peculiarly efficient, autonomous and democratic system has to some degree been accepted by foreign observers. The truth is somewhat different.[12]

Reference has already been made above to the way in which the state has exploited the FAs for its own ends, obliging them to 'perform nearly all the economic services which the government needs to have performed in the rural areas' (de Lasson, 1976, p. 268), and frequently to bear the costs themselves. The FAs operate and mainly finance the much-admired agricultural extension service, including the substantial element of pure political propaganda. To extract these economic and political services from the FAs the state needs to exercise a high degree of political control over them. Some of the more prominent dimensions and mechanisms of this control include: the employment on behalf of KMT candidates in FA elections of manipulative methods which are standard in Taiwan; considerable use, especially since reforms in 1975, of administrative discretion over appointments to posts with FAs; the deliberate fragmentation of the FA system as a whole, such that material resources and thus power are concentrated at the level of the individual township FA, while joint economic activities between township FAs are strongly discouraged and the county and provincial levels are limited to a few relatively small scale economic enterprises;

restricting the economic expansion of FAs by forbidding them to finance investment from any source except their own (meagre) accumulated profits; prohibiting the establishment of competing organisations; making it difficult for farm families not to be FA members; subordinating the FAs to the Ministry of the Interior, the ministry most directly concerned with political control of the population; staffing the apex-level Provincial Farmers Association mainly with Mainlanders; and using FAs as instruments of the KMT policy of trying to keep two factors in balance at each politico-administrative level. The FAs are organised to fit exactly the pattern of administrative and KMT party organisation. A common pattern is for a Mainlander-based local faction to control the township government, and a Taiwanese faction to control the township FA.

Yet the very length of this list of control mechanisms itself gives a strong hint that central control is neither complete nor uncontested. This is true of FAs as well as of other political and economic institutions in Taiwan. The state is less totalitarian and central control less complete than many sources, both pro- and anti-government, like to claim. There are the normal conflicts and contradictions between different levels of political and bureaucratic systems and, in relation to agriculture especially, a very deliberate degree of devolution of power to partly-autonomous local organisations. Local FAs do have some autonomy. Any state which wishes to save itself the expense of a very large and perhaps unwieldly public bureaucracy is obliged to coopt local social and political institutions to do its work at the grassroots level. And any such cooption involves some concessions to local autonomy. The Taiwanese regime has found it convenient to hand over power, of a purely localised and very circumscribed kind, to local and village élites through FAs and Irrigation Associations. The price for the regime has been a continual struggle to restrict these local organisations to their appointed roles.[13] As is indicated in Section 9, Korean governments have taken the more statist path: almost uncompromising hostility to any kind of local organisation except village organisation, outside the narrow confines of the public bureaucracy.

8. THE EMERGENCE OF PLURALISM IN TAIWAN

As is suggested in Section 6 above, there have over the past two decades or so been two major trends in the political-cum-economic relationship between the state and Taiwanese agriculture. One is the general shift from statism to pluralism, and the other, in part very closely related but also in part distinct, has been a shift from 'urban bias' to 'rural bias' in macroeconomic policy.

8.1 From Urban to Rural Bias

Having formerly been a net provider of resources to the state, to the urban population and to industry, Taiwanese agriculture, which is increasingly inefficient relative to both Taiwanese industry and world agriculture because of rising labour costs, has been receiving increasing protection against imports, and is now the net recipient of subsidies from the state. The main beneficiaries of these subsidies have been rice growers. There are a range of factors which help explain this change in policy, most of them stemming from structural changes within agriculture or in the national economy more generally.

In the first place it seems likely that economic growth and structural change have wrought in Taiwan certain changes in the direction and intensity of political pressures from socio-economic groups which can be anticipated from a few axioms of the rational choice approach to political analysis (Bates and Rogerson, 1980). In the 1940s and 1950s the majority of the urban and non-agricultural population were spending a high proportion of their incomes on the staple food, rice. There was therefore a strong if not always overt pressure on government to provide rice cheaply: to extract supplies from farmers at less than market prices or subsidise consumers directly. Higher incomes have led to a much greater diversity in consumer spending patterns, and thus the diffusing (and defusing) of political pressures from consumers. In Taiwan consumers now spend almost as much on pork, for example, as rice, and are increasingly concerned about the quality of rice they buy rather than simply with price. The retail price of rice was almost doubled in 1974 without overt protest.

In the second place, the relative decline of the agricultural sector, especially of cereal production, in relation to the expanding national economy meant both that public revenue from the exploitation of cereal producers was of declining importance and that the potential cost of subsidising rice producers was diminishing in relative terms.

In the third place, farmer dissatisfaction with agricultural policy has been on the increase. Several factors appear to have contributed to this: awareness of growing farm–non-farm income differentials; overall political liberalisation; the increasing ability of native Taiwanese politicians to voice criticisms of aspects of public policy and to lay claim to positions of power; and the increasing responsiveness of the administration to public opinion generally.

Finally, and most visibly and directly, in the late 1960s, pro-agriculture policy-makers could make a strong case for some reduction in the level of public exploitation of agriculture as it became evident that the existing policy was leading to a slow-down in the growth of agricultural production at a time when Taiwan could not yet be confident about its long-term ability to feed itself in the event of some drastic reversal in its international diplomatic and trading position.

The year 1968 constitutes a significant turning point in the recent economic history of Taiwan. For in that year the country found itself moving from a condition of labour surplus to one of labour scarcity. Thereafter, real wage rates began to rise significantly, especially in agriculture, the locus of a reservoir of labour for the industrial sector (Section 6). This scarcity of manpower provided the farm population with a means of escaping the ill-rewarded labour hitherto thrust upon them by government's manipulation of agriculture's terms of trade. Farm family labour could be more easily diverted to non-agricultural jobs, with predictable consequences for farm production. The rate of growth of agricultural output had been declining since the mid-1960s. By the end of the decade it seemed stuck below the rate of population growth, at a time when rising incomes were still generating an increasing per capita demand for food, and when the gap between farm and non-farm incomes has begun to widen rather dramatically as the rising cost of labour had begun to undermine the economic competitiveness of small-scale family farming.

The fact that these concerns were translated relatively rapidly into a new policy for agriculture appears due to the accession to power in 1968 and 1969 of a new generation of political leaders. Chiang Ching-Kuo, the son of President Chiang Kai-Shek, became Vice Prime Minister in June 1969 and assumed control of economic policy. He became Prime Minister in 1972. Chiang Ching-Kuo had very consciously attempted to build up connections and support among rural Taiwanese, and included among his coterie of political associates native Taiwanese politicians representing farming interests.

Chiang Ching-Kuo's initial agricultural policy measures did not directly touch the institutions and policies of statist agriculture. His first initiative, in November 1969, was the announcement of the Accelerated Rural Development Programme (ARDP), a time-bound programme for large increases in public expenditure on rural infrastructure, credit and marketing (Yu, 1978; Ong, 1984). The ARDP has since been extended indefinitely. On the one hand it is an accounting label for rural public expenditures, 'accelerated' in the sense that the rural share of public spending has increased. On the other hand, the ARDP has become the symbolic point of reference for a whole range of policy changes and initiatives affecting agriculture, notably changes in pricing and revenue policies which within a few years were to amount to a switchover from industrial to agricultural bias. Fertiliser prices were reduced in 1970 and again in 1971. Rural taxes were also reduced in 1971. In 1972 the rice–fertiliser barter scheme was abolished. In response to stagnation in rice production, the official purchase price was almost doubled in cash terms in 1974. Subsequent increases meant that by 1976 the official price had become a support price. Rather than delivering obligatory quotas of rice to the state, since 1975 farmers have been privileged to sell to the government an individual quota amounting in total to about a quarter of rice production. The state now incurs a loss on sugar and rice exports, makes no profit on fertiliser distribution, and in a wide range of ways has given agriculture increasingly generous treatment in its fiscal operations.

8.2 From Statism to Pluralism

Space constraints render impossible any detailed elaboration of the shift from statism towards pluralism. All that can be done in this section is to illustrate some features of this transition which are specific to Taiwan or particularly noteworthy.

One important general point is that the crops which formed the foci of statist agriculture, rice and sugar, are no longer in short supply or a source of state revenue. Indeed, to some degree increasing production of these crops involves a drain on public funds. Yet, unlike in the earlier period when firm administrative action was taken to increase production or market deliveries, the state has shown itself remarkably non-coercive and ineffective in its attempts to reduce surpluses and the burden they impose on public finances. While the government imposes a limit on the quantity of rice that it will purchase from any individual farmer, it has not attempted to impose any overall limit on rice acreage. It has similarly shied away from attempting to use its control over irrigation systems to reduce rice production. This could be achieved by refusing to provide sufficient water to grow rice. The only direct disincentive measure has been a small cash subsidy introduced in 1982 for farmers who voluntarily agree to grow crops other than rice on rice land.

More broadly, the government has been talking for the past two decades of a 'Second Land Reform'; aimed at enlarging the size of farm production units to meet the increasing inefficiency of small-scale agriculture. A plethora of schemes have been introduced to encourage various forms of cooperative and collective production, specialisation, farm amalgamation, and the pooling of farm machinery.[14] In comparison with the first land reforms of the late 1940s and early 1950s, it is remarkable that the state has not attempted any kind of coercion during the 'Second Land Reform', but has rather limited itself to offering subsidies and exhortation, has been almost totally unsuccessful, and has created a strong impression of vacillation. In so far as the desired structural changes in agricultural production have begun to occur, these have been almost entirely the result of individuals responding to market forces.

The private market economy has also come to the fore in the sphere of agricultural input supply, in which the FAs were formerly dominant. This is partly the result of all the restrictions which the state has placed on the expansion of the FAs' activities. It seems only a matter of time before the marketing of chemical fertilisers is opened up to private traders. Private traders anyway totally dominate in the rapidly-growing areas of agricultural input supply – farm machinery, animal feed, pesticides, herbicides, etc. They have consequently become a major source of technical advice. Public extension workers feel that they have lost the very considerable authority which they used to exercise over farmers by virtue of their (the extension workers) near monopoly of new technical knowledge. And the Farmers Associations are themselves moving away from any unique connection with farming. Taking advantage of rising rural incomes and population densities, they increasingly concentrate on their small scale retail banking function, and derive almost all their profits from this source.

One area of rapid growth of FAs' agricultural activities has been in the marketing of hogs. Their share of the total hog market increased from 4 per cent in 1971 to 30 per cent in 1981. This is not the result of any special efficiency or enterprise on the part of the FAs, but of a recognition by government that it cannot attain the desired stability in the consumer pork price through direct administrative controls on marketing volumes and retail prices. It has instead tried to match market supply to expected demand, using both the Taiwan Sugar Corporation (see Section 7.1 above) and the FAs as agents. FAs can attract supplies from producers by virtue of their privileged access to pork wholesale markets. This example illustrates that pluralism is not to be equated with a simple reduction in the degree of state intervention in the economy. It involves a reduction in direct administrative regulation of the economy in favour of attempts to regulate markets indirectly by altering the pattern of incentives available to private producers and traders.

The final point about the emergence of pluralism is that the increasing debate and conflict within the state bureaucracy about agricultural policy has been reflected in changes in the public bureaucracy itself. In 1980 a Bureau of Agriculture was established within the powerful Ministry of Economic Affairs. In 1983 a well-publicised attempt to create a Ministry of Agriculture was eventually rejected. But it was decided to amalgamate the Bureau of Agriculture and the Council for Agricultural Planning and Development (the former JCRR) into a new Commission of Agriculture. The government felt obliged to promise that the Commission would have the same responsibilities as a ministry, and the 1983 Agrarian Law, itself the subject of considerable public debate, included a clause giving the Commission the right to have a say in policy over the import of agricultural products – a clear sign of the increasing strength of the agricultural interest. That 'agricultural interest', while having some success in entrenching itself within state agencies, is itself underoing fission. The few large enterprises which increasingly dominate livestock production have direct and relatively easy access to policy-makers. They can offer cooperation in regulating market supplies and thus retail prices in return for favourable treatment in other respects, including a large degree of *de facto* control over the import of feed grains. These imports have been virtually unrestricted. Such liberalism is at least marginally contrary to the interests of ordinary small farmers, who are mainly crop producers, and decreasingly involved in livestock production.

9. STATISM AND PLURALISM IN SOUTH KOREA[15]

The post-war regimes in both Taiwan and Korea have made little concession to the notion that citizens have the right to make economic decisions independently of the state. Although basically similar in this regard, the two countries do differ in that economic *dirigisme* – the direct administrative and political regulation of economic life – is more routinised and apparently more accepted in Korea. This reflects long established differences in political culture. But, in relation to agriculture in particular, it can also be traced to differing circumstances surrounding the establishment of the regimes in the late 1940s and early 1950s (Cumings, 1981).

The Korean war was in part a civil war. A rural radicalism, combining anti-landlordism with nationalism directed against landlords and others who had collaborated with the Japanese colonial regime, was an important component of what was, by force of circumstances, to become the North Korean/Communist bloc. Even before the Korean war this rural radicalism had pushed a reluctant government to begin implementing land reforms which were ultimately considerably more sweeping and egalitarian than those introduced in Taiwan. The combined effect of land reform and the Korean war was to leave rural South Korea with a much simplified class structure and a much attenuated level of political consciousness. The villages were populated almost entirely by small farming families owning their own land. Tenants, landless labourers, radicals and rural élites capable of commanding political support in arenas wider than small localities had, for a combination of reasons, mainly disappeared. Korean villagers came to exemplify the politically disarticulated and dependent peasantry so vividly described by Karl Marx in his *Eighteenth Brumaire*.[16] They have become the electoral 'cannon fodder' legitimating successive Korean regimes. Yet no regime has really trusted them. Unlike in Taiwan, where power was to some degree devolved to local organisations, all agriculture service organisations in Korea, including 'cooperatives', have been run as arms of the central bureaucracy (Aqua, 1974; USAID, 1984; Wade, 1982 and 1983). No concession has been made to the principle of farmer representation or to any idea that farmers might usefully have a say in how agricultural policy is implemented locally. One might also add that Korean regimes have not been so heavily pressured as has the Taiwanese government to create a facade of democratic and participatory institutions in order to maintain a favourable image in the United States.

While rural conditions in Korea have been more conducive than in Taiwan to an extreme form of statism in agricultural policy, at national level the period of more overt and directed statism, in industry and agriculture, began only with the military coup of 1961. This developed into a partial social revolution 'at the top', with the somewhat effete and civilian-based administration being replaced by the essentially military and development-oriented Park regime. The more general point for present purposes is that, because of this and other contingent differences in circumstances between Korea and Taiwan, the chronology of the statist-pluralist trajectory has been a little different. Things have not fitted together so neatly in Korea as in Taiwan. Our Taiwan story began with a period when statism and the exploitation of agriculture went together; there has been a gradual relaxation of both over time. The Korean story is best seen in terms of three overlapping sub-periods.

The first sub-period, covering the 1950s and stretching into the 1960s, was characterised by a relative neglect of agriculture. Many of the familiar features of statist agriculture, including forced delivery of rice by farmers at low prices and exploitative fertiliser–rice barter arrangements, were in place (Moon, 1975). But in comparison with Taiwan, Korean regimes were less interested in agriculture and statism was of a less activist nature. Part of the reason lies in the very strong nationalist reaction against Japanese colonial rule, and the association of agricultural development programmes with the colonial police. The agricultural extension and research services were allowed almost to wither away. More important however was the fact that, for a range of reasons, the Korean government had easier options for feeding the towns than trying to extract sufficient rice from farmers. The Japanese had developed rural Korea far less than Taiwan. Rural transport was very poor, and high yielding rice varieties adapted to Korea's temperate climate were not available. Targets for state rice procurement were rarely achieved. On the other side, the Americans were on hand with large supplies of cheap PL 480 foodgrain supplies. In the 1950s the Korean government exploited farmers mainly by permitting generous imports of grain and other agricultural products, consequently driving domestic agricultural prices down below world levels.

Our second sub-period, that of statist agriculture, has its origins in the Park coup of 1961 and in President Park's own concern at the neglect of agriculture. He made an almost immediate start in rebuilding agricultural research and extension systems, and in beginning to give agriculture some protection against imports by raising tariffs.[17] The apogee of statist agriculture, coming in the first half of the 1970s, was the result of three main factors. One was the termination of cheap American PL 480 food imports in 1970 and the consequent search for domestic sources of supply. A second was the rapid growth in the late 1960s in the gap between average rural and average urban incomes, a result of a sudden tightening in the labour market. This led to the unwelcome growth of shanty settlements of ex-rural migrants in Seoul, and to concerns about the continuing political loyalty of the rural population. The third factor was the introduction in 1971 of a new 'miracle' rice that promised large yield increases.

Unlike in Taiwan, the period of most intensive agricultural *dirigisme*, intended to force farmers to adopt the new rice and 'modernise' their economy and living environment, coincided with a pro-agriculture shift in economic policy. The level of tariff protection for agriculture continued to climb, government spending on rural infrastructure grew rapidly in the early 1970s, and rice procurement prices were increased and fertiliser subsidised such that the Grain and Fertiliser Management Funds became major sources of large public expenditure deficits. The economic campaign to make Korea self-sufficient in basic foodstuffs was inextricably linked with a political campaign to ensure the loyalty of the rural population to the Park regime, to make the Korean village look 'modern' to foreign eyes, and to convert the conservative and status-conscious public bureaucracy into an action-oriented 'development administration'. The Saemaul (New Community) Movement, launched in the winter of 1970, came to provide the ideological and, to some degree, the organisational framework for all these linked projects (Choe, 1978; Brandt and Lee, 1980; Moore, 1985a).

Our third sub-period, beginning around the middle of the 1970s, can in certain respects be seen as a simple reaction against the more 'extreme' aspects of the 'big push' of the early 1970s (Moore, 1985a). Public foodgrain subsidies could not be sustained at the levels attained' in the mid-1970s, and have been reduced. The incomes of farmers have again deteriorated relative to non-farmers. The Saemaul Movement has become a shadow of its former self because high levels of popular and bureaucratic mobilisation could not long be sustained. Government agencies no longer try to force farmers to grow new high yielding rice varieties because of a series of harvest failures caused by disease and the early onset of cold weather illustrated that the new varieties had been over-promoted. From a peak figure of 76 per cent attained in 1978, the proportion of the rice area under high yielding varieties fell to a low of 27 per cent in 1981, and has since recovered only slightly.

There are, however, longer term trends towards pluralism in the agriculture–state relationship which are independent of the fluctuations in the more visible dimensions of policy. Despite severe floods in 1984 and other setbacks, Korea is near the brink of rice self-sufficiency, and the government is now concerned with agricultural diversification and identifying non-farm sources of income for rural people rather than with maximising rice production. The capacity of state agencies directly to influence farmers production decisions has declined as the private sector has emerged as the dominant source of supply of farm inputs. In 1980 the state effectively ended its involvement in the supply of farm machinery. The private sector has recently been permitted a role in fertiliser marketing. The emphasis in public control of retail food prices has shifted from price fixing by administrative fiat to intervention through buffer stocking or linking retail price maxima to wholesale price indices. The large-scale livestock producing (and feedgrain importing) sector has emerged as a well-organised interest group in its own right, and one well-represented in the various public agencies concerned with agricultural policy. It has preserved its very high level of import protection despite bitter opposition from economists with a national perspective who believe Korea has no real future as a livestock producer. The small farm sector has not been able to push its own interests quite so effectively, but also has high levels of import protection and, exactly as in Taiwan, has resisted attempts by government to introduce a 'Second Land Reform' and restructure agriculture in the face of its new-found comparative economic disadvantage.

10. CONCLUSION

The argument of this chapter is that economic structure places greater constraints on the range of efficient modes of state regulation of the economy than is indicated by the voluntaristic tone of most debates on this subject. It is, however, difficult to conclude without making any comment on more practical policy questions, especially the possible 'lessons' of the Taiwanese and Korean experiences. For both governments have after all pursued paths which many would argue are almost automatic recipes for economic disaster, that is the extraction of resources from agriculture to support the state and non-industry, and the extensive bureaucratic regulation of the agricultural economy. Three points are especially relevant to this perspective.

The first is that extraction of economic resources from agriculture without major damage to agriculture itself was possible in part because, in Taiwan even more than Korea, the high level of agricultural development achieved under Japanese rule in the first half of the century did mean that there was a 'surplus' to extract (Chang and Myers, 1963; Cumings, 1984, pp. 8–15).

The second point is that it does not seem justifiable to attribute rapid growth of agriculture to any very special wisdom in public agricultural policy or efficiency in policy implementation. Both countries have made their share of mistakes in agricultural policy. Agriculture has grown fast mainly as a consequence of rapid industrial growth. It is industry which has been the source of growing demand for high value crops and the cause of rising wage costs which have led to the 'modernisation' of agriculture. The main contribution of agricultural policy to agricultural growth has been indirect. The exploitation of agriculture has promoted industry, which has in turn stimulated agriculture.

The third point is that Taiwan and South Korea have not discovered any simple remedy for the problems of bureaucratic self-interest which afflict all statist regimes:

> The typically pervasive state may, however, outlive its historically progressive role and become a bastion of economic irrationality . . . (White, 1984, p. 97)

State agencies which originally played a positive role in mobilising resources for economic growth can easily become impediments to progress in changed economic circumstances. Whereas the market has the power to disregard arguments founded on institutional self-interest and to oblige redundant institutions to find new roles or perish, public agencies entrenched within statist regimes have a tendency to reproduce themselves. This tendency is very evident in the material with which we have been dealing. The Taiwanese Provincial Food Bureau, to take but one example, still survives and employs many people although it has become almost entirely redundant as an agent of food procurement and fertiliser and credit supply. Despite many criticisms of the Bureau, no coalition of agencies or interests within the Taiwan government has had sufficient motivation and strength to have it abolished or amalgamated with the Provincial Department of Agriculture. The Taiwanese and Korean states have not transcended the problem of institutional redundancy within the state itself. The main reason why the continued growth of the agricultural economy was not stifled by the accretion of restrictive and parasitic state agencies serving no useful function is simply that this economy has expanded in areas which the state never attempted to control at all. State capitalism has an advantage over state socialism in that its hostility to market forces is partial, pragmatic and often covert. There is no ideological imperative to subject the whole of the economy to state regulation, and no inbuilt obstacle to the emergence of large areas of relatively unregulated economic activity.

Notes

1. Due to lack of space references are given here only to major sources. Detailed references and statistical sources may be found in Moore (1985b).
2. The term 'statism' is used in preference to the more familiar concept of 'state autonomy' because the latter, while admirably conveying the notion of the independence of the state from social forces and classes, does not adequately connote the equally important idea of the state vigorously and pervasively 'acting on' civil society.
3. Cumings (1984) provides a good overview of these issues.
4. For an unusually sensitive exploration of Korean political culture in comparative context see Pye (1985), especially Chapters 3 and 8. (His account of Taiwan is inadequate and flawed.)
5. The standard source for the information in this section is Lee (1971). For a convenient summary see Amsden (1979), and for an interpretation of the farmers' perspective, Apthorpe (1979).
6. For a useful summary of the history and contemporary operations of the Taiwan Sugar Corporation see Williams (1980).
7. There is no good written account of politics in Taiwan. Clough (1978, Ch. 2) provides a useful introduction, Winckler (1981a, b) a great deal

of insight into political structures, and Gates (1981) an account of ethnic and class dimensions.

8. Lee (1971) is the best single source, but he naturally confines himself to the economic relationships between agriculture and industry, saying nothing about the effect of economic policy in the social and political character of industrial labour. On this dimension see Gates (1979).

9. This appears to be the position put forward by Hamilton (1983).

10. This fear was misplaced because (a) tenants in Taiwan were not very much exploited due to a previous round of land reform under the Japanese, (b) like almost all social groups in Taiwan, tenants have shown little occupational or class consciousness, and were driven to oppose Nationalist rule in 1947 (actively) and since (mainly passively) only under extreme provocation, and (c) farmers actually took little part in the anti-Nationalist uprising of 1947, which was mainly urban-based. (For all these points see Amsden, 1979.) There can be little doubt that the Joint Commission on Rural Reconstruction and a group of American advisers headed by Wolf Ladejinsky played a role, either honest or manipulative, in persuading the KMT that the solution of 'the tenancy problem' was the key to their survival in Taiwan.

11. There is no adequate history of the JCRR. The official history is eulogistic (Shen, 1970). The first few Annual Reports of the JCRR are revealing in an indirect way. In later years they are totally bland.

12. A characteristic eulogy to Farmers' Associations is provided by Kwoh (1964). Stavis (1974) is more balanced, but has limited information. The account here is based mainly on the work of the only foreigner ever to undertake detailed and wide-ranging research into the Farmers' Associations – de Lasson (1976). This has been supplemented by my own research.

13. For example, one of the reasons that the central government asserted direct control of the Irrigation Associations between 1975 and 1982 was that the latter had become bases for local and regional political networks which were insufficiently beholden to the KMT central leadership. The fact that a partial reversal to 'democratic' local control was instituted *before* the central government had achieved all its objectives for reforming the Irrigation Associations is an indication both of the tenacity of local political networks in the face of the central government and of the strength of the pressures on the regime to maintain at least a plausible facade of participatory democracy at local levels (Moore, 1985b, pp. 160–61).

14. For a quasi-official but useful account of the 'Second Land Reform' see Ong, 1984, Chapters 4 and 5.

15. The most useful general sources for this section are Ban *et al.*, 1980; USAID, 1984; and Wade, 1982 and 1983. Contemporary Korean development is far better documented in English than is Taiwanese development.

16. The reference is to the notorious 'potatoes in a sack' image (Marx, 1852, p. 106).

17. Kim and Joo (1983) provide a brief description of agricultural policy since the early 1960s.

References

Amsden, A. H. (1979) 'Taiwan's Economic History. A Case of Etatisme and a Challenge to Dependency Theory', *Modern China*, 5:3, pp. 341–80.

Apthorpe, R. (1979) 'The Burden of Land Reform in Taiwan: An Asian Model Land Reform Re-Analysed', *World Development*, 7 (4 and 5).

Aqua, R. (1974) *Local Institutions and Rural Development in South Korea* (Cornell University Rural Development Committee, Special Series on Rural Local Government No. 13, Ithaca).

Ban, S. H. *et al.* (1980) *Studies in the Modernisation of the Republic of Korea: 1945–1975. Rural Development* (Harvard University Press).

Bates, R. H. and W. P. Rogerson (1980) 'Agriculture in Development: A Coalition Analysis', *Public Choice*, 35(5).

Brandt, V. S. R. and M. L. Lee (1980) 'Community Development in the Republic of Korea', in R. Dore and Z. Mars (eds), *Community Development* (London: Croom Helm).

Chang, H. Y. and R. Myers (1963) 'Japanese Colonial Development Policy: A Case of Bureaucratic Entrepreneurship', *Journal of Asian Studies*, 22.

Choe, Y. B. (1978) *The Korean Model of Rural Saemaul Undong: its Structure, Strategy and Performance* (Working paper No. 4, Korean Rural Economics Institute, Seoul).

Clough, R. N. (1978) *Island China* (Harvard University Press).

Cumings, B. (1981) *The Origins of the Korean War: Liberation and the Emergence of Separate Regimes* (Princeton University Press).

Cumings, B. (1984) 'The Origins and Development of the Northeast Asian Political Economy: Industrial Sectors, Product Cycles and Political Consequences', *International Organisation*, 38(1).

Gates, H. (1979) 'Dependency and the Part-Time Proletariat in Taiwan', *Modern China*, 5(3).

Gates, H. (1981) 'Ethnicity and Social Class', in E. M. Ahern and H. Gates (eds), *The Anthropology of Taiwanese Society* (Stanford University Press).

Hamilton, C. (1983) 'Capitalist Industrialisation in East Asia's Four Little Tigers', *Journal of Contemporary Asia*, 13(1).

Ho, S. P. S. (1982) 'Economic Development and Rural Industry in South Korea and Taiwan', *World Development*, 10(11).

Hofheinz, R. and K. E. Calder (1982) *The East-Asia Edge*, (New York: Basic Books).

Kim, D. H. and Y. J. Joo (1983) *The Food Situation and Policies in the Republic of Korea* (Paris: OECD Development Centre).

Kwoh, M. H. (1964) *Farmers Associations in Taiwan and their Contribution Towards Agricultural Rural Development in Taiwan* (FAO, Regional Office for Asia and the Far East, Bangkok).

de Lasson, A. (1976) *The Farmers' Association Approach to Rural Development – The Taiwan Case* (Sozialokonomische Schriften Zur Agrarentwicklung, No. 19, Verlag der SSIP-Schriften, Saarbrucken).

Lee, T. H. (1971) *Intersectoral Capital Flows in the Economic Development of Taiwan* (Cornell University Press).

Marx, K. (1852) *The Eighteenth Brumaire of Louis Bonaparte* (Moscow: Progress Publications (1972)).

Moon, P. Y. (1975) 'The Evolution of Rice Policy in Korea', *Food Research Institute Studies*, 14(4).

Moore, M. (1985a) 'Mobilization and Disillusion in Rural Korea: The Saemaul Movement in Retrospect', *Pacific Affairs*, 57(4).

Moore, M. (1985b) 'Economic Growth and the Rise of Civil Society: Agriculture in Taiwan and South Korea', in G. White and R. Wade (eds) *Developmental States in East Asia* (Research Report No. 16, Institute of Development Studies, Brighton).

Nolan, P. and G. White (1984) 'Urban Bias, Rule Bias or State Bias? Urban–Rural Relations in Post-Revolutionary China', *Journal of Development Studies*, 20(3).

Ong, S. E. (1984) *Development of the Small Farm Economy in Taiwan* (Taipei: Council for Agricultural Planning and Development).

Pye, L. (1985) *Asian Power and Politics. The Cultural Dimensions of Authority* (The Belknap Press of Harvard University Press).

Shen, T. H. (1970) *The Sino-American Joint Commission on Rural Reconstruction* (Cornell University Press).

Stavis, B. (1974) *Rural Local Governance and Agricultural Development in Taiwan* (Cornell University, Rural Development Committee, Special Series on Rural Local Government No. 15).

Trimberger, E. K. (1978) *Revolution from Above: Military Bureaucrats and Modernisation in Japan, Turkey, Egypt, and Peru* (New York: Transaction Books).

USAID (1984) Korean Agricultural Services: *The Invisible Hand in the Iron Glove. Market and Nonmarket Forces in Korean Rural Development* (United States Agency for International Development, Project Impact Evaluation Report No. 52, Washington).

Wade, R. (1982) *Irrigation and Agricultural Politics in South Korea* (Boulder: Westview Press).

Wade, R. (1983) 'South Korea's Agricultural Development: The Myth of the Passive State', *Pacific Viewpoint*, 24(1).

White, D. G. (1984) 'Development States and Socialist Industrialisation in the Third World', *Journal of Development Studies*, 21(1).

Williams, J. F. (1980) 'Sugar: The Sweetener in Taiwan's Development', in R. G. Knapp (ed.), *China's Island Frontier. Studies in the Historical Geography of Taiwan* (University Press of Hawaii).

Winckler, E. A. (1981a) 'National, Regional and Local Politics', in E. M. Ahern and H. Gates (eds), *The Anthropology of Taiwanese Society* (Stanford University Press).

Winckler, E. A. (1981b) 'Roles Linking State and Society', in E. M. Ahern and H. Gates (eds), *The Anthropology of Taiwanese Society* (Stanford University Press).

Yu, T. Y. H. (1978) 'The Accelerated Rural Development Programme in Taiwan', in *Agricultural Economic Research Papers* (Economic Digest Series No. 23, Joint Commission on Rural Reconstruction, Taipei).

5 State and Market in China's Socialist Industrialisation[1]

Gordon White

The leadership of the Chinese Communist Party (CCP) who assumed power in Beijing in 1949 saw rapid industrialisation as the basic way to strengthen China as a nation and raise the living standards of its people. There was no question of whether or when to industrialise, but how. In this basic aim, they differed little from the late Imperial and Nationalist governments before them. Like their predecessors, moreover, CCP leaders saw the role of the State as *primum mobile* in the process of industrialisation. In the last decades of the Qing dynasty, the imperial government had attempted to foster the growth of modern industry through the so-called *guandu shangban* system (literally 'official supervises, merchant manages'), whereby the government sponsored private industrial and commercial concerns. Similarly the Nationalist (Kuomintang) government in its heyday (1928–37), attempted to lay the foundations of an industrial economy by regaining national economic sovereignty and developing heavy industry through public enterprises with a strategy of 'controlled economy' under state direction (White, 1982a).

Thus the highly statist Soviet model, the only model of realised revolutionary socialism available in 1949, was not incompatible with the modern Chinese tradition of developmental economy. Indeed, the CCP inherited a sizeable state industrial sector from the Kuomintang regime, producing 34.7 per cent of total industrial output value in 1949 (concentrated in basic industries such as metallurgy, coal, electricity, and transport). State control of commerce was weaker, with public enterprises handling 23.9 per cent of wholesale and 14.9 per cent of retail trade in 1950 (Xue, 1981, p. 18). However, the CCP inherited the Kuomintang's control over a major portion of foreign trade through state trading corporations and its commanding financial position through control over the large banks. The new state sector was also swelled by the takeover of all remaining foreign business in China between 1949 and 1952.

SOCIALIST TRANSFORMATION OF CHINESE INDUSTRY

Indigenous private capital was unevenly developed in 1949, was weak overall and weakened further by an outflow of entrepreneurs and managers to Hong Kong and Taiwan. The new regime saw the remaining Chinese bourgeoisie as a valuable resource which could be used to serve the transition to socialist industrialisation. In consequence, their policies towards private capital were far more favourable than their Russian Bolshevik predecessors. Over the longer term, however, the CCP realised that capitalists as a class, and markets as social processes, were potential sources of countervailing power. Transformation of the system of industrial and commercial ownership was thus essential, for political as well as economic reasons.

The 'socialist transformation' of private industrial and commercial enterprises was not executed in one fell swoop; there were two intermediate stages of 'state capitalism'. In the first, dominant up to 1953, the state used various economic measures – monetary policy, price controls, taxation – to redirect the activity of private enterprises. Simultaneously, the state moved rapidly to extend its direct control over the banking system, achieving total socialisation by the end of 1952. In the second phase, from 1954 to 1956, the state gradually converted private enterprises into joint state–private concerns, sending party or government cadres to join or supplant the original managers (Xue, 1981, pp. 25–32, Cheng, 1982, Ch. 5).

By 1956, the modern sector of capitalist industry had been converted into joint enterprises. Though many managers retained their posts and former owners continued to receive fixed interest payments on their capital (until 1967), from 1956 onwards these were *de facto* state enterprises. At the same time, the socialist state sector expanded through the renovation of existing (Kuomintang or foreign) enterprises and an ambitious programme of industrial expansion during the First Five-Year Plan (1953–7). By 1956, all China's modern industry was *de jure* or *de facto* in state hands. Simultaneously, commerce was also socialised: in wholesale trade, state and (state-controlled) joint or cooperative commerce handled

97.2 per cent of total turnover by 1956; in retail trade, the figure was 95.8 per cent (Cheng, 1982, Ch. 5).

THE CENTRALISED SYSTEM OF INDUSTRIAL PLANNING

Adoption of the Soviet Model of Central Planning

The modern industrial sector was gradually incorporated into the new planning system constructed during the First Five-Year Plan along centralised Soviet lines. According to this model (i.e. as it is *supposed* to operate), central planning agencies calculate overall economic balances, and government agencies at different levels specify and transmit orders on output and distribution to subordinate productive units through a hierarchical chain of bureaucratic command (for details of its operation, see Hare, 1983 and Chung, 1955). Though enterprises are formally independent accounting units responsible for calculating their own profits and losses (the Soviet *khozraschet* principle), in reality they are administratively subordinate, responsible for carrying out the plan targets issued by superior state organs. The number of mandatory targets has varied since the mid-1950s, but the most common pattern has been eight: total output value, product mix, quality, consumption of new materials and energy, total wage bill, costs of production, profits (i.e. net revenue) and working capital. Just as capitalist enterprises in competitive conditions are theoretically 'price-takers', so socialist enterprises in such centralised conditions are theoretically 'plan-takers'.

Within this system of planned state industry, markets play a marginal role. In ideological terms, relations between state economic organs and industrial enterprises, and among enterprises themselves, are not based on commodity exchange regulated by the 'law of value', but are subject to unified coordination and control at various levels of the state planning network. The level and allocation are planned, there are virtually no capital markets and the regulating role of interest is minimal; the pattern of industrial output is predominantly determined by state officials (not merely 'planners') not market demand; production functions are set by plan according to relatively unchanging, standardised technical coefficients; most prices are regulated administratively and only marginally subject to pressures of supply and demand; money plays a passive, accounting role, monitored closed by a centralised banking system with cash playing only a marginal role; industrial manpower is administratively allocated by state labour bureaux; inter-sectoral product flows are determined by a balancing process based on physical input–output ratios; supplies of raw materials to industrial enterprises and purchase of their products are both handled administratively by specialised state agencies (the BMA and commercial organs).

In the 'external' relations of state industry, however, markets do play a significant role, most notably in transactions with cooperative agriculture and in retail sales of industrial consumer goods. In the allocation of industrial labour, where the Soviet Union and Eastern European states have made considerable use of (regulated) markets, the Chinese system has remained firmly under direct state control since the late 1950s (White, 1982b, 620–21). Until recently, foreign trade has been relatively marginal; while the Chinese are price-takers in their import and export transactions and thus subject to market pressures, the system of trade regulation (through the Ministry of Foreign Trade and specialised state trading companies) has acted as a partition to screen the domestic economy from international trends.

Chinese Industrial Planning in Operation in the Maoist Era

The above description of Chinese industrial planning is an ideal type. The Soviet model was only partially applied and was modified by successive reforms in the Maoist era, notably during the Great Leap Forward and the Cultural Revolution. Their main thrust was towards decentralisation of planning and management from central to local governments (akin to Khrushchev's regional decentralisation of the Soviet planning system after 1957). In consequence, while the basic principles of non-market regulation were retained, the Chinese system differed from the classic Soviet centralised model, combining elements of both vertical and horizontal integration ('dual rule').

Thus, the planning system appears to have been a complex and often contradictory amalgam of procedures, formal and informal, built up coral-like over three decades. To describe this as 'central planning' begs several key questions. Clearly a good deal of nominal 'planning' took place, but it was only 'centralised' to a limited degree.

How did the system of 'industrial planning' actually work in the

Maoist era and how effective was it? First, the quality of planning was poor due to informational deficiencies, lack of trained cadre and the disruptions caused by the political struggles which raged between 1966 and 1976.

With the single exception of the First Five Year Plan period (1953–7), planning had been conducted mainly on an annual basis. Capacity for framing and enforcing longer-term plans was sorely lacking, even if political circumstances had allowed (Huang Zhenqi, 1982). Second, the authority of the key central planning institutions (the State Planning Commission, SPC, and the State Economic Commission, SEC) was very limited. The eminent economist Xue Muqiao has emphasised the 'semi-planned' nature of the previous system, pointing out that, as of 1979, the SPC only had direct control over 'several hundred products' (out of 'several hundred thousand') and of these only 'dozens' were worked out exactly, the remainder being rough estimations only (1979, p. 15). The degree of central control also varied across sectors, with military-related industries (mostly heavy) being centralised and less strategic (mostly light) industries being left to local administration. The scope of central financial controls was also limited, there being numerous sources of funds outside the state budget (Byrd, 1983, pp. 97–101).

Third, one cannot assume that the formal planning authority of the SPC represented real control. One can roughly distinguish two (ideal) types of planning: 'autonomous planning' whereby the planning agency bases its calculations on priorities defined either by itself or by a superior political authority, and secures compliance from subordinate units; and 'dependent planning' where the agency's calculations are to varying degrees determined by those units which are the recipients of its instructions. Chinese central planners depend heavily on functional departments, notably ministries, which exert considerable influence over the pattern of priorities and allocation of resources by intervening at each stage of the planning process, namely goal determination, goal specification, balancing and adjustment, implementation and monitoring (Barnett, 1967, 440–41).

Fourth, 'planning' took place in a variety of locations (not just the centre), both formally and informally. Functional and regional state agencies and enterprises all had formal responsibility for drawing up their own productive plans. Each unit, through its control over material resources and information, could extend this power in real terms. Though plans at each level were in theory to be coordinated and integrated with national plan priorities, interrelations were loose in 'normal' times and grew looser in times of political conflict or economic instability. The resulting contradictions and ambiguities created a tendency towards *autonomisation* in both administrative and economic units, which reflected their desire to protect themselves against uncertainty. At the regional level, this took the form of 'independent kingdoms' or 'dukedoms' under local party bosses. Though this phenomenon is a natural outcome of central planning systems, it had been encouraged by Maoist emphasis on the virtue of local and enterprise 'self-reliance' (Donnithorne, 1972).

In sum, this system was neither very 'centralised' nor very 'planned.' A good deal of what paraded as 'planning' was in fact merely *administration*. It is important to distinguish an administered from a planned economy, the former obeying the ambiguous logic of complex bureaucracies rather than the rationality of systematic economic coordination and control. In Maoist China, moreover, the political dictates, often of dubious economic value, often shouldered aside processes of *both* administration and planning. Indeed, if we were to rank the real impact of different principles of economic management, the 'politocratic' and the 'bureaucratic' probably outranked the 'planocratic', though their relative salience varied over time.

This system's deficiencies were partly remedied by certain formal and informal mechanisms. At the formal level, the 'down-up' process of plan formulation was more than 'democratic centralist' cant – the Chinese system was arguably less 'top-down' than its Soviet counterpart. Party organisations played a role in improving communications, facilitating coordination and loosening administrative rigidities. The Maoist style of political 'campaigns' had some positive effect in concentrating attention and mobilising initiative. Just as important were the *informal* means of adaptation which developed over the years to unstopper bottlenecks and oil the cogs of the planning machine. There were complex networks of horizontal and vertical links based on 'personal connections' which cut across bureaucratic boundaries. It would be a mistake, for example, to see enterprise managers merely as inert recipients of orders from above. They made strenuous efforts to predetermine the content of these orders through bargaining and deception. They also enlarged their room for manoeuvre by hoarding capital equipment, labour and materials which enabled them to meet and 'overfulfil' plan targets more easily. Enterprising managers could also expand their financial resources by taking advantage of local 'extra-budgetary' funds. Informal links were also made with other enterprises: 'purchasing staff' (in effect 'fixers') ranged far and wide to secure materials or components by purchase or barter. Temporary labour could be taken on through informal contracts with urban neighbourhood organisations, illegal labour gangs, or nearby rural communes. The extent of this 'shadow economy' is impossible to estimate, but retrospective accounts suggest it was considerable and without it the 'official economy' would have been in far worse trouble.

Industrial planning in the Maoist era was thus a complex mixture of administrative regulation, political bargaining, and 'shadow' or 'grey' markets. But it was also a system in which the basic characteristics of markets were absent, weak or driven underground: productive units lacked autonomy, economic linkages were predominantly vertical (state-enterprise), not horizontal (between enterprises), production dominated exchange (i.e. market demands had little impact on the pattern of output) and the allocative role of prices was very limited.

CHINESE INDUSTRIAL PERFORMANCE IN THE MAOIST ERA: PERFORMANCE AND PROBLEMS

The economic results achieved within this cumbersome and contradictory framework over the first three decades should not be underestimated. China maintained high rates of industrial growth and establish a relatively comprehensive industrial and technical base while avoiding dependence on foreign countries. High rates (by international standards)[2] of overall 'accumulation'[3] have been maintained since the early 1950s (for details see *SSB*, 1983, pp. 25–7). Most of state investment funds were channelled into directly 'productive'[4] investment, the lion's share going to industry, especially heavy industry, as Table 5.1 shows.

The annual rate of growth of gross value of industrial output (GVIO – in constant prices) fluctuated sharply but averaged 10.7 per cent between 1953 and 1982, heavy industry (12.2 per cent) outpacing light (9.5 per cent). Agriculture lagged behind, growing at about 3.4 per cent p.a. between 1952 and 1980 (Ishikawa, 1983, p. 245). Industry's share of total (gross) national product more than doubled (from 25.1 per cent in 1949 to 59.6 per cent in 1977) while agriculture's share dropped from 58.6 per cent to 23.3 per cent over the same period.

Table 5.1   Distribution of investment in capital construction[a] by economic sectors (%)

| Period | Agriculture[b] | Industry | Within which:[c] | | Other[d] |
			light industry	heavy industry	
1st FYP (1953–7)	7.1	42.5	6.4	36.1	50.4
2nd FYP (1958–62)	11.3	60.4	6.4	54.0	28.3
1963–5	17.7	49.8	3.9	45.9	32.5
3rd FYP (1966–70)	10.7	55.5	4.4	51.1	33.8
4th FYP (1971–75)	9.8	55.4	5.8	49.6	34.8
1976–80	10.5	52.6	6.7	45.9	36.9
1981	6.6	48.8	9.8	39.0	44.6
1982	6.1	46.9	8.4	38.5	47.0
1983	6.0	47.5	6.5	41.0	46.5
1984	5.0	46.0	5.7	40.3	49.0

[a] 'Capital construction' is defined in *SSB*, 1983, p. 588.
[b] 'Agriculture' includes forestry, water conservancy and meteorology.
[c] 'Light' industry is mainly consumer goods, including industries using both farm and non-farm products as raw materials. 'Heavy' industry usually produces the means of production, with two main branches, mining and felling, and manufacturing (*SSB*, 1983, pp. 585–6).
[d] 'Other' includes construction, transport, communications, commerce, science and public welfare (education, health and culture).

Source: *SSB*, 1983, pp. 324–7.

Certain strategic heavy industries developed very rapidly, notably machine-building (from 11.4 per cent of GVIO in 1952 to 27.7 per cent in 1975), metallurgy, petroleum, chemicals and electric power.

Until the mid-1970s, state industry expanded faster than collective, even taking into account the growth of the rural commune-run sector after the Great Leap Forward as Table 5.2 shows.

This industrialisation took place in the context of a 'self-reliant' strategy of import-substitution with exports treated primarily as a means to procure imported capital goods. Overall, until quite

Table 5.2   Shares of GVIO produced by state and collective enterprises
(measured in constant prices) (%)

Year	Shares of gross industrial output value		
	State-owned enterprises	Collective enterprises	Of which enterprises commune-run
1952	76.2	23.8	
1957	80.1	19.9	
1965	90.1	9.9	0.4
1975	83.2	16.8	2.7
1980	78.7	20.7	5.6
1981	78.3	21.0	6.2
1982	77.8	21.4	6.4
1983	77.0	22.0	6.7
1984	73.6	25.0	7.7

Source: Computed from data in *SSB*, 1983, pp. 214–15; 1985, p. 46.

recently foreign trade has played a small role in the economy, ranging from 5 to 8 per cent of GNP between 1949 and 1979.

However, in spite of these impressive changes, China had hardly been transformed into an industrial society. As of 1982, 84.4 per cent of the total labour force in industry and agriculture worked in the latter. Sutcliffe (1971, pp. 16–26) suggests three criteria of whether a country is 'industrialised': a minimum of 25 per cent of GDP in the industrial sector, a minimum of 60 per cent of the industrial sector in manufacturing and a minimum of 10 per cent of the total population working in industry. China scores highly on the first two criteria, having 46 per cent of GDP in industry in 1981 (World Bank, 1983, p. 152) and about 77 per cent of this in manufacturing in 1982 (SSB, 1983, p. 218), but only 5.8 per cent of the total population was employed in industry as of 1982. Using these criteria, therefore, China could be described as a 'semi-industrialised' country (Sutcliffe's category B).

China's industrial performance during the Maoist era was reasonably impressive by international standards. The figures conceal certain basic problems, however, which grew more serious during the 1960s and early 1970s. Although very high rates of state accumulation may have made some sense in the early period, the developmental logic of this strategy diminished given the incentive costs of constraints on popular consumption and low rates of capital productivity. Per capita earnings and consumption of non-agricultural workers rose sluggishly up to the mid-1970s, stagnating or declining in certain periods (Nolan and White, 1984). Marginal capital–output ratios were falling appreciably (Ishikawa, 1983, pp. 253–60), thus high growth rates were being purchased at increasing capital cost. While capital intensity in industry was steadily rising (White, 1982b, p. 617), labour productivity was stagnant or declining. Capital per worker grew ninefold between 1957 to 1978 while the number of industrial workers increased by less than threefold. The net value of output per industrial worker declined from 2763 to 2593 (current) *yuan* between 1965 and 1975 (cf. Field, 1983).

A number of factors underlay these problems: questionable strategic policy choices about the level and direction of investment; absence of the stimulus which a dynamic foreign trade sector could provide; exclusion or poor absorption of foreign technology and a sluggish rate of domestic innovation; the impact of directive planning methods on industrial efficiency; bottlenecks in key sectors such as energy and transportation; inability to solve the intractable problems of raising agricultural productivity; political instability and international isolation.

All of these factors received attention from Chinese economists after Mao's death (Cyril Lin, 1981). Foremost in their analyses was a critique of the negative impact of the state on industrial development. First, they pointed to a 'state bias' in development strategy which privileged accumulation over consumption, 'productive' over 'unproductive' investment and heavy over light industry and agriculture (for the idea of 'state bias' see Nolan and White, 1984). If accumulation and industrialisation constituted the original *raison d'être* of state control over industry, they were increasingly converted into *raison d'état*, the means whereby the state apparatus (and state workforce) expanded and legitimised their dominance in society. Second, the state sector encroached on the non-state sector, converting formally independent collective enterprises into *de facto* state enterprises. Behind this lay an ideological conviction which equated 'whole people' (i.e. state) ownership with a 'higher' level of socialism.

The Dengist reforms introduced by the Third Plenum of the CCP's Central Committee in December 1978 initiated an economic *'readjustment'* in order to correct these two basic imbalances:

(i) The rate of accumulation was to be reduced and individual and social consumption increased;

(ii) Investment priorities were to be redirected away from heavy towards light industry and agriculture, from extensive to intensive development;
(iii) Greater emphasis was placed on developing collective as opposed to state industry, particularly to generate employment;
(iv) New international links were to be fostered to stimulate the economy, expand employment and absorb foreign technology and management expertise.

The third area of critique ratified by the Third Plenum was directed at the previous system of directive planning and management which was identified as an increasing impediment to economic deficiency and technological dynamism. Reformers proposed basic changes in the ways in which the state should act to direct and regulate industry; it is their critique, policy proposals and practical impact on Chinese industry which is the main focus of this chapter.

In the rest of this chapter I shall cover two topics: first, the nature of the 'market reform' critique of the previous system of industrial planning and the main elements of the reform programme; second, the actual impact of reform policies since 1978, focusing on several key areas of policy. The conclusion examines the political and economic problems associated with the reform process and their implications for the future role of the Chinese state as an effective agent of industrialisation.

I shall base my analysis on primary documents and on the results of three one-month field-trips to China in September 1982, July 1983 and June 1985.

THE THEORETICAL BASIS OF THE ECONOMIC REFORM PROGRAMME

Reform economists have concentrated their fire on the economic irrationalities of the previous pattern of state involvement in industry.[5] They acknowledge that the socialist state *can* play a positive role in regulating (directly or indirectly) the structure and direction of the economy, especially in the early stages of industrialisation. But the economic advantages of planning originally posited by the Marxian socialist tradition are now seen as contingent not automatic, thus raising serious questions about the nature and degree of state involvement.

Specifically, critics have identified two crucial problems in the relationship between state and economy, each of which becomes more acute as the economy grows more complex and the boundaries of state involvement expand: first, between administrative and economic systems as distinct and potentially contradictory social processes and, second, between state planning organs and productive enterprises.

The Conflicting Economic Logics of State and Market

Reformers argue that the previous planning system imposed a statist logic on the economy which impeded economic development. Historically, it was a fusion of two forms of statism: the 'feudal' (i.e. imperial Chinese and Tsarist Russian) and the 'socialist' (i.e. Leninist–Stalinist). In consequence, the economy is transformed into a politico-administrative system giving rise to two basic problems. First, the imperatives of *political* mobilisation and conflict distort economic processes. Reform economists argue that there is an independent economic sphere in society governed by 'economic laws'. Noted economist Hu Qiaomu, for example, accused state officials of taking 'the will of society, the government and the authorities as economic law which can be bent to political expediency' (Hu, 1978 (45), p. 8). For Hu, the function of political leadership is 'to see to it that our socialist economic work operates within the scope of these objective [economic] laws'. This insistence on the 'relative autonomy' of the *economy* in socialist society is a paradoxical inversion of Western Marxist arguments about the 'relative autonomy' of the *state* in capitalist society.

Second, the state imposes its own *administrative* logic on the economy, with several ill effects. To the extent that state power is concentrated and hierarchical, the economy becomes rigidified and its productive elements, the enterprises, are rendered inert. Conversely, to the extent that authority in the state apparatus is diffused and overlapping, 'semi-anarchy' reigns which hampers economic planning. In both cases heavy state intervention is irrational because it imposes 'a "net"-like system of administration whereby countless vertical and horizontal restrictions break up the natural relations of the objective economy' (Ji and Rong, 1979, p. 14).

Skinner (1964–5, part III) has identified the problems caused by this tension between natural and state economic systems in his analysis of the massive disorientations caused by the commune movement in 1958–9. In industry, the economic costs of administrative segmentation are a familiar feature of directive planning systems elsewhere. The Polish economist Balcerowicz, for example (1980, pp. 160–1), points to the problem in an Eastern European context, arguing that it engenders constant tension between the 'material' and 'organisational ties' of the economy, which is particularly harmful to technical innovation.

Reformers have drawn four basic policy conclusions from their analysis of administrative segmentation. First, there should be greater separation between the spheres of administration and economics, the latter having more scope to operate according to its own 'organic' logic. This implies, for example, the formation of 'natural' economic zones crossing administrative boundaries and the promotion of inter-plant integration, particularly through cross-boundary 'companies'. Second, central planning organs should be strengthened to curb branch-based 'departmentalism' and establish a more rational division of labour between central and local governments. Central planners would henceforth concentrate on macroeconomic management, regulating the micro-economy less by directive means and more by 'economic levers' or 'guidance' methods. Third, market processes were to be resuscitated, under the aegis of a new ideological outlook which recognise the 'commoditised' character of socialist economy. Fourth, the bedrock of the reform programme, the decision-making powers of industrial enterprises should be expanded. Let us explore this last proposal in more detail.

The Relationship Between State Agencies and Industrial Enterprises

In analysing state–enterprise relations, the main target has been the overconcentration of economic management power in the hands of state officials. Although successive waves of administrative decentralisation had diffused power to local governments, from the viewpoint of enterprise managers, the identity of their superiors might have changed but the reality of administrative subordination had not. In the view of reform economists, enterprises were virtually powerless. Investment funds were disbursed from the state budget and enterprises had to apply for increments; output levels were assigned and supplies and sales were arranged in a 'unified' way by superior organs which also fixed prices; and most expenditures were provided by, and most profits were returned to, state agencies.

Detailed controls of this kind would be difficult to maintain and monitor with ample information in a relatively simple and small economy; much more so in a large economy like China with a still embryonic statistical system. The situation worsened as the economy grew more complex.

In this supply-driven system, the target of gross output value tended to outrank the others. But output targets set on the 'ratchet' principle gave little incentive for performance above norm in year t because the official target in year $t+1$ would be that much higher. Enterprises were also impelled to seek increased output without concern for cost, quality or customer satisfaction. Although output was theoretically linked to demand, responsibility for selling rested not with the enterprise itself but with state commercial organs which had to 'sell what is produced'. On the supplies side, the enterprise suffered from defects in the system of administrative allocation which caused shortages and delays in production (Ji and Rong, 1979, p. 15).

Enterprises had very little power over the disposition of labour, which was subject to strict administrative controls (White, 1982b). Since the discretionary funds of enterprise managers were so meagre, moreover, they were unable to design incentive schemes to improve labour productivity. Indeed, the financial powers of managers were very limited. A current joke went as follows: 'Question: which enterprises in China have independent economic accounting? Answer: Only one, the Ministry of Finance' (Li and Niu, 1979, p. 2). Expenditures for renewing fixed assets had to be submitted to higher organs for approval, a cumbersome procedure which impeded technical change. Depreciation rates also tended to be set very low (for example, 2.92 per cent at the massive Anshan Iron and Steel Company, a 34-year regeneration cycle) and depreciation funds were often diverted to other uses.

The central theme running through these criticisms was the severe economic cost of a system of industrial management which either reduced enterprises to passivity or, where it did stir them into action, drove them in economically irrational directions. The 'key link' in reform, argued Chinese economists, was the expansion of enterprise decision-making power in an increasingly 'marketised' environment.

The Reform Critique: an Evaluation

Before examining the actual effects of reform policies after 1978, it is important to assess the accuracy of the reformers' critique. The picture they paint of the previous industrial planning system is to some extent a negative caricature designed to dismay. The most irrational features are highlighted, extreme cases are adduced to support general arguments and positive features tend to be downplayed. Indeed, in some accounts this negative stereotype is a mirror image of that idealisation of the market to which some reformers are prone (Riskin, 1981).

While agreeing with their calls for change and accepting their arguments about declining 'economic results' in the early and mid-1970s, one should recognise that, in crude terms of industrial growth and structural change, Chinese economic performance since the mid-1950s had been very creditable. Clearly there was *some* positive dynamic in the old system which needs analysis.

As we have seen, moreover, it would be misleading simply to attribute the economic deficiencies of the previous system to 'central planning' or even to 'planning' – some were clearly also a product of *lack* of centralisation and *weak* or incompetent planning. The very ambiguity of the previous system may also have given room for decentralised initiatives which alleviated the rigidities of a truly centralised system. In fact, in the Chinese context of poor communications, scarce expertise and massive size, 'real' central planning would have brought greater and earlier problems. Nor should the negative model constructed by the reformers blind us to the formal and informal mechanisms, integral parts of the previous planning system, which mitigated some of its deficiencies by improving communications, coordination and flexible adaptation.

In spite of these qualifications, however, the central points of the reform critique are well taken. In the next section, we turn to the nature and impact of the policies deriving from this critique which, have been introduced by a reform leadership under Deng Xiaoping since 1978.

THE IMPACT OF ECONOMIC REFORMS

The transition from diagnosis to cure, theoretical analysis to practical policy, has proven tricky. The policy process since 1978 has proven complex and fortuous, the reform impetus ebbing and flowing in successive waves. I have discussed these policy dynamics in detail elsewhere (White, 1983b, pp. 345–56) and will concentrate here on assessing the amount of reform actually achieved in the mid-1980s in three key areas of policy – finance, labour and trade.

The Financial System

Perhaps the area of reform policy which has had the greatest impact on the urban–industrial economy has been that of finance. Financial reforms set out to redefine the process of capital aggregation and circulation, specifically to diversify sources of capital provision and redefine the terms on which capital is allocated. In this section, I will be interested in the extent to which this has led to the emergence of 'capital markets', characterised by decentralised sources of supply and allocation according to supply and demand conditions measured by variable interest rates.

The first main thrust of reform in industrial finance has been the attempt to impose market-like discipline by moving away from the previous practice of supplying all of the fixed and much of the working capital funds of enterprises as interest-free budgetary allocations. Under the new system, the bulk of capital advances would be in the form of bank loans, subject to repayment and carrying a cost in the form of interest. The previous system, argued the reformers with considerable justification, had generated an essentially political struggle between enterprises to obtain more investment with little pressure to use these funds effectively once acquired (Wang Chuanlun, 1984, p. 61). The scramble for extra investment fostered a tendency towards extensive rather than intensive industrial development, allowed slack management of equipment and raw materials and encouraged managers to conceal their true capital assets as part of their strategy of bargaining with state agencies. The reforms, it was hoped, would raise the efficiency of capital-utilisation by introducing more caution and cost-consciousness into managers' calculations about the acquisition and use of capital.

During 1979–85, therefore, there has been movement towards greater commercialisation of capital provision along several fronts. The role of the banking (as opposed to the budgetary) system was expanded and its autonomy increased. During the Cultural

Revolution decade, the People's Bank of China had effectively been under the control of the Ministry of Finance and the banking system had basically reflected fiscal priorities and processes. In the early stages of the reforms, the People's Bank was allowed to increase its role as a provider of credit. As of 1984, its role was changed to that of a Central Bank in charge of monetary policy and overall financial policy. Most of its commercial functions were transferred to a new Industry and Commerce Bank charged with providing credit for enterprises and managing bank deposits.[6] The banking system underwent further institutional changes: a number of specialised banks were established (to operate under People's Bank supervision), there was a significant devolution of decision-making power from central to local bank branches, and other types of investment trust or corporation were encouraged to set up, at both national and local levels. A special company, the China International Trust and Investment Corporation (CITIC) was also established in 1979 to encourage and channel foreign investment.

Banking institutions were charged with the role of using economic, rather than administrative, methods to stimulate industrial development in two senses. First, they could use their capacity to aggregate and channel credit funds to promote industrial expansion and implement current planning priorities (for example, by directing loans preferentially to light rather than heavy industrial projects, the collective rather than the state sector, and export-oriented rather than domestic enterprises). Second, through their ability to provide or withhold loans, set conditions through differential terms and interest rates and enforce credit contracts through an expanding framework of financial laws, banks could act as a stimulus to industrial efficiency. In effect, they were to play a major role in supervising enterprise finances: they could act to encourage efficient and penalise inefficient enterprises, monitor the implementation of state plans, improve the quality of financial accounting, stimulate technical innovation, speed up the turnover of working capital, curtail unproductive or duplicating investment projects, monitor the level of bonus payments, and so on.

The second major thrust of the financial reforms has been to devolve more financial power to the enterprises themselves by changing the previous practice of syphoning off enterprise revenues into state coffers. This reform has gone through three stages, each of which has brought greater financial power to enterprise managers.

I have discussed these in detail elsewhere (White, 1986b) so I shall be less interested in their precise nature and more in their effects on the system of industrial finance as a whole.

The introduction of these reforms led to claims and counter-claims about their effectiveness in improving industrial efficiency. Though there was some improvement in certain financial indicators of industrial performance, by 1982–3 considerable disappointment was expressed by senior financial officials about the effectiveness of the reforms.[7] In fact, the impact of the reforms was uneven and contradictory. Certain problems arose from their lack of impact. Though the institutional reforms in the banking system did reduce the monopolistic character of the old system to some extent, the new system was still oligopolistic and imposed powerful obstacles to the fluidity of capital. Some economists criticised 'the endless game of administrative changes' and called for decisive steps to establish more lively financial markets.[8] Moreover, many enterprises resisted the move from budgetary to credit provision of investment funds and, in the five years from 1979 to 1984, bank credit only amounted to 10 per cent of the state capital construction budget.[9] The potential for using interest rates as a weapon of economic policy was not exploited and their overall level on industrial loans was too low to have a significant effect on enterprise behaviour (Byrd, 1983, p. 77).[10] Banks also found it difficult to supervise enterprise activities given the difficulties they encountered in enforcing repayment of loans (in the absence of effective legislation on contracts) and in securing accurate information on enterprise activities, their continued vulnerability to political and administrative pressures (for example, to give loans to inefficient enterprises) and their lack of properly trained professional cadre.

Other problems, however, arose from the very effectiveness of certain elements of the financial reform programme. Between 1979 and 1984 there was indeed a major diversification of sources of industrial finance and considerable decentralisation of financial decision-making power: power flowed to individual economic departments, local governments, industrial enterprises, rural co-ops, specialised banks, local bank branches, investment trusts, individuals (in joint-stock ventures) and foreign interests. The proliferation of 'extra-budgetary funds' (EBF) from these sources created what has been called a 'second budget' (Wang Chuanlun, 1984, p. 65) or an 'unorganised capital market'. As a proportion of state budgetary funds, EBF rose from 4 per cent in 1953 to around 60 per cent in

1981. Of total EBF the proportion actually managed by state financial departments fell from 15 per cent in 1953 to 6.9 per cent in 1981 (Wu Renjian, 1983). Apparently a large proportion of EBF were used for investment; already by 1980 EBF provided 55 per cent of gross fixed investment state enterprises (compared with 40 per cent in 1979, 38 per cent in 1976 and only 11 per cent during the First Five Year Plan) (Byrd 1983, pp. 27–8).

The state lost a good deal of its ability to control the money supply in general and the expansion of investment funds in particular. In 1982, for example, gross national investment in fixed assets reached 84.5 billion *yuan*, exceeding the plan by 15 billion *yuan* – a trend which continued into 1983 (Wang Jiye, 1983). 'Overinvestment' was accompanied by 'overdistribution' as enterprises poured money into 'productivity' bonus schemes which were often poorly conceived and outstripped improvements in labour productivity. For example, though full capacity labour productivity in state enterprises in 1982 was 2.3 per cent up on 1981, wages roses 7.6 per cent and the total amount of bonuses and extra piece-rate wages by 19.8 per cent (Rong Zihe, 1983). Along with problematic fiscal policies which created large budget deficits in 1979 and 1980, these financial pressures contributed to the inflation which had risen to alarming levels (by Chinese standards) by 1980 (Dai Yuanchen, 1981). This situation provoked a strong response from the financial authorities who attempted to recentralise financial allocation during 1981–3, with only limited success (Wang Jiye, 1983). There was a concomitant drive to cut back on capital investment programmes particularly by local authorities, again with very limited success. The banks were also impelled to reduce the monetary disequilibrium by limited credit expansion, increasing personal savings and withdrawing currency from circulation. These measures, along with increases in the output of consumer goods and price controls, eased the growth in the money supply and reduced inflation. But with the renewed reform impetus which built up during 1984–5, the same pressures emerged and there were various signs of overheating in the economy in 1985. In fact, there was a rhythm of 'stop–go' financial policy throughout the 1978–85 period: financial liberalisation followed by overheating followed by government attempts to restore controls.

It would be misleading to attribute these problems to an extension of financial 'markets' in any strict sense. To the extent that the role of credit money was expanded, the regulating power of interest rates was increased, sources of investment finance proliferated and investment decisions were decentralised (particularly to industrial enterprises), certain elements of a capital market were introduced. However, many of the sources of investment funds remained bureaucratic (local governments and functional economic departments) and allocations continued to be made on politico-administrative grounds. Moreover the impact of certain key mechanisms of a true capital market – notably variable interest reflecting supply and demand conditions, the vetting of loans on commercial criteria and legally enforceable contracts – still remained weak. Indeed, one could argue that this initial attempt to combine planning and market in the financial sphere led to a situation which combined the worst of both worlds: on the one hand, the state's capacity to control and coordinate capital flows was severely weakened; on the other, the reforms brought much of the disorder of a market system without much of its capacity for self-equilibration and allocative efficiency. However, problems of this kind are to be expected in such an important economic transition. Though they reappeared in the renewed reform push of 1984–5, the CCP leadership pressed ahead undeterred. But this next step involves not merely more decisive steps towards the establishment of financial markets (probably including the appearance of share markets and further erosion of the oligopolistic control of the central banks) but also towards strengthening the capacity of the state to regulate an increasingly complex financial system.[11]

Labour Recruitment and Allocation

As in the case of capital, the issue of 'labour markets' is politically sensitive in China since, in the Marxian classics, the existence of a market in labour-power is a defining characteristic of capitalism. Up till very recently, therefore, economic reformers have been careful to avoid direct advocacy of 'labour markets'. Many of their proposed reforms in the labour system, however, are clearly designed to move in that direction.

They argue that, of all aspects of the previous system of industrial planning, 'the allocation of labour resources is by far the furthest from the market mechanism'. Following the principle of 'unified employment and assignment', state labour bureaux had exercised a virtual monopoly over the allocation of urban labour (including both the state and the 'big collective' sectors) (Zhao Lukuan, 1980: Feng Lanrui, 1981; Ye and Chen, 1979). There was a pressing need to reduce the span of direct controls, simplify the technical and administrative requirements of labour planning by more selective intervention and encourage a greater degree of labour mobility (while retaining a commitment to full employment).

There is considerable evidence that the previous system of administrative allocation had a bad effect on workers' motivations and productivity. It was too 'top down', imposing (often unreasonable) 'plan' requirements on (often unwilling) individuals. Refusal to 'obey allocation' to one's first job assignment could be interpreted as disloyalty to the nation and the socialist cause. After initial job assignment, moreover, the individual found it difficult to move laterally to other units or areas. Administrative labour allocation had also encouraged overmanning, argued the critics. State enterprises had expanded extensively by taking on fresh labour rather than intensively by using technical and managerial innovation to raise the productivity of the existing workforce.

Restrictions on labour mobility meant that most workers and staff on the state payroll had lifetime tenure in their original units with job promotions or wage increments based heavily on seniority. This was the notorious 'iron rice-bowl' which reformers identified as a major impediment to improving labour productivity. Though enterprises could achieve some degree of flexibility by taking on 'temporary' or 'contract labourers' for limited terms, these workers resented the differential, and pressured managers to grant them an 'iron rice-bowl' too. When successful, they became less productive, as senior researcher, Feng Lanrui, points out (interview in White, 1983a, p. 148):

> [All] temporary workers wanted to be full workers; you told them to go and they would refuse. The state tried to control this by allowing *planned* temporary workers to change over, but not those outside the plan, but this approach was ineffective. The trouble is that, when they become fixed workers, they slacked off.

Finally, argued reform critics, state monopoly over urban labour allocation had contributed to unemployment by obstructing the emergence of alternative job agencies and reduced the motivation of the urban unemployed to find jobs for themselves, inuring them to 'dependence on the state'.

Labour reform policies since 1978 have sought to rectify these problems by improving labour planning, changing the degree and forms of state involvement in labour allocation,and encouraging more 'spontaneous' labour mobility. The principle of state planning was to remain the dominant element in a new system of labour allocation: state labour bureaux would determine the overall proportions of the national labour force but would use direct administrative controls more selectively; independent cooperative labour agencies would help people find jobs; enterprises would have a greater say in recruiting and dismissing their own workers; and individuals would be encouraged to find or create their own jobs.

If we turn now to the *impact* of these proposals, progress in the first wave of reform up to 1981 was very slow and disappointing (White, 1983a, 1985). The ability of enterprise managers to select new workers has increased to some extent: for example, enterprises could select individual workers so long as they observed numerical quotas; they made increasing use of advertisements for job vacancies and applicants were vetted by examinations. Very little progress was made in increasing the power of enterprises to dismiss workers. One exception was the 'special economic zones' in the south-east where management powers over hiring and firing were greater than elsewhere. Where the power was exercised elsewhere, it only applied to workers who repeatedly violated labour discipline, relatively infrequent cases. State labour bureaux still controlled numbers of personnel and wage funds, often with little reference to what enterprises themselves wanted. Labour bureaux were under pressure to alleviate urban unemployment; thus they padded their quotas and enterprises had to accept unnecessary labour. Though there had been some progress in diversifying channels of labour allocation through the new labour service companies, their impact on the state industrial sector was negligible and they remained under the control of local labour bureaux. The methods used by central personnel agencies to allocate 'strategic' groups (notably college graduates) had not changed. The degree of individual choice was still very limited and levels of 'misallocation' remained high.

As of early 1982, therefore, labour system reforms in the state sector had been far less effective than their counterparts in finance. State controls were still tight, labour flexibility in the state sector had hardly changed and the 'iron rice-bowl' was as strong as ever. Indeed, in some aspects the situation had got worse: labour productivity was stagnant and even falling in some cases; overmanning actually increased to an extent that by mid-1983, economists estimated that between 20 to 30 per cent of the workforce of state enterprises were unnecessary (White, 1983a, pp. 12, 147); the practice of job inheritance had spread (White, 1983a, pp. 120, 130); the number of 'strategic' categories subject to central state 'unified allocation' had increased (White, 1983a, p. 16). Clearly labour reform remained a pressing priority.

A second wave of reform, more deliberate than the first, began in early 1982, spearheaded by Premier Zhao Ziyang. The aim was to push forward elements of reform which had stalled and launch a frontal attack on the 'iron rice-bowl' through the introduction of a labour contract system. I shall concentrate on the latter here given its importance in increasing flexibility in labour circulation within the state sector. The contract system was designed to change the status of state workers, 97 per cent of whom had previously enjoyed job security. Henceforth they would be employed on contracts of varying length, agreed between themselves and enterprise management and enforceable through new labour legislation. At the end of the contract, if job performance had been unsatisfactory or if the labour requirements of the enterprise had changed, the contract need not be renewed. Ideally, this system would improve productivity by concentrating the minds of the workers; it would give enterprise managers more flexibility in adjusting their labour force to changes in market demand and production process. The enterprise, labour service companies and local governments would each play a role in guaranteeing welfare benefits (sickness or injury pay, pensions, etc. which had formerly been the sole responsibility of the enterprise) and for redeploying and retraining redundant workers. Thus the state's role would become more 'parametric', with the key elements of labour allocation based on the relationships between enterprise and worker (for a discussion of the new form of labour planning by an official of the Ministry of Labour, see White, 1985, pp. 19–21).

This is a radical change in labour policy and is a political hot potato, a fact reflected in the cautious way in which the policy was introduced during 1983–5. By mid-1985, only a very small percentage of state workers were on contracts, mostly the new intakes of 1984 and 1985. There was little movement towards extending the principle to the established workforce. Interviews revealed that, though the Ministry of Labour was apparently committed to generalising the contract system, as of mid-1985 there was still considerable disagreement among policy-makers and their advisers about how to proceed (White, 1985). It was easier in sectors where the contract principle was already established and fitted specific job conditions (notably in mining and construction). Interviews and press reports suggest considerable scepticism and opposition, from academics such as Jiang Yiwei (1985) (then head of the Institute of Industrial Economics in the Chinese Academy of Social Sciences), from state industrial workers and their organisations who could complain of a return to 'wage labour', but also from industrial managers who, like senior managers in a Shenyang woollen mill interviewed in 1983 (White, 1983a, p. 120), or in Taiyuan Iron and Steel Company interviewed in 1985 (White, 1985, p. 32), feel that the system is 'inappropriate' to specific conditions in their own factories.

Political constraints apart, however, successful introduction of the contract system requires local governments to improve their capacity to deal with frictional unemployment and establish complementary systems of social welfare, housing and education. While the contract system further reduces the direct role of the state in labour allocation, it also requires government to take on new functions (along 'welfare state' lines) for which it is as yet ill-prepared.

Economic conditions are also unfavourable for introducing the contract system. So long as there is a significant level of urban unemployment and the rewards for non-state employment remain inferior, state workers will resist the contract principle with vigour. Though official sources claim to have brought the unemployment rate down to 2.6 per cent by 1983, this was certainly an understatement. Pressures on the state workforce, moreover, do not stem merely from unemployment: many workers in the urban collective sector would dearly like a state job, even on a contract basis (because there is always the chance of converting it into a 'fixed' position); and outside and over the cities looms the problem of rural surplus labour, estimated at present to be about one-third of the rural workforce (or about 100 million people) (White, 1985, pp. 2–4).

Thus for these powerful reasons it will be difficult to make headway in improving industrial performance by increasing labour circulation. In the state sector at least, it is unlikely that there will be any significant shift in the direction of labour markets in the near future: the principle of job tenure will be hard to budge, lateral mobility will increase slowly if at all and state labour bureaux will continue to dominate labour allocation. In the non-state urban sector, however, there is much more of a labour market with far greater freedom of entrance and exit, and lower job security. Thus the question of planning and market in labour allocation must be situated in this 'dualist' economic structure, each sector operating according to different economic principles, not unlike the industrial structure of a capitalist economy such as Japan. If the rewards to work in the non-state sector increase (and there is some evidence that this is happening), this will not only reduce the demand for state jobs but will tempt state workers out into the 'informal' sector, trading security for higher immediate incomes. On the other hand, the defensiveness of state workers may be reinforced if greater numbers of peasants are allowed into the cities (an increasing trend), adding a third tier to the dualist urban economy.

Commodity Circulation and Price Policy

We can separate this topic into the two broad areas of commodity circulation and commodity exchange. Taking commodity *circulation* first, the previous system essentially had three components:

(a) A centralised system of materials supply which planned and allocated basic raw materials and capital equipment to state enterprises;
(b) The state commercial network which handled the wholesale and retail distribution of industrial goods;
(c) Rural supply and marketing cooperatives (SMCs) which bought farm produce and supplied industrial goods to the countryside.

Reformers argued that this system had been monopolistic and cumbersome: the materials supply system was prone to the usual miscalculations of centralised directive planning; the state commercial system was an ineffective link between producers and consumers since it had insufficient outlets, was poorly managed, and operated along lines of distribution which followed administrative rather than economic logic (e.g. Wan, 1983); and the SMCs, which were originally envisaged as providing a supplementary channel to state commerce, were 'cooperatives' in name only, in fact being merely appendages of local commercial bureaux.

Reformers proposed several avenues of improvement. The materials supply system should be carefully deregulated, centralised allocation being retained only over a few strategic goods, others being handled by local authorities or marketed freely either by specialised agencies of the Bureau of Materials Allocation (BMA) or by producing units themselves. The degree of monopoly exercised by the state commercial system over the distribution of consumer goods was to be reduced and channels of commercial circulation made more rational (the principle was 'increase the channels and cut down the links'). These aims were to be achieved by encouraging the development of independent cooperative and private trading concerns, by allowing enterprises to market a portion of their output directly, and by organising the flow of commodities according to 'natural' marketing systems, bypassing the bureaucratic network of state wholesale stations (including the move towards city-based 'economic zones'). To improve their capacity to link changing patterns of supply and demand, state commercial enterprises and SMCs were to be granted more independence and put on a better business footing.

Turning now to commodity *exchange*, reformers argued that the previous commercial system failed both to create an effective link between production and sales and to reflect real conditions of supply and demand. They devoted particular attention to the irrationality of 'planned' prices. In the sphere of production, the relationship between the price of a commodity and its costs of production was vague and prices failed to register differences in enterprise efficiency. In relations between state enterprises, prices played a 'passive' accounting role, reflecting 'planned' relationships between physical goods. In the sale of consumer goods, prices were inflexible, too often reflected non-economic considerations and were only seldom used to readjust patterns of production or demand.

Certain fundamental changes were required, argued reform economists. First, planned prices should be *rationalised* to relate them more closely to actual costs of production. Second, prices should be *deregulated* by decentralising price administration from central to local agencies, reducing the range of goods subject to state price controls, and diversifying price forms, with a range from 'fixed' to 'negotiated', 'floating' and 'free market'. Third, the state should use *price policy* more actively as an 'economic lever' to regulate demand and supply. The central aim was to increase the allocative role of price, the main operating principle of 'market regulation'. However, it was still assumed that the state would continue to fix prices for strategic producer and essential consumer goods and be responsible for maintaining overall price stability.

How have these proposed reforms fared? Taking *circulation* first, there was progress on several fronts. First, there were some (limited and uneven) changes in the system of materials supply. Commodities deemed in 'good supply' (for example, in 1982–3, machinery and electrical equipment certain steel products) have been deregulated to some extent (White, 1983a, p. 24). They are increasingly allocated through direct relations between producing and consuming enterprises or by special 'materials trading markets' specialising in certain groups of products (for an account of the Shanghai Chemicals Materials Trading Market, see White, 1983a, pp. 87–93). Deregulation varies considerably across sectors: the First Ministry of Machine-Building has been a pace-setter. Some factories (such as the Shanghai High Pressure Oil Pump Factory which I visited in 1983) (White, 1983a, pp. 58), now purchase most of their own materials. There has also been some progress towards decentralising allocation, with more power going to local governments and greater use of specialised supply stations or 'shops'. Barter trading between local governments also expanded formally (i.e. an undiscoverable proportion of it had existed before informally) with some provinces obtaining as much as 20 per cent, some counties as much as 50 per cent of their material needs through barter (White, 1983a, pp. 65–6).

In spite of this movement, however, the dominance of administrative allocation has been difficult to dent. The materials allocation bureaucracy was still enormous (Peking officials estimated a total staff of 700 000 natonwide!) and, as one BMA official put it, 'some small commodities can be freed, but we really can't open up much' (White, 1983a, p. 30). The central problem is that, as Kornai (1980a) has pointed out for Eastern European economies, the system of administrative allocation of producer goods operates according to a logic of shortage. As long as the basic system is unreformed, the amount of products in 'good supply' will be relatively marginal. Though there has been a certain degree of organisational decentralisation and a number of buyers' markets have emerged over recent years, the principle and practice of bureaucratic allocation and systematic scarcity still dominate. This in turn has hindered progress towards organising the flow of materials along more rational, 'natural' channels of circulation.

On the other hand, there has been more striking progress in improving circulation through management reforms and a diversification of channels in the state commercial system. In the past, state commercial agencies had usually been obliged to sell whatever factories produced, including goods of dubious quality and unsaleable lines. From 1979 on, they were able to exercise greater discretion in choosing factory products, reserving the right to reject unsatisfactory items. Within commercial units, 'responsibility systems' and productivity schemes helped improve efficiency to some degree but, as in the case of industrial enterprises, the overall impact of such measures was disappointing (for a recent critical evaluation, see Wan, 1983).

A much more effective impetus for greater efficiency was the increasing competitive pressure arising from a diversification of marketing outlets. Enterprises were allowed to market a portion of their output independently, they signed contracts with other enterprises, set up their own shops and advertised their own products. The overall level of self-marketed output had reached about 15 per cent of total non-agricultural retail sales by 1983. But the levels of self-marketing vary greatly across regions (much higher in pace-setting cities such as Shanghai and Chongqing), across sectors (higher in consumer than producer goods sectors), across subsectors and individual enterprises within sectors, and across products (varying according to their officially defined importance, Categories 1, 2 or 3 being progressively more marketised). This is all at the formal level, of course; additional informal market procurement and sales may well be substantial.

There has also been a rapid expansion of cooperative and private commercial businesses in the cities. By the end of 1984, they were handling about half the country's total retail sales (urban and rural).[12]

Urban commerce has been enlivened by the spread of farm produce markets where peasants sell their produce in a (regulated) free market environment (for an account of one such in the north-eastern city of Shenyang, see White, 1983a, pp. 109–13). The benefits of this diversification have been considerable: stimulating agricultural and industrial production, speeding flows of circulation, raising levels of service in commerce, and meeting demands arising from the sharp increase in mass purchasing power over the past five years and thus reducing inflation. In spite of successive 'stop-go' clampdowns by the authorities, therefore, the process is likely to continue at a steady pace. In Shanxi province, for example, it was planned, as of early 1983, to reduce the state share to 70 per cent of wholesale and 60 per cent of retail industrial and agricultural trade within three to five years; in the urban service and catering sectors, the state share was set to drop to 30 per cent.[13]

One major dimension of commercial reform, however, is still in an embryonic stage, namely the desire to redirect commercial flows, both state and non-state, from following the logic of administrative regions and departments to 'natural' marketing zones based on principles familiar to economic geographers. While some progress has been made in breaking down barriers to inter-regional trade, the thrust towards 'central city'-based economic regions is in its early stages. The pace-setters are Chongqing in the south-west and Shanghai (as the hub of the Lower Yangtze Region) in the east. While the process is as yet not far enough advanced to hazard a judgement, progress appears to have been slow and patchy so far, dogged by bureaucratic recalcitrance, local rivalries and poor policy coordination.

Turning now to questions of commodity *exchange*, movement on the *price* front has been fitful and slow. Planners have been unwilling to grasp the nettle of comprehensive reform of the official price parities of state industrial products, confining adjustments to a very few cases of (mainly) consumer goods. Moreover, limited attempts to deregulate prices (for example, in 1979–80 and 1985) have fuelled inflation and popular discontent, leading to administrative backlash. Fluctuations apart, however, there has been some limited movement towards granting greater power over price regulation to local authorities, and expanding the range of commodities allowed to circulate at non-fixed 'floating' or 'negotiated' prices, especially for less important consumer items (for a discussion of the different forms of price, see White, 1983a, p. 41). In the producer goods sector, movement towards more flexible price forms has been more cautious. The main experimental unit has been the First Ministry of Machine Building which implemented a system of 'floating prices' for certain types of machinery and electrical goods in early 1980. But this experience has apparently not been generalised.

Though there have been some attempts to use price policy to adjust supply and demand, these have not necessarily been thought through and the results have been ambiguous. The most important measure was a dramatic increase of 40 per cent in agricultural procurement prices between 1978–82, which served to stimulate agricultural production and, through higher peasant incomes, increase demand for industrial (especially consumer) goods. On the other hand, it raised an inflationary wave throughout the economy, which the authorities failed to foresee and found difficult to manage. Compared with this major change, other efforts to use price policy have been more incremental: for example, cutting the price of durable consumer items in oversupply (such as wrist-watches) to clear stocks, reducing the price of synthetic in relation to cotton fibres to reflect changing cost conditions and increase demand for the former. Some price increases (such as cigarettes and wine) were purely for revenue purposes or to reduce inflation by soaking up excess purchasing power (for example, through injections of expensive imported consumer goods such as Japanese cassette-recorders, televisions or refrigerators). In general, however, price policy has been treated with caution like a loaded weapon and used sparingly.

To what extent do these changes in circulation and exchange contribute to 'marketisation' of the Chinese urban-industrial economy? The answer is ambiguous and reflects a basic unclarity in the Chinese conception of 'market regulation' i.e. between the market as a form of commodity circulation and as a method of regulating commodity exchange. In the first sense, the reforms have brought considerable movement by diversifying commercial channels, breaking down administrative barriers and promoting more direct contacts between producers and consumers. Even without significant price competition, the expansion and diversification of the commercial network has been economically and politically important in meeting rapidly rising consumer demands, exerting salutary pressures on the state commercial system and alleviating urban unemployment. Yet periods of dynamic commercial change (such as 1979–80) have tended to provoke official counter-measures; why is this?

In the second sense, the operation of prices as indices of changing conditions of supply and demand for industrial goods has in the event been marginal. But if scarcity prices are the essence of 'real' markets and the economic reforms, to be effective as a package, depend on a properly functioning price system, why has there been so little progress?

First of all, many officials in the party-state apparatus viewed expanding markets (in both senses) with alarm, as subversive forces which spread economic anarchy and social unrest and undermine the plan rather than complementing it. From one point of view, this perception reflects the competing interests of state and non-state economic sectors. Politocratic and bureaucratic interests showed through in various ways. Partly through sheer inertia and red tape. Partly through clashes between state commercial and service agencies which are being undercut and outperformed. Partly through a generalised (and sometimes apparently pathological) organisational ideology, nurtured by millennia of bureaucratic dominance and anti-commercial ideology and by decades of directive planning, which define social fluidity as indiscipline, economic autonomy as potentially subversive, and which has sought to reimpose control before 'chaos' sets in.

From another point of view, the conflicts which have emerged between state and commerce reflect the contradiction between the (still largely unreformed) operational logic of the previous system of planned circulation and exchange on the one hand, and of emerging 'real' markets reflecting actual conditions of supply and demand on the other hand. The state wished to expand markets in industrial goods incrementally, without any significant attempt to free the terms on which they exchanged through price reform. But prices in the new channels of circulation (often in sellers' markets) clashed sharply with the official price system and, to the extent that industrial and commercial enterprises had more autonomy, they could use it to raise prices, formally or informally, directly or indirectly.

There were many manifestations of these tensions after 1978 as repressed 'real' markets burst into the open. Enterprises and trading outlets expanded the frontiers of officially sanctioned 'negotiated' and 'floating' prices. Enterprises were often able to use oligopoly power, sometimes reinforced by local protectionism, to raise prices as a way to increase profits and bonuses. Even if nominal prices were not raised, moreover, real prices were increased by using inferior materials, adulteration, giving shorter measure, etc. In one publicised case in Peking, for example, a snack-bar had responded to increases in the price of pork by reducing the number of meat-balls in their soup from 12–14 to 6–7, while keeping the price the same.[14] There was also a good deal of arbitrage with traders taking advantage of price differentials between localities or between state-fixed and free market prices.

Though sharp practices were no doubt widespread, the basic problems was that the state, for all its talk about the need for 'market regulation', could not manage real markets when they surfaced. There were of course problems which needed corrective action: the rush into profitable lines led to overproduction; enterprises concentrated on their self-marketed, 'floating price' output, directing attention away from planned production tasks and reducing the quality of planned output. Evasion of price controls also fed the general rise in prices during 1979–81 and 1985, contributing to the economic and political problems of inflation to which the CCP has been extremely sensitive.

But the state's reaction cannot be analysed merely as a rational response to 'problems' arising from reform policies; it reflects the conflicting interests and operational logics of state and non-state political economies, planning and market processes. Activities which reflected real patterns of supply and demand and which might, in other contexts, be perceived as normal market behaviour were thus defined as 'speculation', 'profiteering', 'extortion', 'economic criminality', and so on. The resultant policy cycle is depressingly familiar: extension of market freedoms in circulation and exchange; officials complaints about economic 'chaos', illegality and excess, reinforced by public complaints about 'sharp practices'; the reimposition of administrative controls; a stifling of markets which drives them underground, stimulates new forms of evasion and has a harmful effect on public morality; shortages are created which lead to a public unrest; a new attempt to liberalise, etc. One major cycle occurred between 1978 and 1981, the clampdown coming at the end of 1980. It looked like another cycle was under way in 1985. The administrative backlash involves efforts to control price increases and limit the range of commodities targeted for deregulation; reimposition of rationing; controls over the content of advertising; mobilisation of the population to supervise the activities of traders; tightening of the licensing arrangements for non-state trading enterprises; 'corralling' free markets (such as urban farm-product markets) within stout bureaucratic fences; police measures against 'smugglers', 'profiteers', and the like. But much of this bureaucratic furore was rather like someone trying to catch ten fleas with ten fingers. Officials of price control teams complained that they went into shops or factories, lectured the miscreants who promised to be good in future but who reverted to their previous behaviour as soon as the team was out of sight.

A similar logic operated in the specific area of *price policy*; the big bugbear was inflation. The existence of generalised shortages drives up the prices of extra-plan industrial commodities and, given the shallow effect of the reforms overall, the lack of effective competition between state industrial enterprises allows them to pass on price increases to the consumer with impunity. Market blockades between localities help to prevent the entry of competitively priced commodities from more efficient regions such as Shanghai.

Though inflation posed economic headaches for the reformers, the main problem was political. The CCP had been helped to power in 1948 by hyper-inflation under the Nationalist regime and had prided itself on maintaining price stability since then. The ability to control inflation, a phenomenon avowedly characteristic of capitalist economies, was one of the CCP's most significant claims to legitimate rule. The issue was thus very sensitive and when considerable urban discontent over prices emerged (for example, during 1980), the state reacted strongly with a battery of administrative controls.

Inflation thus provided an important political impetus to slow the pace of reform. It also helps to explain the Chinese authorities' reluctance to deregulate prices and use price policy as an 'economic lever'. An even more basic problem, however, was the *politicisation of prices*, an endemic feature of all state socialist societies. Xue Muqiao has pinpointed the problem well (1981, p. 146): '[prices] are a concentrated expression of the contradictions among different social groups which, in their own interests, wish to see certain products sold at prices higher or lower than their values'. Since price decisions can be directly traced to governmental action and not to the impersonal processes of a market, they are politically loaded. Thus the CCP has been very reluctant to tamper with prices, however economically irrational they might be. Consider this familiar policy cycle when price reforms, however marginal, are introduced. Rumours about an impending price increase of commodity x; panic buying of x which drains government stocks and drives up the price of x on informal markets; the government either relents, deciding to postpone the increase (and subsidise the price of x if contributing costs have risen), or goes ahead but attempts to cushion its impact through non-price subsidies to affected groups. Thus when agricultural procurement prices were raised after 1978, price rises were either not passed on to urban consumers or, where they were, a monthly supplement was paid to compensate urban wage earners. In the case of cotton textiles, for example, while the average procurement price of cotton rose by 50 per cent between 1978 and 1982, the price of cotton textiles did not increase. The result was that, in some regions, the price of the finished product was lower than the cost of the raw material. Yet when the price of cotton textiles was adjusted in 1983, it was done with considerable preparation and caution, and sweetened by better prices for synthetic substitutes. Even then, the state paid subsidies to 50 million people living in poor rural areas in eight provinces who relied upon bought cotton textiles.

Public discontent is thus avoided at the cost of increasingly heavy burdens on the public purse. As of mid-1983, subsidies swallowed up about one-third of state budgetary expenditures (White, 1983a, p. 5). The government is thus caught in a vice between price paralysis on the one side and escalating subsidies on the other. For both economic and political reasons, this situation cannot be maintained; yet how to escape from it?

Clearly, if the logic of the reforms is to be pursued consistently and if reform policies are to achieve their desired effects across the board, comprehensive changes in commodity circulation and exchange are necessary and the nub of these is the price question. Steps must be taken to lay a rational basis for price policy, namely to establish an economically sensible foundation for setting official price parities and develop a capacity for flexible adjustment (notably through decentralisation of price decisions to local governments and state enterprises); to clarify the respective spheres of operation of fixed, intermediate and free market prices and establish a complementary rather than contradictory relationship between them (the expansion of enterprise autonomy and the establishment of mutually beneficial relations between state and enterprises is crucial here); to find ways to manage the economic repercussions and reduce the political sensitivity of price decisions; and to draw up a programme of reform which coordinates price with other aspects of the reforms (financial, fiscal, wages and welfare, etc.).

The experience of China and other socialist countries (including Hungary) suggests that progress on the price front will be slow and uneven: the political costs are potentially high and the economic 'ripple' effects potentially unmanageable. The prospect for the short and medium term is that the Chinese government will continue to be reluctant to embark on any comprehensive price reform, will seek policies which are functional substitutes for price policy and are easier to implement (for example, through differential tax rates on enterprise revenues designed to counter profit distortions arising from irrational price disparities) and, to the extent that price reforms are re-introduced, the government will proceed with extreme caution, like infantry in a minefield (using basic level Party organisations and economists as two different kinds of geiger-counter), introducing changes in a relatively marginal and piecemeal fashion. This scenario does not augur well for the future of the economic reform programme as a whole.

CONCLUSON

What is the future likely to hold for the relationship between planning and markets in China's urban–industrial economy? Though reforms have achieved considerable progress over the past years, their impact has been very uneven and, in overall terms, fairly superficial, in sharp contrast to the countryside. The mould of the bureaucratic command economy has yet to be broken. The scope of 'directive' plans has not contracted as much as reformers would have liked; though the importance of 'guidance' planning is strongly asserted, there is still little clarity about what this means in both theory and practice. The fundamental nature of the relationship between state and enterprise has changed little.

Nor have market processes expanded as much as the reform blueprints of 1978–9 envisaged. Though the scope of markets varies across sectors, in general they have not taken on the full characteristics of competitive price systems, have not generated the salutary efficiency pressures and allocational benefits which reform analyses promised. Indeed, liberalisation in a context of partial reforms (in which enterprise budgets are still soft) has proven to be a recipe for profligacy at the micro-level and overheating at the macro-level, imparting a 'stop–go', cyclical rhythm to the reform programme.

The process of moving towards a more productive relationship between state and economy and greater complementarity between plan and market is likely to prove more tortuous. While the experience of post-Mao era has brought greater clarity about the analytical and practical problems of combining plans and markets, the constraints on reform have also become clearer. Efforts to implement reform policies have run into serious *economic* problems, notably budgetary deficits, inflation, and over-investment. There has also been formidable *political* opposition from former supporters of radical Maoism and from entrenched interests both inside and outside the state apparatus. There has also been the familiar clash between 'efficiency goals' and 'socialist ethics' which Kornai has analysed for the Hungarian reforms (Kornai, 1980b). It is much to the credit of the Dengist leadership, however, that they have been willing to brave opposition and court unpopularity in their desire to carry the reforms forward.

Since both state and markets are matrices of differentiated interests, historically and structurally determined, a fundamental change in the state–economy relationship affects the balance of power between social groups. Thus, the problems in building a stable and productive relationship between the socialist state and markets are not merely technical or managerial; they may reflect a structural contradiction at the heart of state socialist political economy.

Indeed, the post-Mao reform era has highlighted one of the basic dilemmas of a socialist developmental state. The record of the 1960s and 1970s suggests the growing incapacity of the state institutions to direct the economy productively through the traditional mechanisms of political mobilisation and bureaucratic control. To respond to escalating economic problems by strengthening traditional methods could only make matters worse. On the other hand, to embrace the reform programme fully would bring about such a radical shift in relations between state and society as to undermine the very basis of Leninist socialism. Thus the 'competitive' view of the state–market relationship may well be vindicated.

What lessons can be drawn from the experience of the Chinese state's role in the industrialisation process? First, it may help to resist any simple, ahistorical generalisations about the economic impact of state intervention and support a case that different forms and degrees of state involvement are appropriate at different stages of the industrialisation process, with traditional directive methods having greater relevance and effectiveness in initial periods of basic construction of structural change. More basically, Chinese experience argues that in *all* stages, not merely in more 'mature' phases of industrialisation, state involvement needs to be more selective in the *scope* of involvement (whether in terms of types of economic decisions or of different economic sectors) and more flexible in the *forms* of involvement adopted (notably between 'directive' and 'guidance' methods). The Chinese case also points to the importance of striking a balance between state agencies and productive units (whether state, collective or private enterprises) and developing a lively micro-economy which can be channelled and not stifled by state actions. Finally, the Chinese experience illustrates the general point that questions of economic management and reform in state socialist contexts are deeply political and not susceptible to merely technical solutions – they are problems of political economy in the full sense of the term.

Abbreviations

BCAS	*Bulletin of Concerned Asian Scholars*
BR	*Beijing Review*, Peking.
CASS	Chinese Academy of Social Sciences.
CREA	Joint Publications Research Service, *China Report: Economic Affairs*.
FBIS	Foreign Broadcasts Information Service, *China: Daily Report*.
GMRB	*Guangming Ribao* (Glorious Daily), Peking.
JJGL	*Jingji Guanli* (Economic Management), Peking.
JJYJ	*Jingji Yanjiu* (Economic Research), Peking.
RMRB	*Renmin Ribao* (People's Daily), Peking.
SSB	State Statistical Bureau, Peking.
SWB:FE	British Broadcasting Corporation, *Summary of World Broadcasts: Far East*.
XH	*Xinhua* (New China News Agency), Peking

Notes

1. This is a shortened version of my more detailed article in G. White and R. Wade (eds), (1985) pp. 315–412.
2. The 1981 World Bank figures on gross domestic investment (as a percentage of GDP) were as follows: China 28 per cent, compared with a weighted average of 24 per cent for all low-income countries, including a weighted average of 26 per cent for China and India and 14 per cent for the other 32 countries; the corresponding figure for middle-income economies was 25 per cent.
3. The 'accumulation fund' is officially defined as 'that part of the national income which is used for expanded reproduction, non-productive construction and increase of productive and non-productive stock. Its material formation is the newly added fixed assets of material and non-material sectors (less depreciation of the total fixed assets) and the newly acquired circulating fund in kind by the material sectors during the year' (SSB 1983, pp. 579–80).
4. 'Productive' accumulation includes fixed and circulating assets 'of productive use . . . in material production sectors'. 'Non-productive' accumulation includes 'newly added fixed assets of non-productive use and residential buildings . . . as well as the increase in stock of consumer goods held by industrial enterprises or commercial departments' (SSB, 1983, p. 580).
5. This section on the reform critique is based heavily on analyses by the following authors: He Jianzhang, 1979; Jiang Yiwei, 1979, 1980; Liu Shinian, 1980; Liu Guoguang, 1980; Sun Xiaoliang, 1980; Ma Hong, 1981; Xue Muqiao, 1981.
6. *XH*, English, 28 September 1983, in *SWB:FE*, 7452. For a detailed analysis of this reform, see Lu and Qian, 1984.
7. For example, see Wang Bingqian, 'Certain Questions of Financial Work', *RMRB*, 26 November 1982, in *FBIS*, 229.
8. *China Daily*, 9 June 1984.
9. *XH*, domestic, 4 July 1984, in *FBIS*, 133.

10. For a discussion of interest rate policy, see Jiang Weijun, 'Forum on Reforming Bank Interest', *RMRB*, 13 August 1984, in *FBIS* 161.
11. For a useful discussion of the latter, see Li Chengrui, 'An Important Question in Macro-economic Management – Strict Control of Issuance of Currency by the State', *RMRB*, 26 April 1985, in *FBIS* 087.
12. *XH*, English, 24 December 1984.
13. Shanxi radio, 15 February 1983, in *FBIS*, 35.
14. *XH*, English, 13 December 1980.

References

Balcerowicz, L. (1980) 'Organisational Structure of the National Economy and Technological Innovations', *Acta Œconomica*, 24, pp. 1–2, 151–67.

Barnett, A. D. (1967) *Cadres, Bureaucracy and Political Power in Communist China* (New York: Columbia University Press).

Brus, W. (1972) *The Market in a Socialist Economy* (London: Routledge & Kegan Paul).

Byrd, W. (1983) *China's Financial System: The Changing Role of Banks* (Boulder: Westview Press).

Cheng, Chu-yuan (1982) *China's Economic Development: Growth and Structural Change* (Boulder: Westview Press).

Chinese Economic Yearbook 1982 (published 1983), Economic Management Magazine, Beijing.

Chung Ch'i-fu (1955) 'Methods in Formulating National Economic Plans', *Jihua Jingji* (Planned Economy) no. 3, in Lardy, *Chinese Economic Planning* pp. 3–11.

Dai Yuanchen (1981) 'The Socialist Economy can Effectively Check Inflation', *JJYJ*, no. 8 (20 August), in *SBW:FE*, W1153.

Donnithorne, A. (1972) 'China's Cellular Economy: Some Economic Trends Since the Cultural Revolution', *China Quarterly*, 52 (Oct.–Dec.), pp. 605–12.

Feng Lanrui (1981) 'On factors affecting China's employment', *RMRB* 16 November, in *SWB:FE* no. 6888.

Feuchtwang, S. and A. Hussain (eds), (1983) *The Chinese Economic Reforms*, (Beckenham, Kent: Croom Helm).

Field, R. M. (1983) 'Slow Growth of Labour Productivity in Chinese Industry, 1952–81', *China Quarterly*, no. 96 (December) pp. 641–64.

Hare, P. (1983) 'China's System of Industrial Economic Planning', in Feuchtwang and Hussain (eds), *The Chinese Economic Reforms*, pp. 185–223.

He Jianzhang (1979) 'Problems in the Planned Management of the Economy Owned by the Whole People and the Orientation of Reform', *JJYJ*, no. 5 (20 May), pp. 35–45, in *CREA*, 5 (3 August 1979).

Hu Qiaomu (1978) 'Observe Economic Laws, Speed up the Four Modernisations', *Peking Review*, nos 45, 46 and 47 (10, 17, 24 November).

Huang Zhenqi (1982) 'Improve the Scientific Nature of Economic Planning', *RMRB* (1 June), in *FBIS*, 4 June 1982.

Ishikawa, Shigeru (1983) 'China's Economic Growth Since 1949 – an Assessment', *China Quarterly*, no. 94 (June), pp. 242–81.

Ji Chongwei and Rong Wenzuo (1979) 'How Are We to Reform the System of Industrial Administration?', *JJGL*, no. 6 (25 June), pp. 8–12, in *CREA* no. 14 (17 September 1979).

Jiang Yiwei (1979) 'A Discussion of "The View that the Enterprise is the Fundamental Unit". . .', *JJGL*, no. 6 (25 June), pp. 20–27, in *CREA*, no. 18.

Jiang Yiwei (1980) 'The Theory of an Enterprise-based Economy', *Social Sciences in China*, no. 1, pp. 48–70.

Jiang Yiwei (1985) 'If all Staff and Workers are on the Contract System, it Will Not Suit the Socialist Nature of Enterprises' (in Chinese), *Jingji Tizhi Gaige* (Structural Reform of the Economy), Sichuan, No. 1, 11–13.

Kornai, Janos (1980a) *Economics of Shortage* (vol. A), (Amsterdam: North-Holland Publishing Company).

Kornai, Janos (1980b) 'The Dilemmas of a Socialist Economy: the Hungarian Experience', *Cambridge Journal of Economics*, 4, 147–57.

Lardy, N. R. (1978) *Chinese Economic Planning* (New York: Sharpe).

Li Ji and Niu Fenghe (1979) 'Are enterprises getting more and the state collecting less? On expanding the autonomy of enterprises', *Gongren Ribao* (Workers Daily), 4 October, in *CREA* no. 41.

Lin, Cyril Chihren (1981) 'The Reinstatement of Economics in China Today', *China Quarterly*, 85 (March), pp. 1–48.

Liu Guoguang (1980) 'The Question of the Reform of the Chinese Economic Management System', *Wen Wei Po*, Hong Kong (8 March), in *FBIS*, 20 March 1980.

Liu Shinian (1980) 'Discussions on the Orientation for Restructuring China's Economic System', *JJYJ*, no. 1 (20 Jan.), in *CREA*, 54 (8 April), pp. 10–25.

Lu Baifu and Qian Zhongtao (1984) 'Establishing a New Socialist Banking System in Our Country', *RMRB*, 1 February 1984, in *FBIS*, 033.

Ma Hong (1981) 'On Several Questions of Reforming the Economic Management System', *JJYJ*, Beijing, no. 7 (20 July), pp. 11–24.

Nolan, P. and G. White (1984) 'Urban Bias, Rural Bias or State Bias? Urban–rural Relations in Post-revolutionary China', *Journal of Development Studies*, vol. 20, no. 3.

Nove, A. and M. Nuti (eds), (1972) *Socialist Economics: Selected Readings* (Harmondsworth: Penguin Books).

Riskin, C. (1981) 'Markets, Maoism and Economic Reform in China', *BCAS*, vol. 13, no. 3 (1981), pp. 31–41.

Rong Zihe (1983) 'The Problems Facing Financial Work', *Caizheng* (Finance), no. 8, in *FBIS*, 178.

Skinner, G. W. (1964–5) 'Marketing and Social Structure in Rural China: Parts I, II, and III', *Journal of Asian Studies*, xxiv, 1–3 (Nov. 1964, Feb. 1965, May 1965), pp. 3–43, 195–228, 363–99.

State Statistical Bureau (1982, 1983 and 1984) *Statistical Yearbook of China 1981, 1982, 1983*, Economic Information and Agency, Hong Kong.

State Statistical Bureau (1985) *Zhongguo Tongji Zhaiyao 1985* (Abstract of China's Statistics), Peking, Chinese Statistics Publishing House (in Chinese).

Sun Xiaoliang (1980) 'Motivating Force, Initiative and Market Economy', *JJGL*, no. 3 (15 March), pp. 11–14, in *CREA*, no. 66.

Sutcliffe, R. B. (1971) *Industry and Underdevelopment* (London: Addison-Wesley).

Wan Dianwu (1983) 'An Inquiry into the Question of Separating Government Administration from Enterprise Management in Commerce', *RMRB*, 20, April 1983, in *FBIS*, 81.

Wang Chuanlun (1984) 'Some Notes on Tax Reform in China', *China Quarterly*, 97 (March), pp. 53–67.

Wang Jiye (1983) 'Appropriately Strengthen the Degree of Centralisation in Financial Work', *RMRB*, 26 August 1983, in *FBIS*, 170.

White, G. (1982a) 'Why Did China Fail to Follow the Japanese Road?', in M. Bienefeld and M. Godfrey (eds), *The Struggle for Development: National Strategies in an International Context* (New York: John Wiley) pp. 111–133.

White, G. (1982b) 'Urban Employment and Labour Allocation Policies in Post-Mao China', *World Development*, vol. 10, no. 8, pp. 613–32.

White, G. (1983a) *Industrial Planning and Administration in Contemporary China*, Transcript of a Research Trip, June–July 1983, Institute of Development Studies, University of Sussex, Brighton.

White, G. (1983b) 'Socialist Planning and Industrial Management: Chinese Economic Reforms in the post-Mao Era', *Development and Change*, vol. 14, pp. 483–514.

White, G. (1985) '*Labour Allocation and Employment Policy in Contemporary China*', IDS Research Report, University of Sussex.

White, G. and Wade R. (eds), (1985) *Developmental States in East Asia*, IDS Research Report, University of Sussex, Brighton.

World Bank (1981, 1982, 1983) *World Development Report* (Oxford University Press).

Wu Renjian (1983) 'National Forum to Discuss Comprehensive Planning of Finance and Credit', *RMRB*, 20 May 1983, in *SWB:FE* 7344.

Xu Dixin *et al*, (1982) *China's Search for Economic Growth*, (Beijing: New World Press).

Xue Muqiao (1979) 'A Study in the Planned Management of the Socialist Economy', *Beijing Review*, no. 43 (26 Oct.), pp. 14–20.

Xue Muqiao (1980) 'A Probe into the Question of Changing the Economic System', *JJYJ*, no. 6 (20 June), pp. 3–11, in *CREA*, 81 (3 Sept.), pp. 1–19.

Xue Muqiao (1981) *China's Socialist Economy* (Beijing: Foreign Languages Press).

Yang Jianbai and Li Xueceng (1980) 'The Relations Between Agriculture, Light Industry and Heavy Industry in China', *Social Sciences in China*, vol. 1, no. 2 (June), pp. 182–212.

Ye Ming and Chen Guangzhen (1979) 'Enterprise Management must Adapt to the Demands of Great Changes', *Caiwu yu Kuaiji* (Finance and Accounting), no. 3 (20 March), in *CREA*, no. 7.

Zhao Lukuan (1980) 'Several Problems of Labour and Employment in our Country', *RMRB* (19 August), in *FBIS*, 4 September.

6 The State and the Rural Economy in the Chinese People's Republic

Jack Gray

INTRODUCTION

In the advanced economies, income elasticity of demand for food is usually low; state intervention in agriculture tends to take the form of subsidies to maintain farm incomes. In the LDCs, it is supply which is inelastic: state intervention in this case has a double task; to provide incentives to agriculture by increasing the profitability of farming, while avoiding increases in retail food prices which would raise wages in industry and so reduce industrial capital accumulation. In theory a policy of subsidising food prices would reconcile these two objectives; in fact the resources seldom exist. In the competition, urban interests usually win, and farm prices are kept lower than market prices by state intervention.

There is no obvious economic rationale behind this policy. The criterion is political: urban interests hostile to high food prices are a more immediate threat to governments than peasants hostile to low farm-gate prices.[1] The alternatives, however, are influenced by the course of economic development and represent different stages of growth. When industry has developed to the point at which industrial workers are no longer spending the greater part of their wages on food, it becomes possible to allow farm-gate prices to rise. At the same time, increasing wealth may permit some subsidisation.

The need to control agricultural prices is not the only motive for state intervention. There are other problems which invite state action. First, there is a widespread lack of confidence in the ability of traditional peasants to modernise on their own initiative. Second, there are difficulties springing from imperfect markets and weak monetisation. Third, there is the fear that spontaneous agricultural development will lead to increased polarisation of rural society. Fourth, given the difficulty which scattered and uneducated peasants face in attempting to organise socially and politically, the state may feel obliged to intervene to encourage and assist organisation. Fifth, state control tends to be increased by another, rather paradoxical, factor. It is much easier to increase industrial than agricultural production; industry more readily provides for import substitution; heavy industry is of direct interest to the state as the basis of defence. Agriculture therefore tends to be treated as the residual sector for investment. If lack of investment perpetuates low production in agriculture, the state may be even more strongly motivated to intervene.

In this context the rural policies and agricultural institutions associated with communist governments are only an extreme form of those pursued in many other LDCs. There is a continuum rather than a contrast. One could make a schedule of increasing degrees of state intervention in agriculture as follows:

- (i) Price controls.
- (ii) State purchase and sale of staple farm products.
- (iii) State planning enforced through the use of economic incentives and disincentives.
- (iv) State intervention in the production process through the manipulation or control of peasant organisations.
- (v) Collectivisation of the infrastructure.
- (vi) Collectivisation of the production process.
- (vii) Detailed authoritative planning of agriculture via control of the collectives.
- (viii) State direction of peasant savings and investment as well as of production.
- (ix) Elimination of the vestiges of private property in the means of production by their absorption into the collective.
- (x) The replacement of collectives by state farms.

The Soviet agricultural system represents a point towards the 'red' end of this spectrum of state involvement. But this system was neither the result of the straightforward application of a theory of development, nor of unambiguous socialist principles. It emerged from expedients adopted in a crisis, a crisis which expressed the dangers of agricultural underdevelopment at their most apocalyptic: a new industrial population threatened by famine.

It would be too simple, however, to see the Soviet system as the result only of improvisation. Ideology played a role in the choice of expedients. Yet the only specific guidance offered by Marx and

Engels was that if any peasants survived the capitalist destruction of the peasants as a class they should, under socialism, be persuaded gradually to form production co-operatives. Coercive collectivisation was explictly and emphatically ruled out.

On the question of the form of the state and its relation to society. Marx and Engels were ambiguous. They made no attempt to reconcile the two contradictory notions of socialism current in their time. One was the Saint-Simonian view, by which the socialist regime would take over the economic resources of society and allocate them in the most rational pattern; its implications are centralist, étatist, and élitist. The other was a view which we may identify with the Owenites, that socialist society would consist of autonomous local working communities only loosely associated with each other. Sometimes the founding fathers wrote as if socialist society would operate as one huge all-embracing enterprise; sometimes (as when they praised the Paris Commune) they seemed to take a view closer to that of Robert Owen. Lenin was equally ambiguous. In his *State and Revolution*, he gave a glowing account of the future in terms of communal socialism but in practice he laid the basis of a system which comes close to the Saint-Simonian model. Communal socialism would have given autonomy to peasant communities, but Stalin chose to subject them to Saint-Simonian etatism while rationalising this in terms of the communalist ideal by describing the new state-directed farms as 'collectives'.

The Soviet Party took advantage of the ambiguity in another Marxian concept, 'the dictatorship of the proletariat', to impose authoritarian rule in the name of the industrial working class. Marx used this phrase epigrammatically: to denote the real democracy which would follow the defeat of the 'dictatorship' of the bourgeoisie under a capitalist system. Used thus, the phrase does not necessarily imply authoritarianism; *a fortiori* it does not justify the dictatorship of a minority working class over a majority peasant class. Nor is there a clear justification in Marxist theory for the idea that in a socialist society there should be only one political party – the working-class party – and that parties representing peasant interests should be suppressed.

Stalin also used the Marxist theory of class struggle to insist that socialist society is harmonious, and thus to justify the outlawing of conflicts which actually took place. It was assumed that the state, once freed from class conflict, could behave with perfect rationality, so that opposition would be by definition perverse. The peasants with their attachment to their unviable plots and their pursuit of petty profits were an obvious affront to rationality.

In this way, a particular interpretation of Marxism, made possible by its ambiguities, could rationalise the treatment of the peasants as if they had neither rights nor interests and to make them subjects not citizens of the workers' state. Yet they were the vast majority of the population.

The place of the peasants and the rural economy was determined primarily by the fact that contrary to Marxist predictions the revolution took place not in an advanced capitalist industrial society but in a pre-modern agrarian society. It had taken place too in a defeated country, faced with bitter international hostility. The socialist state thus had to replace capitalism as the motor of accumulation, and rapidly construct the industrial sinews of defence to protect the revolution. Hostility to the market was natural in such a state, which rapidly underwent a metamorphosis into a military–bureaucratic complex.

If circumstances dictated that the development of industry would take priority over agriculture in the Soviet Union, Marxist theory determined that industry would develop at the expense of agriculture. Marxist historiography held that the original British industrial revolution had been made possible by a process of 'primary capital accumulation', in which capital was ruthlessly concentrated in the hands of a few by the expropriation of the peasantry and that the new industrial labour force was supplied from destitute former peasants. This is wrong at every point. It was in fact the exceptionally high level of mass purchasing power in Britain, rapidly increased by the sharp fall in the cost of food as a result of the agricultural revolution, which touched off the mechanisation of the production of commodities of mass consumption.[2]

Yet this myth of primary accumulation at the expense of the peasants created one of the basic axioms of Soviet economic strategy: to build industry, the socialist government must imitate the capitalists of eighteenth-century Britain, and wrest the means of industrialisation from the peasants. How different the course of economic development in the communist countries might have proved, had the lesson of Marxist history been that the driving force of development is increased mass purchasing power created by the transformation of agriculture.

This alternative view was not entirely absent from the Soviet scene. It was represented in the opposition offered by Bukharin to Preobrazhensky in the Soviet industrialisation debates of the 1920s (Gray, 1973, pp. 112–13).

Mao Zedong was to rediscover these 'rightist' arguments in China, using them to justify the Great Leap and the Communes. They have been inherited by his successors and built into China's new rural policies.

There are two more elements of Soviet theory and practice which have further helped to determine policy towards agriculture. The first of these is an obsessive belief that economies of scale are decisive for the efficiency of agriculture. Prairie farming was regarded as the farming of the future, although its unique factor proportions – plentiful land and capital, scarce and expensive labour – were very different from those of the Soviet Union. Hence collectivised production on a large scale has been maintained for fifty years although its theoretical economies have not been realised. The second element was the belief that economic development requires that producer goods industries must from the beginning have absolute priority over consumer goods in the allocation of investment. The thesis is incorrect, yet this was and is the basis of Soviet economic strategy.

Primary capital accumulation at the expense of the peasants, belief in decisive economies of scale in agriculture, and an obsession with the primacy of heavy industry – these three convictions, none of them valid, became shibboleths of Soviet socialism. It need hardly be said that to force peasants into collectivisation and to keep them there, in order to run agriculture on a scale which is probably counter-productive and in order to appropriate most of the product, is not compatible with a democratic and pluralist political system. Until these three shibboleths go, the democratisation of communist systems is not possible, and they will continue to suffer the inefficiencies as well as the injustices of a forced system.

The background of Soviet agricultural development has been treated here at some length. This is necessary because the course of the evolution of Chinese rural policies since 1958 has expressed the gradual repudiation – sometimes explicit, sometimes implicit – of almost every assumption and assertion involved in the orthodox Soviet system.

CHINESE AGRICULTURAL POLICY IN THE ERA OF MAO (1949–76)

Before Liberation

The Communist Party of China was not founded by peasants but by young intellectuals. Few of them (Mao Zedong being the outstanding exception) had close ties with rural China, and even fewer took much interest in the countryside. They were driven into the countryside after the bloody breakdown of their alliance with Chiang Kai-shek's Nationalists in 1927.

The question of organising the peasants for revolution was no longer merely academic; it became a question of political, and indeed of physical, survival. The Chinese Communist Party thus began a twenty-year apprenticeship in rural revolution, in sharp contrast with the experience of the Russian Bolshevik party, which was almost wholly urban.

Particularly important was their experience in the Border Region revolutionary base-areas during the war against Japan. In striving to maintain resistance to the Japanese invaders from some of the poorest areas of the arid northwest, the Party, now firmly under Mao's leadership, was forced to expedients which soon became established practice. Lacking capital, they substituted labour, settling refugee peasants from the Japanese areas by co-operative labour-intensive land reclamation and irrigation works. Lacking industrial machinery, they improvised. Lacking the power to impose central planning on such scattered guerrilla areas, they had to depend on persuading and assisting the villages to undertake their own development. Their situation thus forced them in the early 1940s to practise policies which by the late 1950s had elsewhere become the pieties of rural development strategy: labour-intensive development of infrastructure, intermediate technology, and community development.

The effects of the Border Region experience on those members of the Party most directly exposed to it increased the gulf between Soviet and Chinese political and economic thinking. Mao and his associates became passionately concerned with rural development, and they had learned that, with help and encouragement, the villages could themselves find the means and generate the initiative. They had learned also that extractive policies, tempting as they were in a desperate military situation, were counter-productive. This led

Mao Zedong to assert that a yearly increase in peasant incomes was the only possible basis of a protracted war.[3] The success of economic development in the Border Regions did not depend upon centralised planning or on state accumulation of capital, but on the ability to mobilise the population for self-help. In this process the Party rather than the state apparatus was the active element, so that thereafter the Chinese Communist Party never wholly forgot the distinction between Party and state, however blurred that distinction became.

Agriculture in the First Five Year Plan (1953–7)

This wealth of special experience, however, was laid aside when the Chinese Communist government in 1953 launched its First Five Year Plan for economic development. The plan was orthodox in its priorities and methods and Russian advisers played a large part in its framing. Industry was given investment priority over agriculture and heavy industry over light industry. Over 50 per cent of state budget investment went to heavy industry, and only 6.2 per cent to agriculture. The state also took over trade in grain and other staples, the producers selling obligatory amounts of grain at controlled prices.

The collectivisation of agriculture began tentatively and proceeded very slowly at first. Farmers were encouraged to pool their labour in the busy seasons and to acquire some common property in so doing, then to form co-operative farms in which a dividend was paid according to land contributed as well as to labour. There was no general enthusiasm among CCP leaders for rapid collectivisation. The achievements of collective agriculture in the Soviet Union and East Europe were not inspiring. In China, moreover, there was a powerful argument against collectivisation, i.e. a 30 per cent surplus of farm labour which made mechanisation seem irrelevant to many leaders. If mechanisation was irrelevant, the main justification for collectivisation did not exist. In 1955 the collectivisation movement actually went into reverse. At this point Mao Zedong intervened to demand rapid collectivisation.[4] Within one year, by mid-1956, Chinese agriculture was collectivised.

The analogy between Mao and Stalin is obvious here, but it is misleading; Mao was already embarked on an intellectual journey which was to take him far from Stalinism. And yet the main reason why Chinese agriculture was so abruptly brought under control by collectivisation differed only in degree from the earlier Soviet situation: the difficulties of ensuring the supply of grain without direct control of its production. A large number of villages were deficient in grain supplies, and grain had to be sold to them, at subsidised prices. Further, without direct control it would be difficult to increase the amount of grain procured as production increased.

Yet Mao's rationale for the collectivisation of agriculture actually represented the first stage of his search for an alternative to the extractive policies which were inseparable from the Soviet strategy. Khrushchev's speech of February 1956 criticising Stalin played a major role in this rethinking. It came at a time when there was already a good deal of disillusionment in China over the Soviet-type First Five Year Plan.

The Plan had been an unambiguous success in its own terms. The rate of industrial growth was 14 per cent per annum and agricultural production (more difficult to measure) expanded at the very respectable rate of about 3 per cent per annum (Howe, 1978, p. xxiii).

However, looked at from the wider point of view, as representing an economic strategy appropriate to Chinese conditions, the Plan had some basic deficiencies. First, the assumption that a high priority to increasing the output of producer's goods would stimulate the other sectors into rapid growth had proven false. As the products of heavy industry were largely directed to the further growth of heavy industry itself, there were negligible linkage effects. Also, the development of heavy industry had even then outrun the market offered by the other sectors, the largest part of which was determined by the level of the purchasing power of the peasantry who were 85 per cent of the population. Although China sought to ensure that peasant incomes increased, that consumer goods were relatively plentiful and that the gap between agricultural and industrial prices was relatively small, there was still a grossly wasteful imbalance between the rate of investment in heavy industry and that in the rest of the economy.

A second problem in the plan was that the development of modern capital-intensive urban industry could not provide new employment at a rate which would even dent, far less eliminate, the rural labour surplus. The man–land ration was expected to worsen, and there was an urgent need to provide rural employment alternatives to agriculture. A third source of discontent was the slow growth of agriculture in comparison with industry. Though the rate of growth of agriculture had been very satisfactory compared with similar countries, the rapid growth of population and a tendency towards a backward-sloping supply curve as peasants used much of their modest increase in output to increase their own consumption, sharply limited any increase in the marketed surplus of agriculture. Finally, in contrast to the Soviet Union, control through collectivisation did not enable Chinese industrial planners to be independent of the harvest. The standard of life of Chinese peasants was too low; belts could scarcely go any tighter. From 1956 Mao realised that a cautious estimate of future harvests would have to be the bottom line of Chinese planning.

The policy response which emerged from the first session of the Eighth Party Congress in September 1956 simply cut back on the planned rate of development by reducing the overall rate of savings and investment; the priority given to heavy industry was also somewhat reduced. It is clear that if the majority of CCP leaders who favoured a more relaxed policy in industry had been able to enforce their views on agriculture, there would have been a parallel relaxation which would almost certainly have involved changes in the collective system: smaller units, a larger private sector, less pressure to secure a high rate of collective accumulation, and perhaps even a return to the 'primary' co-operatives in which dividends were paid on land. There was no hint at the first session of the Congress of the dramatic changes which were soon to occur. However, a radical political and economic alternative was in the making.

In late 1955 Mao and his supporters published a series of reports on the operation of collectivised agriculture which pointed to a new strategy of village regeneration through collective effort.[5] The perspective was that labour-intensive development of agriculture (for example, in irrigation or soil improvement) would *both* increase production *and* increase subsequent demand for labour. It would thus create *both* the means *and* the incentive for a process of gradual mechanisation. Mao saw in this the start of a spiral of development which could modernise and industrialise the village out of its own resources; its labour surplus was its greatest capital.

In 1956, Mao made a confidential speech under the title 'On the Ten Great Relationships',[6] which he later referred to as the CCP's first attempt to distinguish its strategy from that of the Soviets. The speech rejected the orthodox zero-sum view of the basic economic relationships of socialist development (between sectors of the economy, consumption and accumulation, etc.) and insisted on viewing these relationships as dynamic and dialectical. Thus, on the relationship between heavy industry and the rest of the economy, Mao reversed Stalin's priorities, arguing that the probable direction of spread effects was not from heavy industry *to* the rest, but to heavy industry *from* the rest.

The third stage of Mao's intellectual evolution at this time was represented by his speech 'On the Correct Handling of Contradictions Among the People' in early 1957.[7] The speech was at once a response to the Hungarian rising, an attack on authoritarian bureaucracy which suppressed conflict or evaded it, and – as it proved – an invitation to the Chinese people to criticise the Communist Party. The resulting criticisms were devastating, amounting to a widespread condemnation of the Party's monopoly of power and abuse of that monopoly. The Party leadership promptly demanded an end to the free criticism. Mao although shaken, resisted the demand but was overruled.

The critics were punished, but this did not make the authoritarian bureaucracy any more popular. Mao, although in no doubt that the Party must remain supreme, had a profound distaste for bureaucratism. Yet although willing to tolerate criticism and protest up to a point, his alternative to Stalinist authoritarianism was not democracy (in a Western sense) but mass-line mobilisation. It was to the creation of an alternative based on mobilisation that he now turned.

One essential dimension of the movement which followed, culminating in the Great Leap Forward and the Communes, was an attack on Stalinist orthodoxy. Mao's critique of Stalin was not systematically expressed, but his marginal notes to Stalin's 'Economic Problems of Socialism in the USSR' come nearest to full exposition.[8]

(1) Stalin was wrong to assert that there were no conflicts in socialist society; without political conflict, political evolution ceases.
(2) Stalin 'stressed cadres and forgot people . . . stressed technology and forgot people'. But without popular participation, social evolution ceases and a bureaucratic minority takes over.
(3) Stalin overstressed collective incentives and underestimated the value of individual incentives.
(4) Stalin did not appreciate that the satisfaction of short-term interests can serve long-term interests; under him it was always jam tomorrow, never jam today.
(5) Soviet agricultural policy had always 'drained the pond to catch

the fish' and Soviet collective farms had 'perpetuated the counterproductive exploitation of the landlords'.
(6) Stalin's priority for heavy industry had been a counterproductive obsession.
(7) Finally, unlike Stalin, Mao held that agricultural means of production such as tractors should be put in the hands of the collective peasants, not owned and operated by the state. In his view, for example, the Soviet state tractor stations 'held the peasants to ransom' and should not be adopted in China.

As Mao pondered these ideas, he began to reach back into his own experience to find a more satisfactory framework for China's socialism. He found the clues in the policies and institutions of the wartime Communist Border Regions.

THE GREAT LEAP FORWARD AND ITS AFTERMATH (1958–65)

The focus of Mao's new strategy was agriculture, village by village. 'It is not one plan we need', Mao had earlier said, 'but half a million plans.' Its basis was a thorough decentralisation – of state sector enterprises from centre to provinces, and provincial enterprises to the counties; and of decisions on village development to the village. Industries at higher levels were also expected (in Bukharin's earlier phrase) to 'turn and face the villages', and provide the technology appropriate to rural development.

It was Mao's belief that if peasant communities were given the right to make their own decisions, they would (with help and encouragement) find not only new economic opportunities, but also the means to take advantage of them from their own resources. In this way, China's total rate of savings and investment might be maintained at a high level by voluntary means rather than by central taxation and quasi-taxation through procurement pricing. Savings which might otherwise not even have existed would be called forth.

Communal industries (later to be called commune and brigade industries) were the heart of the programme; their profits could provide the capital necessary for the modernisation of Chinese agriculture. Labour-intensive capital construction was another key development, providing short-term gains which would lead to acceptance of longer-term investments. The method was the traditional one by which China's clan estates had been developed, by winter-season construction which paid off in the next harvest.

With decision-making in the hands of the peasants, with development responding naturally to changing local needs, there was less possibility of administrative rigidities and ideological reifications bringing progress to a halt. With the whole village population involved in increasingly successful collective effort, acceptance of collectivism would grow, and from this 'new socialist man' would emerge.

The Great Leap Forward provided the contents of the new alternative; the Commune was its frame. The Chinese phrase for the commune – *gongshe* – does not occur in the pre-modern Chinese language. It is a neologism, invented by the Japanese to refer specifically to the Paris Commune. The choice of this name was significant because to Marx the Paris Commune represented a democratic socialist alternative to the 'bourgeois state'.

The implications of the communes for the nature of the socialist state are interesting. Their basic characteristics were strikingly similar to those of the ideal Owenite communal view of future socialist society which we discussed earlier.[9] This is not to argue that Mao was in any sense an anarchist. The state played a powerful role in the Great Leap Forward; the Leap's purpose was not to substitute decentralised community enterprise for state enterprise, but to develop both – to 'walk on two legs' – and to build a fruitful relationship between them. It is the change in this relationship which is significant; it reflects a determined application to the relation between state and society of Mao's 'mass-line' concept of political leadership.

The state would be one which would respond to initiative from below, through the 'mass-line' activity of local party leaders who would foster and make operational sense of popular aspirations, formulate policies on this basis, and put these policies to the test of mass opinion. State planners would use their knowledge and skills to react flexibly to the changing needs of the communities as they developed. The state would not be a bureaucratic machine standing over and against society, but a part of society, representing the aspirations of the communities at the highest level of generality. As a statement of Marxist ideals, such a view of the socialist state is not very original. What gives it importance is that Mao believed that he had created a process – an economic process – which would produce a political transformation and make a reality of the ideas.

The Great Leap ended in disaster. Why did it fail? Because in fact the relations between state and society were not changed as intended. While the state apparatus lost much of its influence, it was not to grassroots communities but to the Party apparatus, which was as top-down as the state, but less predictable, less limited by its own rules, and out of its collective mind with millennial hopes. The commune, intended to be a collective organisation, instead became an added lower level of the state. Its leaders, although ostensibly elected, were put on the state payroll, and were responsible to their state superiors at county level. Not only was it the first time in history that the Chinese state had thrust itself down to the village level, but it also appeared there not just as governor but as proprietor. As proprietor, it demanded the ownership of all peasant assets right up to and including the fruit trees on the cottage wall.

In the same way, communal construction work was turned into state corvée, and the indiscriminate establishment of commune industries – often no more than the requisition without compensation of the resources of existing craft co-operatives – became yet another means of exaction.

Mao was quick to recognise how badly wrong the movement had gone. He protested but his protests came too late. The damage was done; rural society was demoralised. The Party's authority suffered a paralysing blow. Production dropped to levels so low that, by recent Chinese calculations, as many as twenty million people may have died in consequence. Eventually after two years, defeat was conceded and the Great Leap wound up. The communes remained, but they were articulated into three levels of ownership – commune, brigade and team – with the team as the actual unit of collective ownership and farming; most of the new village industries were shut down.

The period which followed, from 1960 to 1965, need not detain us long. Mao's strategy was replaced by policies which broadly speaking followed the precedents of contemporary East European reform: greater autonomy for enterprises, a larger private sector in agriculture, lower levels of saving and investment, and political relaxation. Many precedents were set for the policies of the present day; but in between, from 1966 to 1976, came the Cultural Revolution. The policies which emerged after Mao's death were much more than a continuation of the reform of 1960–65; they show the influences, both positive and negative, of the Cultural Revolution experience.

THE CULTURAL REVOLUTION AND THE RURAL SECTOR (1966–76)

The Cultural Revolution in the sense of violent protest, factional fighting and seizures of power did not much affect the countryside; there was a tacit understanding that agricultural production must be protected from disruption. There was an apparent paradox here, for the long-term aims of the Cultural Revolution very much concerned the rural sector. The final purpose was to restore Mao's Great Leap strategy, purged of its disastrous faults; but the first necessary step to its restoration was the capture of the urban centres of power.

Although the Cultural Revolution took place mainly in the cities, it had grown partly out of events in the countryside. In 1963 a Socialist Education Movement was launched in the rural areas to repair the damage done to agricultural collectives by the Great Leap (Baum, 1975). Cadre corruption was widespread in the villages. Controversy began immediately over the methods of reform to be employed. Liu Shaoqi saw the problem in legal and administrative terms – crimes had been committed and the criminals must be identified and brought to book by special party work-teams dispatched from outside. Mao took the view that the solution had to be a political one. The poor majority who (he believed) were the victims of the situation, must be assisted in 'seizing power' so that they could control the offenders. Nothing could reveal more clearly the gulf between Mao and Liu as to the proper relationship between state and society. When Liu pursued his own preferred methods, Mao decided that he was an unsuitable successor and moved against him in 1966 as the Cultural Revolution escalated into a struggle for national leadership.

The victory of the left in the Cultural Revolution created a new climate of opinion in which collectivism and egalitarianism were highly valued. Private plots, private trade by individual peasants, large differentials in the remuneration of labour, were criticised. High levels of collective saving and investment were praised. Yet no generalised attempt was made to 'raise the level of ownership' from the team to the brigade or the commune. The personal possessions of the peasants were not collectivised as in the heady days of 1958. The private plot was not abolished, although it was sometimes assimilated to the collective by various devices.

Labour-intensive construction was restored; village industries were developed with great rapidity but with more care than in 1958. By the end of 1976 and the death of Mao, followed by the fall of the 'Gang of Four', they were rapidly becoming an essential part of the rural economy and the principal source of investment in agriculture. Mao's 'great and glorious hope' was gradually being realised.

THE NEW POLICIES: THE STATE AND RURAL SOCIETY UNDER DENG XIAOPING

The Critique of Past Policies

The Cultural Revolution, chaotic as it was, did not arrest (although it may have slowed) the growth of the Chinese economy. Agriculture continued to show an annual rate of growth (4.5 per cent) with which many comparable countries would have been very satisfied.

Yet it is not unreasonable that the Party and Government of China should have been discontented with the progress of Chinese agriculture. Although production has increased at a commendable rate overall and has somewhat more than kept pace with the growth of population, the situation is still far from acceptable. The scarcity of grain is still a tight constraint both on overall development and on the increase of popular welfare. Growth in grain output has been erratic, and the present leaders of China point to the fact that the worst periods have been those when the egalitarian policies of the Left held sway.[10] In Leftist periods, moreover, slower rates of growth in grain were accompanied by even lower rates of growth in most other key agricultural products.

Left-wing insistence on giving absolute priority to grain and neglecting – or even condemning – diversification was also counter-productive from the point of view of grain production itself. This counter-productive effect is ascribed to three causes. First, by depriving peasants of alternative sources of income from other crops and commodities, the incentive to work was reduced, collective labour discredited and grain production adversely affected. Second, concentration on grain prejudiced the ecology of farming, in particular by limiting supplies of manure. Third, the policy limited agricultural profits derived from non-grain production, which could have increased investment in agriculture.

The charges against the Left are somewhat overstrained. They certainly do not apply to Mao himself: peasant that he was, he was second to none in his persistent calls for diversification. Indeed, the Cultural Revolution was the first period in which the diversification of agriculture was taken seriously. Mao's slogan that grain should be taken as the key link in a process of diversification was the first breach in China in the orthodox Communist obsession with grain supplies as the *raison d'être* of collective agriculture. The true criticism of Cultural Revolution policies is that, while it proved easy to ensure by political pressure that grain was made the 'key link', it was far more difficult to induce local cadres to apply new rotations and create new farming ecologies.

A further cause for condemnation of past policies is the disappointing results of the vast campaigns which have since 1949 more than doubled the area of irrigated land. For instance, Zhan Wu, Director of the Agricultural Economics Institute of the Chinese Academy of Social Science, stated that, 'due to failure to link up projects and to poor management', the water utilisation rate was under 50 per cent.[11] Also, in spite of heroic and partially successful efforts to create effective defences against flood as well as drought, China remains vulnerable to natural disasters; the uncertainties of the Chinese climate can still play havoc with the harvest and put millions of lives at risk.

Finally, the new regime, while conceding that agricultural production continued to rise – though more slowly – during the period of the Cultural Revolution, point out that peasant incomes failed to rise in proportion, and in some areas even decreased in spite of increases in production. Average rural incomes remained far below urban incomes; the rural 80 per cent of the population received only 20 per cent of national income. It has been estimated that some localities – about one in six of China's two thousand or so counties – had not had a good year since the 1950s. The peasants there had 'lost faith in the collective', and where this was so, they should be allowed to return, for the present, to family farming.[12] The current diagnosis of past failure is as follows:

(1) Levels of investment in attempts to improve agriculture had been unrealistically high and produced poor results. Zhan Wu has pointed out that while from 1965 to 1977 the capital invested in farm machinery had increased over eight-fold and chemical fertiliser supplies by almost two and a half times and while farm costs had increased 130 per cent, production had only risen by 80 per cent. He attributed this relative failure – costly in terms

of peasant incomes – to 'an irrational economic structure and low levels of management', and emphasised that 'increased investment is not the only way to speed up development'.[13]

(2) The level of management ability among many rural cadres was very low.[14] Their notion of management was 'to ring the bell and count heads'. Proper accounting was scarce; many teams had little idea about their level of expenditure and no means of judging the returns on expenditure. There was little or no democratic discussion of the accounts. Since 'today's cadres are yesterday's peasants', rural cadres had little knowledge of modern scientific methods. Cadres were often incapable of taking decisions for themselves, and the institutional framework actually discouraged initiative; the safest course was to obey orders. Many of them were ignorant of simple local market possibilities which could have increased both peasant incomes and the accumulation of capital.

(3) The burdens imposed on the peasants were too heavy and unpredictable.[15] In some cases the total handed over to the team, brigade, commune and state in taxes, levies, accumulation, etc., was over 50 per cent of gross production; in this respect the poorer teams – less able to support this wasteful superstructure – suffered most. The first burden was wasteful investment; the second was the swollen administration, with cadres often enjoying incomes two or three times as high as the peasants. The third burden arose from the abuse of the state monopoly of trade: procurement norms were raised in good years or prices reduced so that 'the more enthusiastic you have been, the greater your burden'.[16] It was in fact normal for over 30 per cent of gross production to be siphoned off before any distribution of the product was made to the peasants. This was about the same proportion of total farm incomes taken by the landlords from their tenants before the revolution.

(4) The problem of implementing the principle of distribution 'to each according to his labour' had never been solved. The piecework and job-contract systems used in imitation of traditional Soviet methods were not satisfactory; the quality of work could not be controlled. The egalitarian Leftist policies of the Great Leap or the Cultural Revolution were also ineffective since a worker received much the same income whether he or she worked hard or not. Productivity on private plots, where incentives are not impaired, has been much higher than on the

collective fields, and represents the intensive and meticulous cultivation which China must achieve on all her farmland.

(5) The suppression of private plots, rural fairs and family sideline occupations severely limited peasant incomes. The obsession with growing grain prevented the team or the brigade from pursuing alternative sources of profit collectively. These restrictions, by reducing incomes, also reduced possibilities for accumulation; this in turn limited the improvement of arable farming; this was reflected in a slow growth of incomes which depressed incentives still further. 'Who wants to do unprofitable work?' said the peasants and many of them deserted the collective farm for itinerant peddling or craft work.[17] National figures for overall increases in agricultural output conceal the near total failure of some areas to improve production while population continued to rise.

The New Agricultural 'Responsibility Systems'

The new system of farming is based on contracts. Staple arable crops (grain, cotton, oil seeds and sugar) are now for the most part grown by individual farm families, under contract to the collective (in the first instance, the team leadership), which thus secures its assigned deliveries under the state plan. For the most part, the collective provides farm families with the main means of production. The farm household, having fulfilled its contractual responsibility, is free to use its assigned resources for its own profit; no contracts or quotas are imposed on this additional production. The members of the collective are encouraged to specialise either individually or in associations. This allows many peasants to leave arable farming and concentrate on stock-raising, horticulture, forestry, handicrafts, small workshop industries, or services.

One main reason for giving peasants freedom to leave arable farming is the need to diversify, a goal which is also sought by offering peasants larger private plots comprising up to 15 per cent of the collective arable (formerly 5 per cent), with in addition up to 20 per cent of the non-arable land, usually in the hills, for forestry and stock raising (the other 80 per cent of this being assigned for the same purposes under contract). The contracts for staple field crops and collective hill land are for 15 years at least, while the 'private' hill plots are for 30 years in the first instance, and inheritable. The assignees of hill plots do not contract for output, but simply pay in respect of the assigned land their due share towards collective revenues, in effect a rent collected by the team leadership.

The contract system has been extended to commune and brigade enterprises (about half of these are industrial) which have now become virtually worker-managed enterprises under contract to the collective. In addition, any citizen or group of citizens can now create new enterprises, subject to approval and to the duty of contributing to local revenues. These new 'economic combines' vary enormously; they may be simply co-operative groups of peasants and/or tradesmen, or operated jointly with the public authorities or marketing organisations. Enterprises which serve farming are especially encouraged; they spray crops, raise hybrid seeds, provide transport, or trade in chemical fertilisers etc. Many of these have been formed by joining members of official scientific and technological institutions with peasants to create new private associations responsible for their own profits and losses.

The commune has been abolished, its political powers transferred to new township governments and its economic responsibilities taken over by local trusts which play a supervising and enabling role in relation to local farming, industry and commerce.

There has been a concomitant effort to encourage the spread of 'specialised households' (for example, raising pigs, poultry, rabbits and sheep and keeping bees). These are usually families with particular skills; they need little capital and have negligible overheads. Thus a single family can often produce more than a collectively-organised enterprise. The state supplies fodder and buys the products under contract.

The rationale for specialisation is not concerned solely with the fact that in such lines a particular family may be more productive. Specialisation contributes to the diversification of rural production, as important for ecological as for market reasons. Above all, however, it provides a possible line of attack on one of rural China's most intractable problems, the existence of surplus rural labour, which is still about the same as in the 1930s.

In fact the low marketed surplus of agriculture, the growing demand for non-grain foods and for consumer goods, and the need to increase the labour productivity of agriculture by removing the surplus of labour on the farm, all point to the need for the rapid development of a division of labour in the rural economy. Without this, it is pointless to expect the modernisation of production or to anticipate economies of scale. The specialised household (including the specialised arable farmer) is the first step, the second is the encouragement of 'new economic combines'. It is envisaged that economic combines having ties with rural households farming on contract and with specialised households, and which develop joint ventures, will become 'a main form of the co-operative economy, providing comprehensive service'.[18]

The advance of specialisation also means that some farm households, especially those with more labour power, are ready to contract for more than their share of land, while others who have chosen other specialisations or occupations want to farm less land or none. The spread of these 'grain households' is now not only permitted but positively encouraged.

Some of them now produce 40 000 or even 100 000 *jin*, which implies contracted holdings up to about 10 hectares – an enormous farm for China.[19] Clearly such a scale implies the use of employed labour. In early 1983 the CCP Central Committee ruled that peasant households could hire seasonal labourers, professional-technical workers and 'assistants', or take on apprentices subject to certain policy regulations.[20] The Central Committee stopped short of permitting long-term hiring of labourers by peasants engaged in arable farming, and subsequent documents are carefully vague, referring to the employment of wage labour on the farms as 'a difficult problem'. Yet it certainly exists in practice.

From the point of view of increasing production, the agricultural responsibility system and the policies surrounding it have so far been highly successful, as far as one can judge at this early stage. It spread steadily from 1979 but it was perhaps fully operative only from 1981. Table 6.1 gives a general indication of its impact up to 1983. Agricultural output value has increased since 1980 by about 7 per cent per annum. Excluding 1980 which was a year of natural disasters, the average rate of growth of the production of grain and tubers from 1981 to 1983 was about 6.4 per cent per annum, and almost 9 per cent per annum in 1982 and 1983. Cotton production has grown much faster, at an average rate of 22.7 per cent.

A new policy to allow peasants into forestry and to associate state forestry administrations with local production teams produced an extraordinary leap in afforestation in 1983. Oil-bearing crops increased with such rapidity that, as a matter of policy, rape acreage was sharply reduced in 1983. The relatively slow growth in animal husbandry products conceals a steady rise in the production of pork. Except in the mountain provinces and on the steppe country of the north-west, China has no tradition of cattle or sheep raising. However, an extensive breeding programme is well under way and its results should soon show up in the national figures, provided the responsibility system is as effective in this field as elsewhere.

In general, these growth figures are remarkable, although to a large extent they represent the use of slack resources, encouraged by improved incentives, and are unlikely to be sustained indefinitely at this high level. Still, an increase in agricultural output value of one-third in four years is a valuable advance, and there are still ample slack resources to be taken up.

Between 1979 and 1983, rural per capita incomes are calculated to have risen by about 70 per cent. We are on less certain ground here because the figures are based on small samples of peasant households and because the constituents of income measured are not always uniform; but there is no reason to doubt that per capita incomes have risen by roughly that order of magnitude. The main contributor to increased incomes has undoubtedly been local enterprise rather than agriculture, and within agriculture diversified production rather than grain.

Altogether the results of the new policies are a matter for congratulation.

Table 6.1   Agricultural output, inputs, and incomes, 1980–83
(percentage increases)

	1980	1981	1982	1983
Agriculture, total o.p.v.	2.7	5.7	11.2	7.9
Grain and tubers (tonnes)	−4.2	1.4	8.7	9.2
Cotton	22.0	9.6	21.3	28.9
Oil-bearing crops	19.5	32.7	15.8	−10.7
Pork, beef and mutton	13.5	4.6	7.1	3.8
Aquatic products	4.5	—	11.9	5.9
Afforestation, increase in area planted	1.4	−9.7	9.4	40.7
Inputs				
Large and medium tractors	11.7	6.3	2.5	3.5
Small and hand tractors	12.1	8.7	12.3	20.2
Powered drainage and irrigation equipment	4.8	0.45	2.3	2.3
Chemical fertiliser inputs	17.0	5.2	13.4	9.7
Rural electricity consumption	13.5	15.3	7.3	9.6
Per capital rural income	2.5	16.8	15.2	14.7

Sources: Annual Communiques of the State Statistical Bureau on China's National Economic Plans.

Implementation Problems

The introduction of responsibility systems encountered many problems arising from bureaucratic recalcitrance and residual leftism among local cadres. Some local government agencies, complained the official media, were only interested in plan targets, taking no account of local conditions or peasant wishes and neglecting the diversification of production outside the state plan. They also showed no respect for contracts, and changed them arbitrarily.[21] Some local cadres thought that 'since they act on behalf of the state and the collective, they can order peasants about and change or tear up contracts at will'.[22]

Abuses of, and misunderstandings of, the new system by local cadres (as well as exploitation of it in their own personal interest) have led in many places to an actual increase in peasant burdens through arbitrary financial exactions. These included levies for public works, salaries for non-productive staff, energy supplies, maintenance of roads, etc. In some cases, these impositions drove peasants out of farming into less onerous activities.[23] The sums deducted from peasant incomes for various types of accumulation and welfare funds or reserves was also too high in many places.[24] The main reason given was that cadres, unable to calculate costs, erred on the safe side to ensure that the collective would not suffer loss. Figures were also 'enlarged level by level' as various local authorities each added their own supplementary levy.[25] Peasants sent letters of complaint to the newspapers and Party authorities responded by laying down rules to prevent further exactions. In Nanjing, for example, it was stipulated that, during procurement, no money beyond that specified in the contract should be taken from the peasants; the debts of the collectives should not be shared among the households; peasants who had bought equipment from the collective on credit should not be asked to pay back more than 20 per cent of the debt in any one year.[26]

There were cases also of peasants who broke their contracts or evaded their responsibilities, but such reports were much less frequent than those of cadre misdemeanours.

The problem of neglect of farming and abandonment of land is widespread, partly as a result of the burdens sometimes imposed under the new system and partly of the new opportunities for non-farm employment. In one commune, the setting up of a government market resulted in 70 per cent of the labour force of some brigades switching to garment making and refusing to farm, so that the teams had to hire labour to till and harvest. Elsewhere there has been a shift away from grain growing to other crops, such as rape, which are much more profitable; indeed, grain growing is the least profitable of rural activities in spite of substantial increases in the prices offered to farmers.

A further series of difficulties has arisen from the speed with which production and marketing have grown. The changes which have taken place in the system for the marketing of agricultural and other rural products are almost as significant as the changes in the organisation of production. The contract system is itself a part of this in that it substitutes a relationship of mutual advantage arrived at through negotiations for the former relationship of command. The new rules on rural marketing permit peasants to leave agriculture for commerce; they allow peasants to sell their produce at rural fairs at negotiated prices; they permit individuals and collective enterprises to trade anywhere in China; they allow sellers dissatisfied with the terms offered by local state purchasing organisations to seek a better deal elsewhere; they encourage competition, although for more important commodities this is over design and delivery rather than price; and they encourage local enterprises to go out and look for markets, even abroad.

Progress in developing the new commercial system has been relatively slow, however. By 1983 almost 75 per cent of rural trade was still in the hands of the state, almost 20 per cent in the hands of the supply and marketing co-operatives, and only a residual 7 per cent was conducted by individuals.[27] The main obstacle is the hostility of local cadres who continue to identify trade with speculation and free marketing with capitalism.

The most convincing change which has taken place in the marketing system is the handing back of the supply and marketing co-operatives to the peasants. These were founded on peasant subscriptions soon after the revolution, but became parastatal institutions responsible to the state and party, not to their members. The original peasant shares had come to represent only 8 per cent of the co-operatives' assets; they never paid a dividend. In 1977 they were formally taken over by the state. In 1983 they became peasant co-operatives again. Subscriptions have been reopened and over 80 per cent of peasants have bought shares. They are governed by a representative congress of shareholders, and their tasks are defined in terms of the peasants' needs: prompt supplies and expanding markets.

In this new and democratised form, the supply and marketing co-operatives loom very large in Deng Xiaoping's perspective of rural development through voluntary co-operation. They will supply, advise, offer contracts, provide production services, process and market produce. They will, it is hoped, offer 'a comprehensive service to their members before, during and after production'. They will be responsible for their own profit and loss. Special emphasis is put on the stipulation that they are village-level organisations, and not branches of the county-wide co-operative, which is now to be only a federation of the independent grass-roots institutions.[28]

It remains to be seen whether the supply and marketing co-operatives actually attain so much independence. For this, two things are necessary: that their peasant shareholders can withdraw their funds without penalty, and that there are alternative channels through which they can buy or sell if they are dissatisfied with the co-operative. In the present proliferation of enterprise of all kinds in the Chinese countryside this is possible, but not yet certain.

The New Role of the Collective

There has been much misunderstanding abroad as to the significance of the new responsibility system in Chinese agricultural organisation. It is generally represented as a return to individual farming and the end of collectivisation. When the system gradually was introduced, there was much misunderstanding within China also; and the new Communist Party leadership has had to exert itself to show that the new system represented a re-articulation of the collective, not its overthrow.

Especially in the first years when the new system was being rapidly extended, both cadres and peasants in many places concluded that the era of collectivised agriculture was over. Collective property was neglected, split up and distributed, or deliberately destroyed.[29]

In the first three years, 1979 to 1981, the emphasis was on decentralisation to small groups or individual households; but by 1982 the stress shifted to publicising the continuation of collective tasks and responsibilities.[30] It was laid down that contractors (group, family or individual) must recognise the rights of ownership of the collective. The transfer, lease or mortgage of collective land was forbidden. Regulations proscribed certain uses of collective land; if these were flouted, the collective had the right to resume its property and seek compensation for damage in the courts.

The official position is that the new agricultural system is a form of collective agriculture in which the collective authority owns the means of production and determines the uses of collective property and division of the product according to plans implemented through the contract system.

According to one detailed analysis from Shanxi, the continuing responsibilities of the collective leadership (i.e. the production team leadership) are as follows:[31]

(1) The collective is responsible for equitable distribution of the land under contract, ensuring that it is allocated to families capable of cultivating it while taking into consideration the position of large families with a small labour force. It must ensure that the land is well cultivated, adequately fertilised, and properly maintained.
(2) The collective must ensure that the quantity, quality, and variety of crops demanded by both the state and the collective are guaranteed through the contract system under a unified plan.
(3) The collective owns and is responsible for the use and maintenance of agricultural machinery, and for the administration of irrigation water. These tasks may be carried out by giving contracts to groups or individuals, but the contracts should be properly framed to ensure, for example, that tractors are used for cultivation and not merely for transport and that the profit remitted by the contractors is sufficient to cover depreciation and maintenance.
(4) Plant protection, seed care and the control of pests and diseases are the responsibility of the collective, as is the related duty of popularising modern farm technology and science.
(5) Large-scale capital construction remains a major responsibility of the collective and all contracts should stipulate that male labourers should provide 30 days' work a year, and others 15 days, in communal construction work. The costs are to be met from the profits of commune and brigade enterprise and household ancillary occupations.
(6) Contracts should be offered not only for arable farming but for forestry, animal husbandry, industry and household ancillary occupations. Funds for depreciation and for re-investment

retained by the contractors should be paid to the collective. Part of the collective funds accumulated from the contracted enterprises should be used to subsidise agriculture.

(7) The collective is responsible for paying various welfare benefits (for example, to the sick and disabled), gathering agricultural taxes, generating communal accumulation funds, paying allowances or salaries for cadres, 'barefoot doctors' and school teachers, and for purchasing state-procurement and surplus grain.[32]

Collective leaderships are also encouraged to act as entrepreneurs: for example, developing new lines of agricultural production, setting up new industrial, commercial and service enterprises, or stimulating technological improvements. Substantial benefits have been claimed but cadre entrepreneurship does have its dangers. There have been reports of a growing tendency for cadres to take advantage of their connections with authority, which assist in getting contracts and materials, to become partners in the 'new economic combines', doing no work but enjoying a share of the profits.[33]

There is no question of the abolition of collectives in China; the collective has not relinquished its role but changed it. Rural cadres nowadays probably have more to do, not less. Their jobs are more complex and they have to do them by exercising economic judgement rather than issuing orders. They are themselves now in relations of contract with their superiors, within the new framework of local economic management which has replaced the communes.

Abolition of the Commune

The restructuring of the commune began experimentally in early 1982 in the provinces of Sichuan and Anhui, spreading steadily throughout China from then on, and being basically completed by early 1985.

Official accounts admitted that 'the communes had been successful in organising large-scale capital construction and water-conservancy construction, and in running rural ancillary occupations by pooling labour and capital'.[34] However, the fusion of economic and political organisation in a single institution has produced 'insurmountable contradictions' which could only be resolved by separating these functions, reviving the township as a political organ and leaving the commune as a purely economic institution. The advantages were described as follows.

First, the reform would eliminate administrative interference in the operation of local economic enterprises and the practice of requisitioning labour and funds without remuneration. Second, with increasing diversification of the economy and the spread of horizontal economic ties across commune boundaries, the commune in its existing form was 'no longer apposite'. Third, the commune had too many functions and its cadres often could not cope with the demands of their jobs. Moreover, they were paid by the government regardless of economic performance. Finally, with the development of the responsibility system, the work of the commune cadres had shifted from direct economic management to more purely governmental and supervisory functions: mediating disputes, maintaining public order, collecting taxes, supervising village welfare services and local construction. They could not do these jobs properly if they were still directly involved in economic management.

The separation of administration from economic management, it was felt, solved many of these problems: it defined responsibilities more clearly, eliminated the concentration of power in a few hands, and opened up the possibility of democratic management within the economic enterprises.

Essentially, the change was a division of responsibility: the revived township (*xiang*) is responsible for the political and administrative tasks of a normal organ of local government, while the commune becomes a sort of trust of which brigades, teams and industrial and commercial enterprises are the constituent firms. The criteria on which the township operates are primarily political and social; the criterion of the new commune is profit and loss.

This, however, is too simple a division. The township retains important economic functions. Although these do not in theory include the right to direct or intervene in the operation of local enterprises and collectives, in fact they are widely defined, and may leave ample scope for direct intervention. This ambiguity is visible in the following extract from an authoritative article on the subject in the *People's Daily*:

> The township should administer the economy. Rural economic organisations are not on a par with the township government but are economic entities under its leadership.
>
> On the other hand, the township government cannot interfere in

concrete marketing and operational activities of collective economic organisations as in the past.[35]

The actual economic responsibilities of the township will depend less on these definitions and more on the new context in which they will work, a context created by the responsibility system and the new stress on more democratic organisation. The first implies that the township government must fulfil its economic plans by economic as opposed to administrative means, that is through contracts which offer economic inducements rather that threaten political penalties. The second is the political obverse of the contract system, the acceptance of the fact that the new economic system inevitably creates a pluralism of interests which must be reflected – if only for the sake of efficiency – in a system of political decision-making which gives due weight to the expansion of those interests.

There is in fact a strong political content in the reform. It is linked explicitly with the strenghtening of local democracy and 'socialist legality'. At times, this is specifically linked to the Paris Commune.[36]

A thorough attempt has been made to create institutions which will guarantee a degree of democratic control, though detailed arrangements vary from place to place. A common pattern is for the township government to be elected by a representative assembly; under it, the previous production brigades are transformed into villagers' committees, 'basic-level mass organisations of self-government'. These village-level organisations are not regarded as a 'special agency' of the township but as a separate level of local government with their own elections and executive committees. The villagers' committees elect their own team leaders and accountants. The tasks of village-level government are quite broad: 'to organise programmes of self-education, self-management and self-service; to operate village public utilities and welfare programmes; and to help the township government to make a success of village administration, construction and production'.[37]

Moreover, it is envisaged that the personnel of township governments should not be totally divorced from production, but should be both 'officials and people'. Contemporary reports suggest that township and village elections have produced new groups of leaders, many in their thirties or late twenties, and most with at least a junior-middle school education. Unlike their predecessors, these new officials will not enjoy life tenure.

An attempt is also being made to redefine the role of the

Communist Party, with great emphasis on separating the Party from the state.

The role of the new economic institutions which have inherited (perhaps in a limited sense only) the economic powers of the former commune is still somewhat unclear. There has been a variety of experiments. In some places they are still called 'communes'; in others, the old name has been rejected. In some areas the three-level system of ownership has been maintained; in others the brigade has been abolished like the commune. In some cases the team has been replaced by more flexible institutions; in others the team has been abolished and the old agricultural producers' cooperative revived. Where the commune name has been abolished, its economic successor is most commonly called the 'agriculture-industry-commerce combine'. In some areas this is a unified organisation; in others it consists of three companies acting in coordination.

In this rather complex picture, a few points seem to emerge clearly. First, the 'new commune' is expected to act in much the same way as the team, as part of the collective economy. Whatever changes take place, moreover, commune and brigade property must remain intact and pass intact to any successor institution.

Again, like the township, definitions of the new commune's rights and duties are less important that the change in context. The new commune is not a government organ whose officials are members of the state *nomenclatura*; it is once more a collective, as it was when first created in 1958. Instead of being able to mobilise the resources of lower levels by political pressure, it must now induce cooperation by offering acceptable contractual terms. While it retains its previous acquisitions, its future development must be based on inducement through the offer of economic advantage.

Theoretically at least, the success criteria for the new commune are commercial; profit is the measure of efficiency. In practice, it is difficult to see how a losing commune could be shut down, though it might be restructured. However, the new commune is clearly regarded as an enterprise, not an administrative organ. It is responsible for its own profit and loss; it accumulates its own capital; it borrows from the banks; it enters into contracts with suppliers and with marketing institutions. It is not a single firm, but a sort of trust or holding company for the collectives and enterprises of the area. It draws funds from two sources: the profits of enterprises under its own ownership, and a share in the profits of other enterprises (most notably some of the 'new economic combines') in which it is a shareholder. These funds enable it to invest in improved infrastructure, and to impose on the local economy a degree of coordination aimed first at fulfilling its duties to the state (represented by the township plan) and second at the general development and diversification of local economic activity.

Problems of Inequality

There are fears in China that the new system, with its rewards to individual or small-group enterprises, will increase inequalities among the rural population and perhaps lead to a new 'polarisation'. Deng Xiaoping has advocated the policy of allowing individual peasants to pursue prosperity. He has admitted that this may in the short term increase disparities of wealth in the rural areas, but argues that the demonstration effect of higher incomes achieved by a minority through hard work and enterprise is vital for China's development.

The fears nevertheless remain and the new regime has had to try to allay them. Deng's opponents can certainly point to plenty of examples of individuals, families and groups who are now earning many times the average rural income; indeed, these successful peasants are lionised by the media. A very small minority of the rural population have become rich beyond the dreams of peasant avarice.[38]

Although official ideological analyses try to justify this in socialist terms, they do not really deal with what for socialists must be the most critical point: that peasants can now invest individually, that some have the means to invest and some have not, and that a process of capital accumulation in the hands of a rich minority of peasants may be put in train – especially if, as is now the case, contractor peasants may employ labour.

Chinese accounts tend to be optimistic, arguing that these increased disparities will not lead to polarisation, but 'on the contrary will arouse initiative, promote a great increase in social wealth and lay the material foundations for all to become rich'.[39]

In Chinese circumstances this optimistic view may be justified. First, the individual ownership of capital is not the most critical factor in the development of Chinese agriculture. It may be some advantage to a peasant to own his own walking tractor, for example, but the collective provides tractor services for the rest. The same is true for other inputs. Second, as Griffin and Saith have shown (1981), the returns to investment in modern agricultural inputs at the lower range of Chinese agricultural productivity are very great, but diminish substantially at higher levels. The process of agricultural investment therefore tends to decrease rather than increase disparities. Third, in so far as Chinese agriculture still remains labour-intensive, increased rewards are closely related to labour inputs. Fourth, the new stress on agricultural diversification and non-agricultural employment provides alternative sources of income, some of which are directed to the needy. Fifth, the major investment out of local collective accumulation is in water conservancy; this is redistributive because vulnerability to flood or drought is a major cause of poverty. Finally, redistributive policies are still a very strong factor in the Chinese rural scene and increasing wealth – generated by individuals but shared by the collective – will provide greater resources for such redistribution.

Nevertheless, there are some risks inherent in the new system. The problems faced by those families which lack labour power in relation to the number of their dependents, or who lack even the simple means to participate productively in the contract system, are sufficiently serious for the State Council and the Party Centre to have issued a joint decree on the importance of a systematic effort to assist poorer families.[40] There is a further long-term risk. Rural Party members are being urged to set an example of individual and co-operative enterprise. At the same time successful non-Party rural entrepreneurs are being offered Party membership. If these two groups should coalesce into an élite, in control of the allocation of local resources, then a process of polarisation might begin. Yet present policies actually encourage such a coalescence.

On the other hand, Chinese explanations of the new policies are unambiguous in their existence that the 'socialist orientation' of rural development remains unimpaired. The elements of individual enterprise, it is argued, exist in a collective context; individual rewards are won in the service of collective welfare.

New Economic Combines

These are seen as new forms of co-operative enterprise which differ from the old in that peasants join them voluntarily and create them to further their own perceived needs. For agricultural specialists such as Du Runsheng, they are to serve as an embryonic form of 'a specialised and socialised agriculture'.[41] They reflect the process whereby peasants pool their surplus labour, funds and skills in order to develop commodity production, specialised production based on the division of labour.[42]

While the creation of such enterprises is meant to be voluntary, some controls are necessary in order to prevent 'blind development, duplication and waste', and to guard against conflict with state plans. However, such control must be exercised by economic means and disincentives, not through administrative orders. Proposals for new enterprises should be examined by local industrial and commercial departments which, if satisfied, will issue a licence. This entitles the enterprise to the same treatment with respect to taxes and loans as commune and brigade enterprises.

The agricultural responsibility system, by limiting and defining the obligations of farmers to the state and the collective, leaves them time and energy for other work. The new economic combines provide a channel by which this energy can be used in projects which require more than the labour of one household or which enable one person's skill to be put to use by others who have labour or funds to offer. The stress is on activities which service agriculture. In many cases services and processing previously undertaken by collectives, but done inefficiently, have been offered out to tender by groups of peasants.[43]

Many of the new economic combines have links with state or collective organisations, sometimes by contract, sometimes in the form of joint ownership. These links bear various interpretations: some see them as ways to provide services to privatised rural enterprise; others as a means of reasserting direct state or collective control. All are agreed, however, that the return to peasant enterprise is a policy of *reculer pour mieux sauter*. Such enterprise is intended to work within an evolving new system of voluntary cooperation and indicative planning.

Township and Village Industry

There has been one indisputable continuity with the Maoist past, the encouragement and growth of commune and brigade enterprise (now referred to as township and village enterprise). As these have been China's most characteristic contribution to development, this continuity is of great significance. Their development was the central plank in Mao's strategy, and if they continue to develop on the same lines, then the break with Maoism has been far from complete, and there may indeed prove to have been no fundamental change at all.

The economic arguments for the encouragement of rural industry in China are simple and familiar (Gray & White, 1982). By far the most important argument is its capacity to provide, out of its profits, the means of modernising agriculture.

To Mao and his successors, these enterprises have also great value from the point of view of wider socialist aims: as providing the best opportunity for peasants to participate in the development process. The growth and proliferation of village-based industries, moreover, starting with the processing of crops and the manufacture of tools and small machines, would initiate the elimination of the 'three great differences' – between town and country, industry and agriculture, and mental and manual work, differences which in Marxist theory are regarded as a contributory cause of class divisions. These industries are an important part of the creation of self-reliant, self-developing local communities which could create a countervailing power to the centralised socialist state, or even an alternative to it. Mao's successors have accepted this rationale with the qualification that they deny that party and state bureaucrats form a new exploiting class. But they are as ready as Mao to see local and communal decision-making as a necessary means to minimise bureaucratic power.

Thus township and village enterprises as the backbone of local self-development are of critical importance to the emergence of a new relationship between the state and the rural economy.

The direct economic contribution of local industry is also of great importance. For example, they supply over half the total output of chemical fertilisers, and 20 per cent of coal. Local industries provide an average of 20 per cent of all rural employment, and in the areas where they are most developed this may rise to 70 per cent. As their labour productivity is far higher than that of agriculture, they provide considerably more than 20 per cent of rural incomes; in a large and growing minority of China's 2000 counties, local industries and non-agricultural enterprises already provide over 50 per cent of total rural income. Seventy-three per cent of investment in agriculture comes directly from their profits (especially in irrigation and flood control), as well as the greater part of investment in local roads.

Taxation policies encourage their growth. State enterprises are pressed to sub-contract to village industries, and some small locally-based state enterprises are being handed over to township management. A strenuous effort is being made to ensure that village industries are given equal treatment with state enterprises in access to finance markets and professional expertise. Finally, a renewed effort is being made to encourage the local processing of farm produce, a form of development which has been stalled by the resistance of state enterprises and state buyers.

There has, however, been one major change since the Cultural Revolution. The left-wing regime was anti-market. It has been a paradoxical characteristic of left-wing communism that its adherents, while being passionate about communal and workers' self-management, have also been passionately anti-market. But without some market freedom, self-management is an illusion. The Chinese left wing, although they rapidly developed commune and brigade enterprise, saw it as a constituent of a planned local economy in which markets played little or no part. Though the local *authority* enjoyed greater powers of decision-making, the lower levels of the commune and the enterprises themselves had little or none.

The new policies on the contrary stipulate autonomy for the enterprises and encourage them to seek out their own markets; thus a market dimension has been added to the Maoist strategy of rural development.

Interviews with village leaders and with managers and workers of local industries in China leave the author in no doubt that to them the main significance of village enterprise is that it contributes strongly to increasing rural purchasing power. Interviews with leaders at higher levels showed the same; Mao's conviction that peasant purchasing power is the main motive force of development is now conventional wisdom.

It must be emphasised that these enterprises are owned by the community, as represented by the township or village government, and not by their workers. Most enterprises now work on contracts and the community receives the major part of the profits, disbursing them on the basis of a unified local plan. This is the main strength of the Chinese system of local development.

CONCLUSIONS

We are now in a position to sum up the nature of the new Chinese farming system, and to draw some wider conclusions as to its significance.

The theoretical rationalisation of the restoration of family-scale farming, that the change in production relations had been allowed to outrun the development of the forces of production, would seem to be valid in China. In the commune system, the economies of scale of mechanisation were not realised, while the diseconomies were considerable. The return to small-scale farming eliminates these diseconomies, while the freedom of peasants to seek other occupations makes it possible to reduce the labour force in agriculture and thus allow mechanisation to increase the incomes of those who remain in farming.

Recent changes in Communist agricultural policies elsewhere have taken a similar direction, though the Chinese have gone much further. In China, as elsewhere, collective agriculture is not likely to win the support of farmers unless it can offer a technology which brings such superior rewards that it would be irrational to return to individual production.

In the communist world the tractor has always symbolised this compelling new technology. However, as long as the tractor was used as an additional instrument for state extraction of surplus from agriculture, it could hardly act as a stimulus to the acceptance of collective cultivation. In Chinese conditions the tractor was no genie out of the bottle. Mechanisation is irrelevant except in so far as it can help to increase production and incomes. It could do this to some extent by ensuring more timely completion of certain farm tasks; but this hardly provided a compelling argument, from the peasant's point of view, for collective cultivation. The tractor could also be used to speed up farm capital construction but this did not dictate the necessity of its use in day to day cultivation.

There are two other relevant points. First, at the present stage when the means of agricultural mechanisation are still scarce and expensive, Chinese policy has wisely concentrated resources on irrigation, threshing and ploughing, leaving transplanting, inter-row cultivation, and harvesting, etc. to hand labour. The result is a weak argument for collective cultivation. Second, the readier availability of small walking tractors has made mechanised cultivation possible on a family scale. There is thus, in most parts of China, no technological imperative for collective production. This being so, the diseconomies of scale tend to outrun the economies.

In this respect there is a contrast between China and Vietnam on the one hand and the Soviet Union and Eastern Europe on the other. Typically in the communist countries of Europe there is now a shortage of agricultural labour, industrial development having reached a stage when it is both possible and attractive for most young people to leave the countryside and seek employment in industry. In China on the other hand, with a still massive rural labour surplus and with employment possibilities in urban industry still very restricted, there will be no significant net economies of scale until alternative employment can be found for surplus rural labour, and found by means involving the least possible investment of capital. Hence the role of commune and brigade industry, of the new economic combines, and of licensed individual rural enterprise.

The Chinese have not yet produced any systematic economic theory on their new rural policies, but there is clear resonance with Western theories of the linkage effects of agricultural growth and the role of agriculture as the leading sector in economic development. One might tentatively rationalise Chinese policy as follows.

To start with a somewhat extreme but simple theoretical case: suppose that, in a population spending 80 per cent of its income on a subsistence diet, the cost of the subsistence diet falls by 25 per cent because of decreasing farming costs. Disposable purchasing power would thereby be increased by 100 per cent.

The key question is, what will that increased purchasing power be spent on? We have no systematic statistics from China on demand schedules at different levels of income, but observation over the years suggests the following:

Phase I: greater consumption of grain, tubers, etc., to the extent that the existing diet was low in calories.

Phase II: greater consumption of other agricultural products – meat, fruit and vegetables, dairy produce, and natural fibres.

Phase III: larger purchases of simple modern garments and footwear, traditional craftwares, furnishings, bicycles, electric fans.

Phase IV: improved and extended traditional housing.

Phase V: acquisition of refrigerators, media receivers, tape recorders, cameras, watches and more expensive traditional craft products.

Throughout this process one would also expect increasing investment in modern agricultural inputs: irrigation pumps, chemical fertilisers, pesticides and appliances, walking tractors, and small trucks, broadly in that order. There would also be an increasing demand for agricultural services.

Note that up to and including Phase IV, most of the goods purchased can be produced without much resort to modern capital-intensive industry. In fact, in China since 1970 local and commune and brigade industry has proved capable of producing almost all the consumer goods listed, as well as chemical fertilisers, building materials, farm tools, small machines and machine-made textiles.

As the market grows, labour productivity rises rapidly in these small local industries as the first simple machinery is applied to production, thus increasing purchasing power further. This in China's case has been at least as important as improvements in agriculture in increasing rural purchasing power.

It is clear that the capacity of improved agriculture to generate new purchasing power, and on that basis to generate a wide range of labour-intensive enterprises, does depend to some extent on the growth of large-scale modern industry to supply certain inputs. In China, however, if one includes industries at county level, local communities have proved already capable of producing a large range of energy supplies, raw materials and modern inputs; dependence on the capital-intensive state sector has therefore been minimal.

Of course the Chinese still walk on two legs. Almost 90 per cent of industrial production still comes from the larger-scale state enterprises, although the proportion is gradually falling. In fact China still has a dual economy. But everything is being done to ensure that the rural economy has the means to accumulate and invest, by changing the terms of trade in favour of agriculture, by moving as much of industrial production as possible down to the villages, and by giving the maximum of freedom and incentives to the peasants. Moreover, the Chinese economy is not as dualistic as it appears. About one quarter of current investment in Chinese agriculture is still provided by the state. More important is the strong sense in China that the modern industrial sector depends on the fortunes of the rural sector, with its rapidly growing purchasing power. This is the fundamental linkage from which all particular linkages are derived.

It is clear that orthodox Communist attempts to manage agriculture as nearly as possible directly by the state run into the same problems which plague state-directed industry, but that the problems are much more severe. Supervision of the labour force is much more difficult; discipline cannot to the same extent replace or supplement incentives. The division of labour on an industrial model cannot be applied, because the farmer must respond to all contingencies produced by weather and other natural variables; piecework on the farm is useless for anything more complicated than picking strawberries. Conditions vary from farm to farm and even from field to field; they cannot be rendered uniform as they can between factory and factory. Local knowledge is everything, and so the problem of information, which is severe enough in centrally planned industry, is infinitely more severe in agriculture. All these factors produce diseconomies of scale which can easily outgrow the potential economies offered by large-scale mechanised farming. Hence the irony that labour productivity in Soviet agriculture still drags along at the level of the peasant agriculture of Spain or Ireland while productivity per acre is in every case lower than that of modern individual farming in comparable natural conditions.

If the obsession with scale has been a major factor in the poor performance of collectivised agriculture so too has the thesis of 'primitive capital accumulation' and the extractive policies deduced from it. However rational the internal arrangements to sustain individual incentives might have been, they could have had little effect so long as taxation and procurement destroyed incentives for the collective unit as a whole. Without incentive prices, there is a chronic contradiction in collective farming. While the main object of the state's agricultural policy is to increase the marketed surplus of agricultural staples, the collective peasants have no interest in doing more than ensuring that collective grain production meets their subsistence needs and minimally fulfils their obligations to the state. Having achieved this, they turn their attention to more profitable individual production on the private plot. The existence of the private plot reconciles them to the collective, but at a heavy cost to the state's ambition to maximise the marketed surplus of field crops. The private plot does not solve the contradiction; it merely condones it.

As the differentiation of the East European collective system widens, and as policies become more complex, general judgements are increasingly difficult to make. On the whole, however, the results of varied recent experiments tend to confirm the judgements made here. Romania's vast agro-businesses are far too large for efficiency, whereas East Germany's smaller-scale undertakings of the same kind are the most efficient in the communist world. The Soviet Union's move from collective towards state farms has done little if anything to improve output, whereas Hungary's opposite move towards much greater freedom for her peasants has had very positive effects. Those countries, such as Bulgaria and Hungary, which have acknowledged the importance of developing agriculture in its own right, have been able to develop quite profitable and efficient operations.

Although quantitative comparative analysis of agriculture in the Soviet Union and East Europe, taking all variables into consideration, is not possible, one can provisionally conclude that decentralised systems work best; that the maximisation of peasant initiative gives results well worth the relaxation of planning control involved; that incentive prices (providing collective incentives) are a necessary but not a sufficient condition of improved efficiency; that the problem of individual incentives has not been solved within a collective context, and that increased investment in agriculture in itself solves little.

The Chinese have reached much the same conclusions. They have gone further, however, in their denial that, in Chinese conditions at least, economies of scale in farming are automatic, and that collective production as opposed to collective infrastructure is an ideological necessity. They have rejected the analogy of primitive capital accumulation and asserted the primary importance of increasing peasant purchasing power. They have relinquished the belief that planning and the market are antithetical. They can now assert that peasants have rights and interests as well as obligations, and that agricultural policy must be based on these rights and interests – not only for the sake of justice but also efficiency. Finally, they are attempting to base economic life on the principle of free contracts – the only possible basis of a free society, capitalist or socialist.

From a broader historical viewpoint, the issue of central state direction versus local autonomy and voluntary associations is one of the oldest issues in Chinese political life. It goes back to the controversy, centuries before the birth of Christ, between Legalists and Taoists. In the seventeenth-century crisis of the collapse of the Ming dynasty, patriotic scholars produced the paradoxical argument that China was strongest when her local communities were strong, and weakest when the central government was too strong. These men (Gu Yanwu, Huang Zongxi, Wang Fuzhi) were to become the heroes of twentieth-century Chinese nationalism, and the young Mao Zedong, in common with the rest of his generation, was steeped in their ideas. When he became a Marxist it was almost inevitable that he would interpret the ambiguous ideas of Marx on the nature of post-revolutionary society in terms of his passionately held belief in community self-government. The discrediting of Stalinism in 1956 provided the opportunity to apply these ideas but his continued stress on egalitarianism and on collectivism, and the conventional hostility to the market, ruined the experiment.

These inibitions have now been removed. The resulting system is one which bears the marks of traditional Chinese political culture. The classical compromise in imperial China between central direction and local (and private) initiative was one enshrined in a number of stock phrases such as 'government supervision, local management . . . official supervision, civilian management'. This concept was applied in China's first government-inspired attempts at industrialisation. It reappeared in the formula of 'central supervision, co-operative management' which Mao applied to the Border Region economy. It was ambiguously applied in the Commune system. It has now reappeared in Deng's economic reforms, with contract as the link between government and rural community. It has its analogies across the Taiwan Straits, for it expresses traditional Chinese expectations as to how the national economy ought to work. It fulfils the expectations shared by almost all Chinese radicals since the late nineteenth century, that China must be renewed from the bottom up. It points up the contrast between the Russian-Byzantine political culture which has shaped the Soviet system and the Confucian political culture which is now, in this and other ways, reasserting itself in Deng Xiaoping's 'socialism with Chinese characteristics'. These Chinese characteristics may indeed be more Chinese than Deng himself knows.

Abbreviations

FBIS	Foreign Broadcasts Information Service, *China: Daily Report*.
GMRB	*Guangming Ribao* (Glorious Daily), Peking.
RMRB	*Renmin Ribao* (People's Daily), Peking.
SWB	British Broadcasting Corporation, *Summary of World Broadcasts: Far East*.
Xinhua	*Xinhua* (New China News Agency), Peking.

Notes

1. For a discussion of these political factors in the African context, see White and Mars (1986).
2. For an introduction to modern historical scholarship on the Industrial Revolution, see Crouzet (1972); Taylor (1975); Hartwell (1967); Musson (1972).
3. Mao Zedong, 'Economic and Financial Problems', *Selected Works, Vol. III*, p. 33: 'Appropriate steps must be adopted to help the people

develop their agriculture (etc. . . .), so that they give, and, moreover, gain more than they give; only thus can we sustain a long war against Japan'.

4. Mao Tsetung, 'On the Question of Co-operativisation', *Xinhau Yeubao* (New China Monthly), vol. 73, 1955, no. 11, pp. 1–8.
5. *Zhongguo Nungcun de Shehuizhuyi Gao Chao* (High Tide of Socialism in the Chinese Countryside), Peking 1956, 3 vols. For a brief analysis of this material, see Gray (1974).
6. *On the Ten Great Relationships* (Beijing, 1977). This was not published officially until after Mao's death.
7. *RMRB*, 19 June, 1957.
8. Mao Tsetung, 'Critique of Stalin's "Economic Problems of Socialism in the USSR"', in *Miscellany of Mao Thought*, vol. 1, p. 191.
9. Mao was introduced early to the two contrasting views of the future nature of socialist society: the Saint-Simonian etatist and Owenite communal views. The first book on socialism he read was by Thomas Kirkup, who dealt with this contradiction. Young Mao favoured, as did Kirkup, the communalist version and it is reflected in his conception of the commune system.
10. *Hong Qi* (Red Flag), Peking, 5 March 1980.
11. *GMRB*, May 1980, in *SWB* 6437.BII.5.
12. *RMRB*, 14 May 1980, in *SWB* 6427.BII.1.
13. *RMRB*, 3 November 1980, in *SWB* 6568.BII.5.
14. On the deficiencies of grass-roots rural cadres *RMRB*, 3 November 1980 in *SWB* 6568.BII.5; *RMRB*, 13 December 1980, in *FBIS* 253.L.42; *Ming Pao*, Hong Kong, 6 December 1981, in *FBIS* 238.W.2.
15. On peasant burdens, see *RMRB*, 6 November 1979, *FBIS* 225; Guizhou Radio, 20 July 1980, in *SWB* 6479.BII.1; *RMRB*, 11 July 1981, in *FBIS* 145.T.1; *Xinhua*, 5 August 1981, in *SWB* 6814.BII.1; *Xinhua*, 4 September 1981, in *SWB* 6826.C.3; *RMRB*, 17 September 1981, in *SWB* 6843.BII.2.
16. *RMRB* 1 September 1981, in *FBIS* 174.K.7.
17. *Ming Pao*, Hong Kong, in *FBIS* 238 W.2.
18. *Hebei Ribao* (Hebei Daily), 25 January 1983, in *SWB* W.1217.A.4.
19. *RMRB*, 21 March 1984, in *SWB* 79291.BII.6.
20. For a striking example of the employment of wage labour in farming, see Henan Radio, 12 October 1984, in *FBIS* 208.P.2.
21. *RMRB*, 18 September 1982, in *SWB* 7139.BII.12.
22. *RMRB*, 3 April 1983, in *SWB* 7304.BII.2.
23. For example, see *RMRB*, 3 July 1983, in *FBIS*, 139.K.6, re Mianyang county in Hubei.
24. For example, Heilongjiang Radio, 20 March 1983, in *SWB* 7289.BII.2.
25. For example, see Ningxia Radio, 25 February 1984, in *SWB* 7580.BII.16.
26. Jiangsu Radio, 4 July 1983, in *SWB* 7383.BII.9.
27. Communique of the State Statistical Bureau on the 1983 Plan, *Xinhua*, 29 April 1984, in *FBIS* 085.K.11.
28. *Xinhua* (in Chinese), 7 March 1983, in *SWB* 7386.B.II.6; *Jingji Ribao* (Economic Daily), 7 March 1983, in *SWB* W.1232.A.11; Hunan Radio, 19 April 1983, in *SWB* W.1236.A.3; *Xinhua* (in English) 1 September

1983, in *FBIS* 175.R.1; *RMRB*, 20 November 1983, in *FBIS* 227.K.15; *Xinhua* (in English), 2 January 1984, in *FBIS* 005.K.23; *Heilongjiang Ribao*, 19 January 1984, in *SWB* W.1276.A.5; *Xinhua* (C) 20 February 1984, in *SWB* 7576.C.3; *China Daily*, 23 February 1984, in *FBIS* 037.K.6.
29. For example, see Hunan Radio, 11 June 1982, in *SWB* 7055.BII.6; Guizhou Radio, 22 July 1982, in *SWB* 7090.BII.14.
30. *Hong Qi* (Red Flag), 1982, No. 13, 1 July 1982, in *SWB* 7100.BII.3.
31. *Shanxi Ribao* (Shanxi Daily), 23 July 1982, in *SWB* 7102.BII.4.
32. For a model brigade, see Henan Radio, 4 July 1982, in *SWB* 7075.C.1.
33. *Xinhua*, 13 October 1983.
34. For example, see *Beijing Review*, No. 29, 19 July 1982.
35. *RMRB* 30 March 1984, in *FBIS* 066.K.1.
36. For example, see *Guangming Ribao* (Glorious Daily), 19 September 1983, in *FBIS* 193.K.3.
37. *Dazhong Ribao* (Great Masses Daily), 30 December 1983, in *FBIS* 013.0.4.
38. For example, see *Hong Qi*, 1982, No. 13, 1 July, in *SWB* 7100.BII.8.
39. *RMRB*, 22 January 1983, in *FBIS* 016.K.6.
40. *Xinhua*, 18 December 1983, in *SWB* 7219.BII.5.
41. *Xinhua* (E), 10 June 1982, in *FBIS* 113.K.2.
42. *RMRB*, 24 February 1983, in *FBIS* 045.T.1.
43. *RMRB*, 12 April 1983, in *FBIS* 074.K.10.

References

Baum, R. (1975) *Prelude to Revolution* (London: Columbia University Press).

Crouzet, V. F. (1972) *Capital Formation in the Industrial Revolution* (London: Methuen)

Gray, J. (1974) 'Mao Tsetung's Strategy for the Collectivisation of Chinese Agriculture', in E. de Kadt and G. Williams (eds), *Sociology and Development* (London: Tavistock).

Gray, J. and G. White (1983) *China's New Development Strategy* (London: Academic Press).

Griffin, K. and A. Saith (1981) *Growth and Equality in Rural China* (Geneva: ILO).

Hartwell, R. M. (ed.) (1967) *The Causes of the Industrial Revolution in England* (London: Methuen).

Howe, C. (1978) *China's Economy: A Basic Guide* (London: Elek).

Musson, A. E. (ed.) (1972) *Science, Technology and Economic Growth in the Eighteenth Century* (Oxford: Oxford University Press).

Schram, S. (ed.) (1973) *Authority Participation and Cultural Change in China* (Cambridge: Cambridge University Press).

Taylor, A. J. (ed.) (1975) *The Standard of Living in Britain in the Industrial Revolution: Debates in Economic History* (London: Methuen).

White, G. and T. Mars (eds) (1986) 'Developmental States and African Agriculture', *IDS Bulletin*, vol. 17, no. 1 (January), Institute of Development Studies, University of Sussex.

Author Index

Subject Index